Preface

Course Technology is the world leader in information technology education. The New Perspectives Series is an integral part of Course Technology's success. Visit our Web site to see a whole new perspective on teaching and learning solutions.

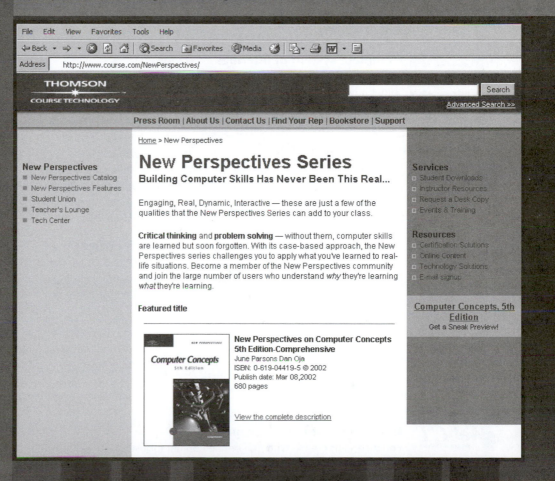

New Perspectives—Building Computer Skills Has Never Been This Real

Why New Perspectives will work for you.

Critical thinking and **problem solving**—without them, computer skills are learned but soon forgotten. With its **case-based** approach, the New Perspectives Series challenges students to apply what they've learned to real-life situations. Become a member of the New Perspectives community and watch your students not only **master** computer skills, but also **retain** and carry this **knowledge** into the world.

New Perspectives catalog
Our online catalog is never out of date! Go to the Catalog link on our Web site to check out our available titles, request a desk copy, download a book preview, or locate online files.

Complete system of offerings
Whether you're looking for a Brief book, an Advanced book, or something in between, we've got you covered. Go to the Catalog link on our Web site to find the level of coverage that's right for you.

Instructor materials
We have all the tools you need—data files, solution files, figure files, a sample syllabus, and ExamView, our powerful testing software package.

How well do your students know Microsoft Office?
Experience the power, ease, and flexibility of SAM XP and TOM. These innovative software tools provide the first truly integrated technology-based training and assessment solution for your applications course. Click the Tech Center link to learn more.

Get certified
If you want to get certified, we have the titles for you. Find out more by clicking the Teacher's Lounge link.

Interested in online learning?
Enhance your course with rich online content for use through MyCourse 2.0, WebCT, and Blackboard. Go to the Teacher's Lounge to find the platform that's right for you.

Your link to the future is at
www.course.com/NewPerspectives

New Perspectives on

MICROSOFT® WINDOWS® 2000

MS-DOS Command Line

Brief Enhanced

HARRY L. PHILLIPS

ERIC SKAGERBERG

THOMSON
COURSE TECHNOLOGY™

Australia • Canada • Mexico • Singapore • Spain • United Kingdom • United States

THOMSON

COURSE TECHNOLOGY

New Perspectives on Microsoft® Windows® 2000 MS-DOS Command Line—Brief Enhanced is published by Course Technology.

Managing Editor:
Rachel Crapser

Senior Editor:
Donna Gridley

Senior Product Manager:
Kathy Finnegan

Product Manager:
Karen Stevens

Technology Product Manager:
Amanda Shelton

Associate Product Manager:
Brianna Germain

Marketing Manager:
Rachel Valente

Production Editor:
Danielle Power

Composition:
GEX Publishing Services

Text Designer:
Meral Dabcovich

Cover Designer:
Efrat Reis

COPYRIGHT © 2003 Course Technology, a division of Thomson Learning, Inc. Thomson Learning™ is a trademark used herein under license.

Printed in the United States of America

1 2 3 4 5 6 7 8 9 QWD 06 05 04 03 02

For more information, contact Course Technology, 25 Thomson Place, Boston, Massachusetts, 02210.

Or find us on the World Wide Web at: www.course.com

ALL RIGHTS RESERVED. No part of this work covered by the copyright hereon may be reproduced or used in any form or by any means—graphic, electronic, or mechanical, including photocopying, recording, taping, Web distribution, or information storage and retrieval systems—without the written permission of the publisher.

For permission to use material from this text or product, contact us by
Tel (800) 730-2214
Fax (800) 730-2215
www.thomsonrights.com

Disclaimer
Course Technology reserves the right to revise this publication and make changes from time to time in its content without notice.

ISBN 0-619-18552-X

What you need to know about this book.

- Students learn the essentials of the Windows 2000 and Windows XP Command Line through a practical, step-by-step approach

- The Appendix contains an overview of Windows XP and addresses any differences a student may experience if using Windows XP while learning from this book

- Technically-oriented students will enjoy learning to open a command line session and working with commands, files, directories and subdirectories in the command line interface

- Coverage provides a basis for comparison of the DOS, Windows 2000, and Windows XP operating system command-line environments

- Designed to provide a hands-on technical addition to a full-semester Windows 2000 or Windows XP Operating Systems course

CASE	TROUBLE?	SESSION 1.1	QUICK CHECK	RW
Tutorial Case Each tutorial begins with a problem presented in a case that is meaningful to students. The case sets the scene to help students understand what they will do in the tutorial.	**TROUBLE? Paragraphs** These paragraphs anticipate the mistakes or problems that students may have and help them continue with the tutorial.	**Sessions** Each tutorial is divided into sessions designed to be completed in about 45 minutes each. Students should take as much time as they need and take a break between sessions.	**Quick Check Questions** Each session concludes with conceptual Quick Check questions that test students' understanding of what they learned in the session.	**Reference Windows** Reference Windows are succinct summaries of the most important tasks covered in a tutorial. They preview actions students will perform in the steps to follow.

www.course.com/NewPerspectives

TABLE OF CONTENTS

Acknowledgments

Dedicated to Neal Stephenson, author of *In the Beginning ... was the Command Line*

Many people were involved in all stages of the planning, development, and production of the original version and revised update of this book, and their combined efforts reflect Course Technology's continued commitment to the instructors and students who use this textbook.

We would like to thank our reviewer, Floyd Winters, Professor of Computer Science, Manatee Community College, whose valuable comments and insight helped shape this book. We would also like to thank him for providing us with photos of jumper blocks and DIP switches for use in Tutorial 1.

Thanks to all the members of the New Perspectives team who helped in the development and production of the original version of this book: Catherine Donaldson, Product Manager; Sandra K. Kruse, Developmental Editor; Rachel A. Crapser, Series Technology Manager; Greg Donald, Managing Editor; Donna Gridley, Senior Editor; Melissa Hathaway, Associate Product Manager; Rosa Maria Rogers, Editorial Assistant; John Bosco and Alex White; QA Managers; Anne Valsangiacomo, Production Editor; Nancy Ludlow; and the QA testers, John Freitas, Justin Rand, and Nicole Ashton, for their contributions in their areas of expertise. We would like to extend our special thanks to Ellen Skagerberg, who freely offered her invaluable time and expertise as a copy editor.

—Eric Skagerberg and Harry Phillips
28 August 2000

My deepest and heartfelt thanks go to my parents, David and Wanda Skagerberg, and my sister Andrea, for their love and immeasurable support through the years. My profound love and gratitude goes to my wife Ellen, for the astounding extent of practical support and encouragement she provided me throughout this process.

Thanks as well to Gary Brown, who saw some potential in a young man and hired him to teach a DOS class at Santa Rosa Junior College's CIS department over a decade ago, and to Lloyd Onyett, who gave so generously of his time and materials to mentor and work with me through those early years. I am grateful to each person in SRJC's CIS department who helped to create a warm, sharing, and cooperative working environment, particularly department chairs Metha Schuler, Cyndi Reese, and Ellindale Wells, and fellow UNIX instructors Pat Grosh and Sean Kirkpatrick.

—Eric Skagerberg
28 August 2000

Thanks to all the members of the New Perspectives team who helped in the development and production of the revised update of this book: Amanda Shelton, Technology Product Manager; Donna Gridley, Senior Editor; Rachel A. Crapser, Managing Editor; Kathy Finnegan, Senior Product Manager; Brianna Germain, Assistant Product Manager; Emilie Perreault, Editorial Assistant; Danielle Power and Jennifer Goguen, Production; Paul Griffin, Copyeditor; John Freitas, John Bosco, and Heather McKinstry, Quality Assurance; and the QA testers, John Freitas and Burt LaFountain, for their contributions in their areas of expertise.

—Harry Phillips and Eric Skagerberg
16 September 2002

New Perspectives on

MICROSOFT® WINDOWS® 2000

MS-DOS Command Line—Brief Enhanced

Read This Before You Begin

To the Student

Data Disk

To complete the Tutorials, Review Assignments, and Case Problems in this book, you need a Data Disk. Your instructor will either provide you with the Data Disk or ask you to make your own.

If you are making your own Data Disk, you will need a blank, formatted high-density diskette. You will need to copy a set of files from a file server or standalone computer or the Web onto your disk. Your instructor will tell you which computer, drive letter, and folders contain the files you need. You can also download the files by going to **www.course.com**, clicking Student Downloads, and following the instructions on the screen. If you download the Data Disk from the Course Technology, Inc. Web site, then you will find that there is an executable program file for the Data Disk. This file is a self-extracting image file that contains an exact image of all the files for the Data Disk stored in the order in which they were originally placed on the disk.

To extract the files and folders for the Data Disk, insert a blank, formatted high-density diskette in drive A, and then double-click the image file's icon. In the resulting command-line window, press the letter **A** (for drive A). The utility then extracts the files to the diskette in drive A. When the operation is complete, close the command-line window if it does not automatically close.

Data Disk 1

Write this on the disk label:
Data Disk 1 – Tutorials 1, 2, 3, and 4

Contents – The self-extracting image file will put 41 files on the disk.

See the inside front or inside back cover of this book for more information on Data Disk files, or ask your instructor or technical support person for assistance.

Appendix

The Appendix at the end of the book will help you complete the tutorials in this book if you are using Windows XP Professional or Windows XP Home Edition. The Appendix contains information on new Windows XP features related to what is covered in the textbook for Windows 2000. The Appendix also contains updates and Help information to assist you with the tutorials. As you step through each tutorial, you can consult the corresponding section in the Appendix for additional topics, updates, and Help. At the end of the Appendix is a supplemental glossary with additional terms covered in the Appendix.

Using Your Own Computer

If you are going to work through this book using your own computer, you need:

- **Computer System** Windows 2000 Professional, Windows XP Professional, or Windows XP Home Edition must be installed on your computer. This book assumes a standard installation of Windows 2000 Professional, Windows XP Professional, or Windows XP Home Edition.
- **Data Disk** You will not be able to complete the tutorials or exercises in this book using your own computer until you have the Data Disk.

Visit Our World Wide Web Site

Additional materials designed especially for you are available on the World Wide Web. Go to **http://www.course.com**.

To the Instructor

The files for the Data Disk are available on the Instructor's Resource CD for this title. Follow the instructions in the Help file on the CD-ROM to install the Data Disk files to your network or stand-alone computer. For information on creating Data Disks, see the "To the Student" section above.

You are granted a license to copy the Data Files to any computer or computer network used by students who have purchased this book.

The Instructor's Resource CD and Test Bank have been updated for Windows XP Professional and Windows XP Home Edition.

In this tutorial you will:

- Examine the role and importance of operating system software

- Learn about the importance of command line skills to Windows 2000 users

- Examine some of the basic functions of operating system software

- Open a command line session

- Identify the version of the operating system installed on a computer

- Set the date and time

- Use the Help switch

- Format a diskette

- Open a Command Prompt window

OPENING
COMMAND LINE SESSIONS IN WINDOWS 2000

Building MS-DOS Command Line Skills at SolarWinds Unlimited

CASE

SolarWinds Unlimited

SolarWinds Unlimited is a California corporation that uses state-of-the-art turbines to harness wind power—the world's fastest growing energy source—so it can provide clean energy to its growing base of environmentally conscious customers. Several months ago, Isabel Navarro Torres, the company's computer systems specialist, supervised the installation of Windows 2000 on computers at SolarWinds' southern California headquarters. To increase the background skills of the company's technical resource staff, Isabel recently scheduled a series of workshops on the use of command line sessions under Windows 2000. This investment in staff training will provide the company's technical support staff with the skills they need to set up and configure computers, and troubleshoot computer problems. Because Isabel recently hired you to provide technical support to other staff members and to assist her with administering the company's network, she asks you to participate in the workshops along with the rest of the company's employees.

SESSION 1.1

In this session you will examine the role and the importance of operating system software, the types of operating systems used on PCs, and the importance of developing a skill set that enables you to work with different operating systems in today's multifaceted business environment.

The Role and Importance of Operating System Software

At the start of the first workshop, Isabel provides an overview of the role and importance of operating system software on the different types of computer systems used by businesses, entrepreneurs, "dot com companies," and individuals.

An **operating system** is a software product that manages the basic processes within a computer, coordinates the interaction of hardware and software so all components work together, and provides support for the use of other types of software such as application software, utilities, and games. Although specific operating systems vary in the scope of tasks they manage, all operating systems play a role in the following tasks:

- **Booting a computer** The operating system participates in the later phases of the boot process. **Booting** refers to the process of powering on a computer system and loading the operating system into memory so it can configure the computer system and manage the basic processes of the computer, including providing support for other software.

  After you power on a computer, and before the operating system is active, the microprocessor executes a series of startup **routines**, or programs, stored on a special type of computer chip called the **ROM BIOS (Read-Only Memory Basic Input/Output System)**. The first routine, the **Power On Self Test** (or **POST**), checks to make sure your computer contains the components necessary for booting the computer and that these components are functional. The next routine searches the outside sector of the boot devices to locate the operating system and start the process of loading the operating system into memory. After the core operating system files are loaded into memory, the PC's operating system loads the remainder of the operating system and completes the boot process. From this point on, the PC's operating system manages the computer system.

- **Configuring a computer** During booting, the operating system configures itself by loading the additional software it needs to interact with the hardware and software on the computer. Newer operating systems can detect hardware automatically and load the appropriate device drivers. A **device driver** is software used for managing a specific type of hardware component and is essential for the proper functioning of your computer.

- **Customizing a computer** Near the end of the booting process, the operating system loads specific types of software that you install and use on the computer. For example, if you have installed antivirus software on your computer, the operating system will load that software during the latter stages of booting so it can check your computer for the presence of viruses as early as possible during the boot process. **Computer viruses** are programs designed to interfere with the performance, or even damage, of your computer. The antivirus software then continues to monitor your computer while you work. Although the operating system can function without this software, users increasingly depend on antivirus software, and other types of software, to customize their computers. Software for configuring your computer is required by the operating system, whereas software for customizing your computer is optional software.

■ **Displaying a user interface** Once your computer boots, the operating system displays a **user interface**, the combination of hardware and software that lets you interact with the computer. This interface has become increasingly important to users because they rely on it to simplify the tasks they perform on the computer. Current operating systems typically display a **graphical user interface** (**GUI**) that uses **icons**, or images, to represent system components such as hardware and software; separate **windows** for displaying the interface used by application software and for viewing portions of documents; **menus** with task-related options for performing different types of operations, such as opening a software application; and **dialog boxes** with options for completing tasks, such as changing the appearance of the user interface; as well as colors, fonts (character styles), and special design elements, such as shading, which all provide a visually rich working environment. The different versions of the Windows operating system also require a mouse.

■ **Providing support services to programs** The operating system provides important support services to programs that you use. Since almost every program must provide an option for saving files to disk and for retrieving files from disk, it makes sense to delegate this function to the operating system to avoid duplication and to provide consistency across different programs. Whether you are saving or retrieving a file, you must provide the program with the names of the disk drive, folder (if applicable), and file that contains your data. When saving data to a file on disk, the operating system handles the transfer of a copy of the document from Random Access Memory (RAM) to the disk. This document may be a new document you created from scratch, or it may be a document you opened and modified. **RAM**, the predominant type of memory within a computer, stores programs that you open and documents you create or open, and therefore provides a temporary workspace for you, the user. Because this memory is **volatile** (dependent on the availability of power), it is important to periodically save data to disk. When retrieving a file from disk, the operating system handles the transfer of a copy of the file from disk to RAM so you can use the data in that file with a program.

■ **Handling input and output** The operating system manages all input and output. In addition to retrieving files from disk (input) and saving files to disk (output), the operating system also interprets keyboard and mouse input, and assists with other types of output, such as printing and displaying the image you see on the monitor. For example, when you press a key on the keyboard, the keyboard produces an electronic **scan code,** which the operating system interprets so the program you are using displays the correct character on the monitor. When you print a document, operating systems use a process called **spooling** to store the processed document in a temporary file on disk called a **spool file,** and to transmit the spool file to the printer in the background, so you can continue to work in your program, or even start a new task. Also, with spooling you can send several documents to the printer at once. The operating system stores the documents in a **print queue** (a list of print jobs) and prints the documents in order. Without spooling, you would have to wait until each document printed before you could do anything else.

■ **Managing the file system** The operating system manages the disks, drives, directories (or folders), subdirectories (or subfolders), and files so it can find the software and documents you need to use. Disks are divided into one or more **partitions** (sometimes called drives), which provide storage for subdirectories and files. **Subdirectories** group related directories and files.

A **file** is the storage space on disk allocated to a program or data, such as a word processing document or a spreadsheet.

■ **Managing system resources** The operating system manages all the hardware and software so everything works together properly. This is a major feat today because of the wide spectrum of hardware and software products installed on any given computer. One important resource managed by the operating system is memory, or RAM. When you open a program, the operating system looks for that program on disk and allocates memory to the program as it loads that program. When you exit a program, the operating system should reclaim the memory used by that program so it can allocate that memory to the next program you open. Some applications leave program code in memory, however, and the operating system does not reclaim that memory. As a result, the amount of available memory actually decreases (a problem called a **memory leak**) overtime, and you need to reboot your computer system to clear memory and start fresh.

■ **Resolving system errors and problems** The operating system must handle and, if possible, resolve errors as they occur. For example, if you save a document to the floppy disk drive, but do not put a diskette into that drive, the operating system informs you of the problem so you can resolve it by inserting a diskette and trying again. If you print a document, but forget to turn the printer on, the operating system may inform you that the printer is off, off-line, or out of paper.

■ **Providing Help** Operating systems typically include a Help system that provides you with information about the use of the operating system and its features. Some Help systems provide troubleshooting assistance by stepping you through operations with wizards and hyperlinks. A **wizard** is a tool that asks a series of questions about what you want to do, what settings you want to use, or what problems you are experiencing; suggests options from which to choose, and then completes the operation for you or provides suggestions of options you should try. A **hyperlink** is a link to an object on your local computer, such as a Help Troubleshooter, a document, or a Web page.

■ **Optimizing system performance** Operating systems typically include a variety of **utilities**, or programs, for optimizing the performance of your computer. For example, you might use a utility to check the file system and the surface of the hard disk for errors and, where possible, to repair those errors. You might use another utility to improve the speed of accessing data on a disk by rearranging how folders, software, and document files are stored on it. Although these utilities are optional, many users depend on utilities to maintain and optimize the performance of their computer.

■ **Providing troubleshooting tools** The operating system on your computer provides you with a variety of tools for troubleshooting problems. For example, you can prepare a **boot disk** (also called a **system disk**) that contains the core operating system files needed to start your computer from drive A, so you can troubleshoot problems with the operating system (such as a failure to boot from drive C), or with the hard disk itself (such as a failure of the hard disk), and if necessary, replace your hard disk and reinstall the operating system. You can view settings assigned to hardware and software components if you need to troubleshoot a problem.

The operating system is an indispensable component of your computer. You cannot use a computer without an operating system. As you work with software, the operating system manages the moment-to-moment operation of your computer in the background, from the point you turn the power on until you shut down your computer. Furthermore, because the operating system handles important operations, such as disk, drive, directory, and file management, as well as all input/output functions, software can focus on what it is designed to do, and the operating system can focus on core functions required of all programs.

PC Operating Systems

Like many other businesses today, SolarWinds relies on a wide variety of computers, software, and PC operating systems. Some staff members use one operating system at work, and another on their home computer. Many of the technical staff members at SolarWinds set up a multi-boot configuration on their work and home computers so they can use one of several different operating systems. Because of the company's dependence on different operating system technologies, Isabel decides next to present a quick overview of the important operating systems that staff members use.

The predominant operating systems used on PCs today were developed by Microsoft Corporation. They share a common history, similar features and ways of working. Therefore, it's important for you to be familiar not only with Windows 2000, but also with other operating systems, such as Windows 98, Windows 95, Windows NT Workstation 4.0, and DOS.

Note: This book assumes that the student already has a working knowledge of the Windows 2000 operating system from a comprehensive Windows 2000 course. While the tutorials provide some summary information for context and step the student through certain operations in the graphical user interface, it is beyond the scope of this book to instruct the student in the operation of Windows 2000. Rather, this book focuses primarily on the features and uses of the MS-DOS subsystem under Windows 2000.

The DOS Operating System

Following the explosion of mass-marketed computer technology in the early 1980s that made PCs indispensable in offices, schools, and homes, the most commonly used operating system was **DOS**, an abbreviation for Disk Operating System. Disk refers to one of the more important hardware resources managed by this operating system. DOS is actually a generic name for three related operating systems: PC-DOS, MS-DOS, and IBM-DOS. PC-DOS is designed specifically for the hardware in IBM microcomputers, whereas MS-DOS is designed for the hardware in compatible PCs.

In 1981, IBM contracted with Microsoft Corporation (then a small company in Washington State) to provide the operating system for its first IBM PC. Over the years, Microsoft and IBM worked cooperatively to develop different versions of PC-DOS and IBM-DOS for use on IBM microcomputers, while Microsoft also worked independently to develop different versions of MS-DOS for use on compatible PCs, or IBM compatibles. IBM now develops its own versions of IBM-DOS for IBM microcomputers, but Microsoft no longer develops new versions of MS-DOS. However, Microsoft provides an MS-DOS command line system as an application within different versions of Windows, including Windows 2000. Although there are subtle differences between PC-DOS, MS-DOS, and IBM-DOS, all manage the hardware and software resources within a computer in similar ways, provide access to similar types of features, and include similar utilities for enhancing the performance of a system. Once you know how to use MS-DOS, you can also use PC-DOS and IBM-DOS, and you have a head start on working with command line sessions under the different versions of Windows, including Windows 2000.

DOS and other operating systems, such as UNIX, VAX/VMS, and Linux, use a **command line interface**, in which you communicate with the operating system by typing a command after an **operating system prompt**, or **command prompt**, as shown in Figure 1-1. A **command** is an instruction to perform a specific task, such as format a disk. Once you see the operating system prompt (usually C:\>), you know that the computer booted successfully, that the operating system loaded into memory, and which drive the operating system uses as a reference point (usually drive C). There are no other on-screen visual clues to help you figure out what to do next. You must know what command to use, the proper format for entering each command, and what options are available for modifying how each command works. After you enter a command, DOS attempts to locate and load a **routine**, or program, that enables you to perform a specific task. When you exit that routine or program, DOS redisplays the command prompt so you can enter another command to start another program. For these reasons, in the past, users commonly relied on technically oriented coworkers or friends to customize their computers so DOS automatically started Windows 3.1 or displayed a menu from which a user could open an installed program, or perform some task, such as formatting a disk.

Figure 1-1	MS-DOS COMMAND LINE INTERFACE

operating system prompt → | **command line**

```
C:\>FORMAT A: /S /U
Insert new diskette for drive A:
and press ENTER when ready...

Formatting 1.2M
Format complete.
System transferred

Volume label (11 characters, ENTER for none)? BOOT DISK

    1,213,952 bytes total disk space
      198,656 bytes used by system
    1,015,296 bytes available on disk

          512 bytes in each allocation unit.
        1,983 allocation units available on disk.

Volume Serial Number is 3236-07CC

Format another (Y/N)?
```

switch for performing an unconditional format under MS-DOS

switch for copying system files to a disk under MS-DOS

program output

command

drive to format

Unlike Windows and other graphical user interface systems, command line interface operating systems operate in text mode rather than graphics mode. In **text mode**, the computer monitor displays only text, numbers, symbols, and a small set of graphics characters, using either white, amber, or green characters on a black background. Because text mode does not display a user interface with graphics, DOS functions were performed quickly and required far less memory or RAM than present-day operating systems that display a graphical user interface.

DOS still is important today. If Windows 2000 will not boot, you must work in a DOS-like command line interface to fix the problem. This is important especially for network administrators, specialists, and *technicians*, as well as telephone support *technicians*, troubleshooters, computer consultants, trainers, and tweakers (people who specialize in fine-tuning and optimizing computers). All of these professions find knowledge of DOS an invaluable resource. Furthermore, as noted earlier, the different versions of the Windows operating systems support the use of DOS commands in an MS-DOS command line window, or in a full-screen mode that emulates the DOS operating environment.

UNIX, Linux, and GNU

DOS and Windows owe much to UNIX, a command line operating system whose development began in 1969 at AT&T's Bell Laboratories by Ken Thompson and Dennis Ritchie. Many of its features have been adopted by DOS, particularly its hierarchical, directory-oriented file system and related commands. If you have used UNIX before, you will find many elements similar to, or derived from UNIX, as you learn more of the Windows 2000 command line interface.

In 1991, Linus Torvalds of Finland created Linux as a **kernel**, or core operating system program, that works like, or is a **clone** of, UNIX. The full operating system actually consists of the Linux kernel and software from the GNU (GNU's Not UNIX) project of Richard Stallman's Free Software Foundation. (GNU is a recursive acronym and an example of programmer wit.) The system is therefore more accurately referred to as GNU/Linux. A worldwide network of volunteers maintains and revises it, and GNU/Linux is freely distributed under the GNU Public License (GPL), which requires that programmers who distribute changes to Linux also make their source code public. (**Source code** is the original human-readable program code prepared by a programmer.)

GNU/Linux is a complete multitasking network operating system, which provides a powerful, stable, and inexpensive alternative to Windows 2000.

The Windows Operating Environment

In 1985, Microsoft introduced the Windows operating environment. An **operating environment** is a software product that performs the same functions as an operating system, except for booting a system and handling the storage and retrieval of data in files on a disk. Windows 3.1—the most commonly used version of the Windows operating environment in the past—was dependent on DOS to handle basic file functions in the background. Instead of displaying a command line interface in text mode, Windows 3.1 (and previous versions) used a graphical user interface. See Figure 1-2.

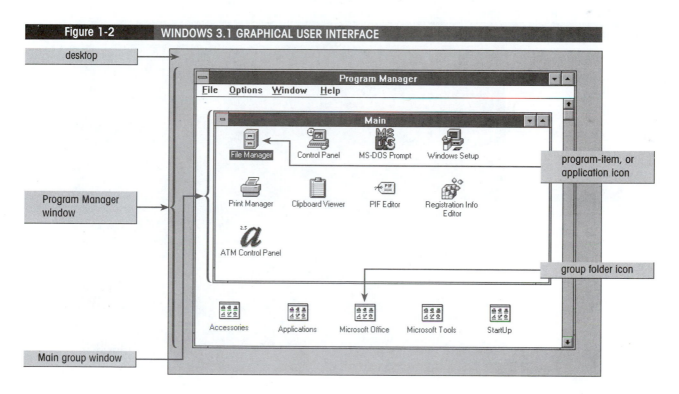

Figure 1-2   WINDOWS 3.1 GRAPHICAL USER INTERFACE

Over the years, many people used Windows 3.1, Windows 3.11, or earlier versions of Windows in conjunction with the DOS operating system. Although DOS was the predominant PC operating system from 1981 through 1995, the Windows 3.1 operating environment led to the development of the newer operating systems that most people depend on today. These new operating systems, including Windows 2000, no longer require DOS to boot and manage the computer.

The Windows 95 and Windows 98 Operating Systems

Microsoft's release of Windows 95 in the summer of 1995 marked a revolution in operating system technology, and opened the door to the development of more sophisticated operating systems like Windows NT Workstation 4.0, Windows 98, and Windows 2000. When you install Windows 95 onto a computer that contains DOS as the operating system, Windows 95 completely replaces DOS (and your previous version of the Windows operating environment) as the new operating system, unless you specify a dual-boot configuration. For example, in a Windows 95 **dual-boot configuration**, your computer would have two operating systems (such as Windows 95 and MS-DOS), and you can choose which operating system you would want to use during booting. If you chose MS-DOS, you could then launch a previous version of Windows (such as Windows 3.1). One important advantage of a dual-boot configuration is that you can still boot your computer if one of the operating systems does not work.

Like previous versions of Windows, Windows 95 displays a graphical user interface, as shown in Figure 1-3. Although its graphical user interface is different in appearance from those of previous versions of the Windows operating environment, you still interact with the Windows 95 operating system and other software using icons, windows, menus, and dialog boxes. In Windows 95, Microsoft added many new features to the operating system, some of which are available in Windows NT Workstation 4.0, and all of which are available in Windows 98 and Windows 2000.

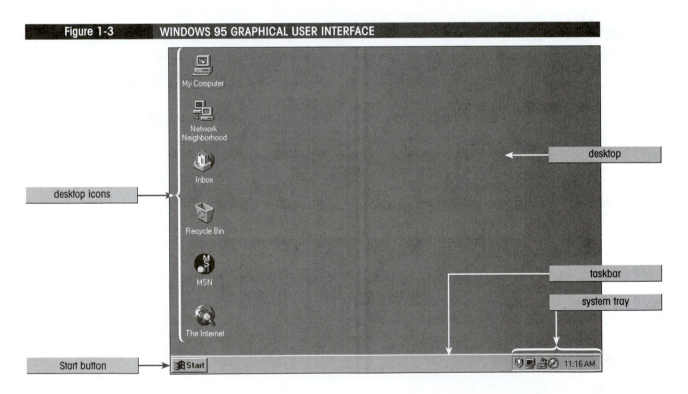

Figure 1-3   WINDOWS 95 GRAPHICAL USER INTERFACE

After introducing the original version of Windows 95, Microsoft introduced four other versions, listed in Figure 1-4. The first upgrade, Microsoft Windows 95 Service Pack 1 (also called OSR 1 or Windows 95a), included fixes to the original version of Windows 95, as well as additional components. OSR 2 (OEM Service Release 2 or Windows 95B), included Internet Explorer 3.0 and support for newer types of hardware, as well as a new file system called FAT32 that maximized the use of storage space on a hard disk. The FAT32 filing system, however, was not compatible with the FAT16 filing system used in previous versions of

Windows 95. Therefore, you could not upgrade your computer from the original version of Windows 95 (or Windows 95a) to Windows 95B by attempting to install it over your existing copy of Windows 95 (or Windows 95a). Instead, Windows 95B was installed only on new computers starting in the fall of 1996. Because some of the components in Windows 95B also worked in Windows 95 and 95a, Microsoft posted those components (called downloadable components) on its Web site. When added to Windows 95, the downloadable components make the Windows 95 interface similar to that of Windows 95B and Windows 98. OSR 2.1, a minor upgrade of Windows 95B, adds support for the universal serial bus (USB)—a high-speed communications port. OSR 2.5, or Windows 95c, included Internet Explorer 4.0, support for other online services (including an MSN 2.5 upgrade), another USB upgrade, and Internet components now found in Windows 98 and Windows 2000. (**MSN** is an abbreviation for The Microsoft Network, an Internet Service Provider, or ISP.)

Figure 1-4	VERSIONS OF WINDOWS 95		
WINDOWS 95 VERSION	**POPULAR NAME**	**WINDOWS VERSION**	**RELEASE DATE**
Original	Windows 95	Windows 4.00.950	August, 1995
OSR 1 (Microsoft Windows 95 Service Pack 1)	Windows 95a	Windows 4.00.950a	December, 1995
OSR 2.0 (OEM Service Release 2)	Windows 95B	Windows 4.00.950 B	August, 1996
OSR 2.1	Windows 95B		November, 1996
OSR 2.5	Windows 95c		January, 1998

Microsoft introduced Windows 98 in the summer of 1998. The Windows 98 graphical user interface, shown in Figure 1-5, is very similar to that of Windows 95. With Windows 98, Microsoft included all of the service pack/service release additions and expanded the role and capabilities of the Windows operating system.

Figure 1-5	WINDOWS 98 GRAPHICAL USER INTERFACE

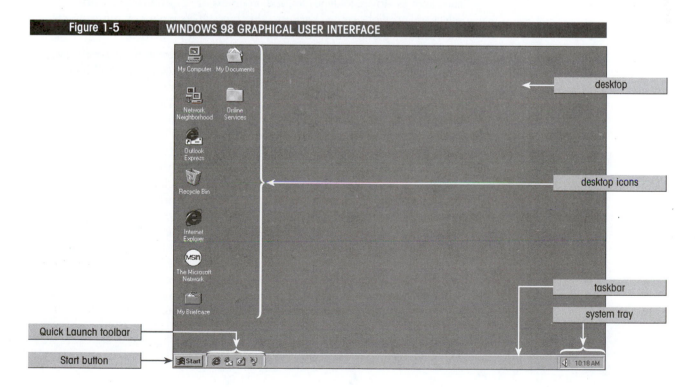

The following features are available in both Windows 95 and Windows 98:

- **Enhanced graphical user interface** The enhanced graphical user interface in Windows 95 and Windows 98 starts with the desktop. The desktop, which appears right after booting, replaces Program Manager in Windows 3.1 and is simpler in design and use. The desktop icons, such as My Computer, Network Neighborhood (or just Network), and the Recycle Bin, represent specific components of the Windows 95 and Windows 98 operating systems. The **taskbar** at the bottom of the desktop displays buttons for open programs and windows. By clicking the Start button on the taskbar, you can display a Start menu from which you can access programs, accessories, folders, files, and the Internet.

- **Document-oriented** The graphical user interface facilitated the use of a document-oriented approach rather than a program-oriented approach to opening documents. When using a **program-oriented** approach (also referred to as an application-oriented approach), you first open the software program you want to use, and then locate and open the document you want to use. This approach was required with the DOS operating system. Using a **document-oriented or docucentric** approach, you locate and open the document you want to use, and then the operating system opens the program associated with that type of document. Although this approach was available with earlier versions of Windows before Windows 95, most individuals were not aware of this approach, and therefore used the same program-oriented approach they had used under DOS. Under Windows 95, Windows 98, Windows NT Workstation 4.0, and Windows 2000, the document-oriented approach has become increasingly important to the ways in which individuals work.

- **Object-oriented interface** Windows 95 and Windows 98 (as well as Windows NT Workstation 4.0 and Windows 2000) treat components of the graphical user interface and computer as **objects**, each having discrete **properties**, or settings, that you can view and change. Hardware and software components, such as disks, drives, folders, files, and programs, are objects. As you work, you select and open objects and perform other types of operations on those objects, such as moving or renaming them, or changing their properties.

- **New system architecture** Microsoft introduced a new **system architecture**, which is the internal design and coding of an operating system, in Windows 95 and continued it in Windows 98, Windows NT Workstation 4.0, and Windows 2000. The improved system architecture takes advantage of newer types of microprocessors, such as the Pentium III, Pentium MMX, and Pentium II, as well as providing support for operating modes of earlier microprocessors, such as the 8088, 8086, 80286, 80386, and 80486 microprocessors. This system architecture also supports **multitasking**, the simultaneous or concurrent use of more than one program; **task-switching**, the ability to switch from one open task to another; and **multithreading**, the processing of separate segments of program code (called **threads**) within the same program. Multithreading is important because it allows the same program to perform multiple tasks at the same time. Even the operating system depends on multithreading for operations it performs. For example, every time you open a new window, Windows spawns a new thread from the same program (Explorer). Although you could multitask and switch from one task to another under versions of Windows earlier than Windows 95, those earlier versions of Windows did not support multithreading.

To further increase the effectiveness and reliability of Windows 95 and Windows 98, the system architecture included new design features that increased the **robustness**, or stability, of the operating system and protected important system resources. For example, the operating system allocates memory to each program you open and provides protection for that memory, so other open programs cannot access the memory used by another program. Also, each time you open a DOS program, Windows creates a **virtual DOS machine** (**VDM**), which is a complete operating environment for that particular program. The DOS program thinks it is the only program running on the computer, and that it has access to all the computer's hardware—a feature typical of DOS programs. These features ensured that a single malfunctioning program did not crash other running programs or the entire computer.

■ **Backward compatibility** Windows 95 and Windows 98 support the use of DOS programs, utilities, and games developed for all microprocessors from the original 8088 to the newest type of microprocessor. Both versions also support the use of software designed for prior versions of Windows, as well as older types of hardware devices. This ability to handle hardware and software designed for earlier systems is called **backward compatibility**. Windows 2000 continues to support the use of DOS programs, utilities, and games, as well as DOS commands.

■ **Plug and Play** Windows 95, Windows 98, and Windows 2000 support Plug and Play hardware and legacy devices. **Plug and Play** (**PnP**) refers to a set of specifications for automatically detecting and configuring hardware. Once you add a Plug and Play hardware device to your computer, the operating system automatically detects and configures the hardware device during booting, with little or no intervention on your part. In contrast, **legacy devices** are older types of hardware components that do not meet Plug and Play specifications and often require manual installation through setting jumpers or DIP switches. A **jumper** is a small metal block used to complete a circuit for two pins on a circuit board, which specifies a configuration. See Figure 1-6.

Figure 1-6	SCHEMATIC OF A JUMPER

pin

jumper (small metal block)

In contrast, a **DIP (dual in-line package) switch** is a set of toggle switches mounted on a chip, which is in turn mounted on an add-in board. See Figure 1-7. You flip a switch on or off to specify a setting. In some cases, you have to set a combination of switches to specify a setting, such as a **baud rate** (the transmission speed of a modem).

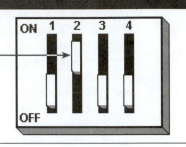

Figure 1-7	SCHEMATIC OF A DIP SWITCH

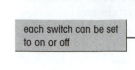

each switch can be set to on or off

DIP Switch

It is important to note that, depending on the type of hardware support built into your version of Windows 95 and Windows 98, these operating systems may or may not automatically detect legacy hardware devices during booting. If legacy devices are detected, then the operating system may only be able to configure the device as a generic, or standard device. Although the device will more than likely work, you will not have access to all the features included with that specific model.

- **Multimedia support** Windows 95 provided increased support for the use of multimedia programs and multimedia hardware (such as CD-ROM drives and sound cards), video and audio recording and playback, and the integration of graphics, video, sound, and animation within documents, as well as the user interface. Windows 98 supported even newer technologies for improving gaming, multimedia, and 3-D rendering. It also included broadcast software to receive television programming via cable, satellite, or the World Wide Web.

- **Hardware support** Windows 95 and Windows 98 provide support for existing hardware, as well as for newer types of hardware technologies. Both provide increased support for display adapters, monitors, printers, modems, and CD-ROM drives, as well as support for new Plug and Play hardware devices, **PCMCIA** (Personal Computer Memory Card International Association) devices (credit-card sized interface cards), and ECP (enhanced capabilities port) devices, such as modems.

  Windows 98 also supports new features of the Pentium III, Pentium MMX (Multimedia Extensions), Pentium II, and later microprocessors; the accelerated graphics port (AGP) for handling 3-D graphics **throughput** (the speed with which a device processes and transmits data); the **universal serial bus** (USB) for connecting multiple devices and for fast data transfer rates; digital video discs (DVDs) for storage and playback of movies; IEEE 1394 ports (also called FireWire) for connecting multiple devices and for handling throughput of video cameras, VCRs, stereos, and other consumer electronic devices; IrDA (infrared) ports for wireless communication; multiple display (the use of up to nine monitors for a "SurroundView" effect); and improved power management of desktop and portable PCs.

- **Network support** Both Windows 95 and Windows 98 are network operating systems that provide enhanced support for connecting to networks and working with network operating software, including Novell NetWare. These operating systems can interact with network program software and hardware, and access documents, e-mail, and other types of information on networks. By using Windows 95 and Windows 98, you can set up a **peer-to-peer network**, a simple network in which each computer can access other computers and share hardware, such as printers, hard disk drives, removable storage devices (such as CD-ROM, Zip, and DVD drives), as well as software, folders, and files.

A peer-to-peer network does not require a server. A **server** is a high-performance computer that manages a computer network with the use of network operating system software, such as Novell NetWare or Windows NT.

- **Support for portable computers** Windows 95 and Windows 98 include support for Dial-Up Networking (DUN) so employees traveling on business or working out of a home office can connect their portable computers to their company's network. They also include a component for linking Direct Cable Connection to a portable and desktop computer by means of a parallel or null modem cable, file synchronization between computers using My Briefcase, Advanced Power Management for managing power on a portable computer, Quick View for viewing the contents of files, Microsoft Exchange (and later Windows Messaging) for e-mail access, Microsoft Fax for sending and receiving faxes, and deferred printing.

- **Support for online services** One of the features introduced with Windows 95 (and still available in Windows 98) is the inclusion of software for access to Microsoft's own online service, The Microsoft Network (MSN). By joining MSN (or any other online service or Internet service provider), you gain access to the Internet, the World Wide Web and to other features such as e-mail, online chat rooms, and file libraries with downloadable software and multimedia files.

- **Web integration** Microsoft integrated Internet Explorer 3.0 into the Windows 95B user interface, and later integrated Internet Explorer 4.0 and 5.0 into the Windows 98 user interface. As a result, you have the option of switching the user interface to **Web style**, which supports single-click selection and launching of programs. Using Active Desktop technology, you can place the active content of Web pages on the desktop. **Active content** refers to information provided from a content provider's Web site and delivered to your desktop. For example, you may subscribe to The Weather Channel, and that Web site will periodically deliver updates on weather conditions in your local area to your desktop and display the information within a window. These versions of Windows also include other tools, such as Outlook Express, an e-mail tool; FrontPage Express, a personal Web page editor; NetMeeting, for Internet conferencing; and NetShow, for delivering streaming multimedia across the Internet. If you have an earlier version of Windows 95, you can download and install a more recent version of Internet Explorer and enjoy the benefits of Web style as well as the Active Desktop technology.

In the summer of 1999, Microsoft introduced Windows 98 Second Edition (or Windows 98 SE) as an upgrade to the original version of Windows 98. Windows 98 SE included Internet Explorer 5.0; **Internet Connection Sharing** for setting up and configuring computer networks at home so more than one computer can share a single Internet connection; new and improved hardware support such as USB modems and improved support for other types of hardware, such as IEEE 1394 and USB high-speed connections for peripherals; new and improved accessories, including a new version of NetMeeting; as well as improved support for WebTV, DirectX, and ACPI (Advanced Configuration and Power Interface), Year 2000 patches, and Service Pack 1 with "bug" fixes.

The diverse range of features in Windows 95 and Windows 98 not only expanded the role of an operating system, but also emphasized the importance of integrating programs and features to optimize the performance of a computer, to more effectively manage its resources, and to increase productivity.

The Windows NT Workstation 4.0 Operating System

In 1993, prior to the release of Windows 95, Microsoft introduced an advanced network operating system named Windows NT (for "New Technology") that supported computers with different types of microprocessors and different types of file systems. Unlike prior versions of Windows, Windows NT was an operating system in its own right and it did not require DOS to boot and manage the computer. Over the years, this operating system gained a favorable reputation, particularly in corporate and industrial programs, for its security features and its stability, as well as its ability to handle multithreading in real time.

In the summer of 1996, a year after it released Windows 95, Microsoft introduced Windows NT Workstation 4.0 for use on desktop computers. Microsoft included the Windows 95 interface in Windows NT Workstation 4.0. After you boot, you see the Windows NT Workstation 4.0 desktop which looks identical to the Windows 95 desktop. However, parts of the user interface, such as Administrative Tools, look and respond like the Windows 3.1 interface and therefore are not object oriented (you cannot right-click). Because Windows NT contains extensive security features for protecting the file system, such as not permitting DOS programs to write directly to disk, running DOS programs under Windows NT Workstation 4.0 is more difficult than under Windows 95 and Windows 98. Furthermore, Windows NT Workstation 4.0 does not support Plug and Play, has limited multimedia support, and does not support as many hardware devices as Windows 95. This release, however, introduced a network operating system for use on desktop computers that was previously used only on servers. Because of the security features available in the Windows NT product line, its history as a stable operating system, and its advanced networking features, businesses preferred Windows NT over Windows 95 and Windows 98 for use on employees' desktop computers.

The Windows 2000 Professional Operating System

The Windows 2000 Professional operating system originally started out as Windows NT 5.0, an upgrade to Windows NT Workstation 4.0, but Microsoft changed its name to Windows 2000 Professional Edition. Windows 2000 Professional incorporates the features of the different versions of Windows 95 and Windows 98 into the Windows NT product line for use on desktop computers. Among the many new features now available in Windows 2000 are the following:

- **Improved graphical user interface** All of the components of the Windows 2000 graphical user interface are similar to those of Windows 95 and Windows 98. The entire user interface is now object oriented. Like previous versions of Windows 95 and Windows 98, Internet Explorer 5.0 is integrated into the user interface so it supports Active Desktop technologies and features.

- **Support for Intel's Pentium III and Pentium III Xeon processors** Windows 2000 provides support for newer processors as well as other emerging hardware technologies. In fact, rapid changes in hardware technologies now require frequent upgrades to operating systems so the operating systems support these newer technologies.

- **Plug and Play support** Unlike its predecessor, Windows NT Workstation 4.0, Windows 2000 now supports Plug and Play hardware devices.

- **Advanced power management** Like Windows 98, Windows 2000 allows you to select or define power management schemes that control power to components on your computer, such as the monitor and hard disk, as well as consumer devices (such as VCRs) attached to your computer.

■ **Device Manager** Windows 2000 now includes Device Manager, a tool for examining the hardware configuration of your computer. Device Manager was available in Windows 98 and Windows 95, but not in Windows NT Workstation 4.0.

■ **Support for different file systems** Windows 2000 supports NTFS, the Windows NT native file system, as well as the FAT16 and FAT32 file systems supported by Windows 98 and Windows 95. If you are using NTFS, you can set disk quotas that control the amount of space used on a hard disk by individuals and workgroups.

■ **Utilities for system maintenance and system recovery** Windows 2000 includes Disk Defragmenter, a utility for optimizing the arrangement of programs and data on disks. This utility is not available in Windows NT Workstation 4.0, but is available in Windows 95 and Windows 98.

■ **Windows Update** Like Windows 98, Windows 2000 includes a Windows Update wizard that connects you to Microsoft's Web site, examines the installed software on your computer, and recommends software updates, device driver updates, and add-on components for your computer.

Upgrading to Windows 2000 from Windows NT Workstation 4.0, Windows 98, or Windows 95 affects users in other important ways as well, such as:

■ **Computer compatibility** Before you install Windows 2000 on your computer, you should check Microsoft's Windows 2000 Update Web site to determine if your computer can run Windows 2000.

■ **BIOS compatibility** In order to take advantage of the new power management features in Windows 2000, your computer must have an ACPI (Advanced Configuration and Power Interface) BIOS. You might need to obtain a BIOS update from the manufacturer of your BIOS.

■ **Hardware compatibility** Windows 2000 has strict hardware requirements. In fact, prior to installing Windows 2000, you need to compare the information you have about your computer's hardware components with Microsoft's Hardware Compatibility List (HCL) (on the Windows 2000 CD or at Microsoft's Windows 2000 Update Web site) to make sure Windows 2000 will support those hardware devices. Windows 2000 does not support the use of Windows 98, Windows 95, Windows 3.x, and DOS device drivers, but instead requires new device drivers for many peripheral devices and hardware controllers. When you install Windows 2000 as an upgrade to Windows 95 or Windows 98, the Setup program examines your computer and prepares a report that identifies which hardware devices will not work with Windows 2000 and recommends that you obtain upgraded drivers from the manufacturer of those hardware devices. If you are upgrading from Windows NT Workstation 4.0, Setup identifies hardware that is not supported by Windows 2000 at the beginning of the upgrade process.

■ **Software compatibility** You might need to upgrade your software and obtain versions designed specifically for Windows 2000. Programs that work under Windows 95 or Windows 98 might not work under Windows 2000. When you install Windows 2000 as an upgrade to Windows 95 or Windows 98, the Setup program examines your computer and prepares a report that identifies which programs and utilities will not work with Windows 2000.

You can download and install a program called the Readiness Analyzer from Microsoft's Windows 2000 Update Web site to check whether your computer is compatible with Windows 2000. The Readiness Analyzer will analyze the hardware and software on your computer, and provide a detailed report on incompatibility problems that it finds.

Windows 2000 Professional is the next important step in operating system technology and, not surprisingly, it builds on the successes of previous versions of Windows.

The Importance of the Command Line

Before upgrading the company's computer systems to Windows 2000, Isabel learned that Windows 2000 not only offers many new features for enhancing and optimizing the performance of computers, but also provides support for the DOS programs that businesses and companies have used over the years.

As noted earlier, from 1981 through 1995, DOS was the primary operating system used on PCs by both businesses and millions of home users around the world. During that time, DOS programs, utilities, and games proliferated.

Here are some reasons why an understanding of DOS and command line skills remains important:

- **Understanding Windows 2000 concepts and features** Windows 2000, like all other versions of Windows, relies on a feature called the full path to locate and open programs and other types of files, such as documents, on the hard disk. The **full path** identifies the exact location of a file and includes the name of the drive, and the sequence of folders to locate and open that file. For example, when you click a program shortcut on the desktop, Windows 2000 uses the full path of that program to locate and open the program. The full path is a feature first introduced with the DOS operating system, which is essential to the proper functioning of Windows 2000 (and all other versions of Windows). You will examine the full path in more detail in Tutorial 4.

- **Backward compatibility with DOS program** Windows 2000 provides backward compatibility with the DOS operating system, as well as software originally designed for DOS and Windows version 3. Some DOS programs did not function properly under Windows 3.1 because they needed direct access to system resources, including memory, and therefore you had to start the program from the DOS prompt rather than from Windows 3.1. DOS games, in particular, did not function well under Windows 3.1 because the software for these games assumed they were the only program running on the system. Furthermore, they placed heavy demands on the resources within a computer. Although DOS and Windows 3.1 handled access to hardware within a computer, the software for DOS games attempted to bypass DOS and Windows 3.1 and interact directly with the computer's hardware, thus creating conflicts with Windows 3.1. Under Windows 2000, you can open DOS programs from a Command Prompt window (known as the MS-DOS Prompt window in Windows 98 and Windows 95). Depending on how you set up your system, you can even open DOS programs from the Start menu or by using a desktop shortcut.

- **Configuring legacy devices** The MS-DOS subsystem is important in configuring legacy devices, or what are now called non-Plug and Play devices, for use under Windows 2000. Although Windows 2000 provides support for Plug and Play technologies, many individuals still have legacy devices, such as CD-ROM drives, modems, and sound cards, installed on their computers. For these legacy devices to work properly, you may need to configure these devices by using Device Manager and perhaps even by modifying the MS-DOS system startup or configuration files (called Config.sys and Autoexec.bat) and the Windows 2000 system startup or configuration files (called Config.nt and Autoexec.nt). Also, knowing how DOS interacts with hardware components is invaluable when using Windows 2000 components, such as Device Manager, to evaluate and assign resources to hardware.

■ **Removing computer viruses** With some operating systems, if a computer virus infects your hard disk drive, you may need to start your computer from a boot disk in drive A, and then run a DOS-based program from a command line interface to scan drive C and remove the computer virus. Because many programs and utilities cannot run from either a command line interface or from a disk with limited storage space, you may need to rely on a program that operates in a command line environment to clean your system. However, you need to make sure that program supports the use of long file-names and the type of file system used on the drive you check.

■ **Troubleshooting system, software, and hardware problems** Command line skills are important for troubleshooting Windows 2000 problems. If Windows 2000 does not start or if you experience a problem with your hard disk drive, you can boot your computer to a command prompt from the Windows 2000 Advanced Options Menu. Then you can attempt to troubleshoot problems, make backups, and restore important Windows 2000 system files. If you use Windows 2000 Help Troubleshooters (for example, to identify and resolve a printing problem), you may find that it recommends you open a Command Prompt window and use DOS commands to troubleshoot the problem. If you contact technical support to help you with a problem, you may be asked to examine, and perhaps change configuration settings and configuration files, and work with a command prompt. Likewise, if you have to rebuild a computer system from scratch, you need to know how to work in a DOS environment, use DOS commands, configure your startup system files, and install device drivers in order to gain access to your computer and reinstall Windows 2000.

■ **Managing the use of different types of computer systems with different operating systems** To maximize their investment in computer systems, businesses typically retain computer systems as long as is feasible, and then gradually replace much older systems with newer ones. Therefore, some employees work on older computer systems that do not support more recent versions of Windows, which require a minimum type of microprocessor (such as a Pentium chip), a minimum clock speed (such as 133 MHz), and a minimum amount of RAM (such as 64 MB). **Clock speed** is the speed at which a microprocessor executes instructions, and it is measured in megahertz (MHz)— millions of cycles per second. Technical support staff and employees, therefore, must be familiar with different operating systems, including MS-DOS.

■ **Training** If you are a corporate trainer or an educator, you should know how to use the command line in the event you need to troubleshoot problems on computers used for training employees or students; you may be the only person with the knowledge of the command line necessary to resolve problems that occur immediately prior to, or during, a training session.

■ **Network administration, setup, installation, configuration, and troubleshooting** If you are a network administrator, specialist, or technician, you will need to know MS-DOS commands and how to work in a command line environment under Windows 2000 so you can install, configure, and troubleshoot network problems. At many colleges, knowing command line skills is a requirement for taking a networking course and learning how to use network operating systems—including Windows NT, Novell NetWare, and UNIX.

■ **Professional certification** To acquire certification in certain specialties, such as a microcomputer specialist, a network specialist, or even as a Windows 2000 specialist, you have to prove competency in the use of DOS commands and a command line operating environment.

■ **Power user skills Power users** are more advanced users who gradually develop a broad base of skills that are invaluable in many different types of situations, such as designing and automating the use of custom programs, troubleshooting problems, providing support for other users, and setting up computer systems from scratch.

Since the introduction of Windows 95, there has been a gradual transition from computers that use the DOS operating system to those that use Windows 95, Windows 98, Windows NT Workstation 4.0, and now Windows 2000. DOS concepts and skills, however, still remain important no matter which operating system you use.

The Windows XP Appendix at the end of the book provides additional information about the Windows ME, Windows XP Professional, and Windows XP Home Edition operating systems. The Appendix also includes updates to the topics covered in this textbook, and Help information on how to complete the tutorials with Windows XP. As you step through the tutorials, you can turn to the Appendix if you have questions about completing part of a tutorial and to also learn about new features in Windows XP.

Session 1.1   QUICK CHECK

1. A(n) _____ is a software product that manages the basic processes that occur within a computer, coordinates the interaction of hardware and software, and provides support for the use of other types of software.

2. _____ refers to the process of powering on a computer system and loading the operating system into memory.

3. Operating systems typically include a variety of _____, or programs, for optimizing the performance of your computer.

4. The DOS operating system uses a(n) _____ interface in which you communicate with the operating system by typing a command after a(n) _____.

5. In a(n) _____ configuration, your computer has two operating systems (such as Windows 2000 and MS-DOS), and during booting, you can choose the operating system you want to use.

6. The _____ identifies the exact location of a file on a disk, and includes the name of the drive and the sequence of directories to locate and open that file.

7. The ability of an operating system to handle hardware and software designed for earlier systems is called _____.

8. A(n) _____ is a complete operating environment under Windows for a DOS program.

9. In _____, the computer monitor displays only text, numbers, symbols, and a small set of graphics characters, using white, amber, or green characters on a black background.

10. A(n) _____ is an instruction to perform a specific task, such as format a diskette.

SESSION 1.2

examine the difference between internal and external commands, and you will use both types of commands in the command line session. You will customize the Command Prompt window, display the current Windows 2000 version, change the date and time, clear the window, and format a diskette. After evaluating the use of storage space on the formatted diskette, you will make a copy of a diskette. Finally, you will close the Command Prompt window, and then log off your computer.

Starting Windows 2000

So her technical support staff and other employees can develop the practical skills they need for working in command line sessions under Windows 2000, Isabel asks you and the other employees in the workshop to start Windows 2000 and set up your computer for the hands-on portion of the first workshop.

How you start Windows 2000 will depend on whether your computer's power is already on, whether your computer uses a dual-boot (or multi-boot) configuration, whether you are connected to a network, whether Windows 2000 requires you to provide a user name and password to log onto a network, and whether someone else has already powered on or logged onto the computer previously (if you are working in a computer lab or an environment where users share the same computer).

If you need to power on your computer first, complete the next section, entitled "Powering On Your Computer." If your computer is already on, and if you see the Windows 2000 desktop, then skip the next section ("Powering On Your Computer"), and complete the section entitled "Logging Onto a Network."

Note: As mentioned earlier, this book assumes that the student already has a working knowledge of the Windows 2000 operating system, such as logging on to Windows 2000 under different user accounts.

Powering On Your Computer

Complete this section only if you need to power on your computer. If your computer is already on, skip this section and continue with the next section, entitled "Logging On to a Network."

To power on your computer and start Windows 2000:

1. Turn on the power to your computer. During the boot process, your computer may display technical information about your computer (such as information about the drives in your computer) as well as startup operations (such as the results of the POST memory test) before the operating system actually starts loading.

2. If you see a Startup Menu prompting you to select the operating system to use, select **Microsoft Windows 2000 Professional** from the menu (it may already be selected as the default operating system to use), and then press **Enter** (it may automatically start after 30 seconds). Then, you will see a Windows 2000 progress indicator. The next screen displays the Microsoft Windows 2000 Professional logo and another Starting up progress indicator. The following screen displays a Please wait dialog box, and you finally see a Log On to Windows dialog box that prompts for your user name and password.

3. If your computer does not require you to log on, and if you see the Windows 2000 desktop, skip the next section, entitled "Logging On to Windows 2000," and continue with the section entitled "Opening a command line Session"; otherwise enter your user name (if necessary) and password, and then press Enter (or click OK)."

REFERENCE | WINDOW   **RW**

Powering On Your Computer and Starting Windows 2000
- Turn on the power switch.
- If you see a Startup Menu prompting you to select the operating system, select "Microsoft Windows 2000 Professional" from the OS Choices Startup Menu (it may already be selected as the default operating system to use), and press Enter (it may automatically start on its own after 30 seconds).
- If Windows 2000 displays a Log On to Windows dialog box, enter your user name and password, and then press Enter (or click OK).

Logging On to Windows 2000

If you work on a shared computer, or if you are using a computer in a computer lab, you may need to log off that computer and then log on to the network under your own user account so you have access to the resources and files you need to use. Rather than restart your computer, you can use log off, and then log on again under your user account.

To log off, and then on to, Windows 2000:

1. Click the **Start** button and, if there is a Log Off option on the Start menu, click **Log Off**; otherwise, click **Shut Down**.

2. If you chose the Log Off option, click **Yes** in the Log Off Windows dialog box. If you chose Shut Down, click the **What do you want the computer to do?** list arrow in the Shut Down Windows dialog box, click the **Log off** option for your user name, and then click **OK**.

   TROUBLE? If the Shut Down Windows dialog box does not contain an option for logging off the current account (whatever its name may be), click Cancel to interrupt the Shut Down process and return to the desktop.

3. If you are prompted to "press Ctrl-Alt-Delete to begin", press and hold the **Ctrl** and **Alt** keys, press the **Delete** key, then release all three keys.

4. After Windows displays the Log On to Windows dialog box, enter your user name and password, and then click the **OK** button or press **Enter**. You may see a Restoring Network Connections dialog box before Windows 2000 displays the desktop, shown in Figure 1-8. Because you can customize the Windows 2000 desktop, your desktop view may differ from that shown in this figure.

   TROUBLE? If you are working in a computer lab, your instructor and lab support staff will tell you what user name and password you should use. Your network connection may also require a server name.

   TROUBLE? If Windows 2000 displays a "Welcome to Windows 2000" dialog box with options for registering Windows 2000, connecting to the Internet, discovering Windows 2000, and maintaining your computer, click the Close ☒ button.

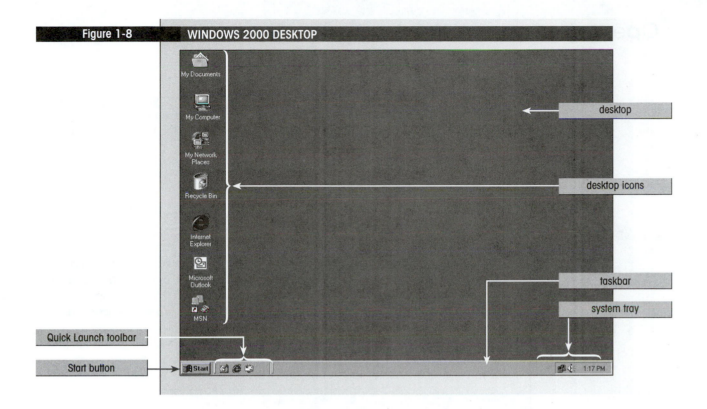

Figure 1-8   WINDOWS 2000 DESKTOP

REFERENCE WINDOW   RW

Logging Off, and Logging On to, Windows 2000

■ Click the Start button and, if there is a Log Off option on the Start menu, click Log Off; otherwise, click Shut Down.

■ If you chose the Log Off option, click Yes in the Log Off Windows dialog box. If you chose Shut Down, click the "What do you want the computer to do?" list arrow in the Shut Down Windows dialog box, click the Log off option for your user name, and then click OK.

■ After Windows displays the Log On to Windows dialog box, enter your user name and password, and then click the OK button or press Enter.

As noted earlier, if you work on a computer network, it's important to log on to the network under the proper account so you can access the resources you need. Windows 2000 supports different user logons (or accounts) and different user groups. For example, if you are working in a college computer lab, the network administrator may set up your class logon for a Standard User or a Restricted User. Both types of users can use software and create and save documents. A **Standard User** is part of the Power Users Group and can modify computer settings and install software. In contrast, a **Restricted User** is part of the Users Group and cannot install software or change system settings. Finally, an **Administrator** is part of the Administrators group and has complete access to, and control over, all parts of the Windows 2000 system, including creation and management of user accounts and permissions.

Opening a Command Line Session

Next, Isabel shows you and the other workshop participants how to open a command line session under Windows 2000.

There are several ways in which you can start a command line session, or work in a command line environment under Windows 2000. The most common way is to open the Command Prompt window from the Accessories menu. Then, you can work from within a window on the desktop.

To open a command line session:

1. Click the **Start** button, point to **Programs**, point to **Accessories**, and then click **Command Prompt**. Windows 2000 opens a Command Prompt window. See Figure 1-9. Within the Command Prompt window, you first see the name and version of the operating system—in this case, the original version of Windows 2000. As noted earlier, C:\> is called the operating system prompt, or command prompt, and it is your reference point as you work in this command line interface. This command prompt, which used to be known as the **DOS prompt**, is now called the **Windows prompt**. Many people also referred to this prompt as the "C prompt." To the right of the command prompt is a small blinking underscore called a **cursor**. The cursor identifies your current working position on the screen. If you type a character, that character is displayed on the screen where the cursor was positioned. The cursor then appears after the character you typed.

Figure 1-9	COMMAND PROMPT WINDOW

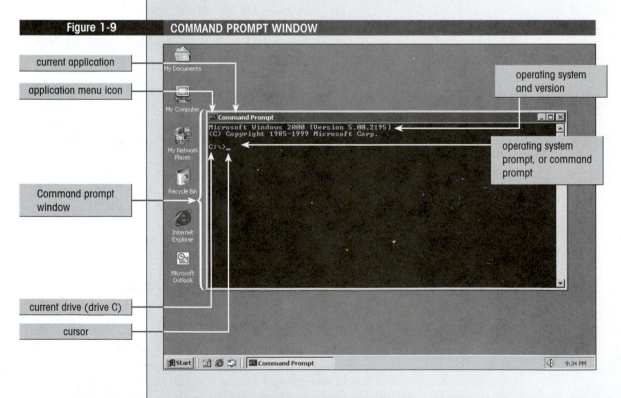

current application

application menu icon

operating system and version

Command prompt window

operating system prompt, or command prompt

current drive (drive C)

cursor

The operating system prompt identifies the default drive and default directory. The **default drive** is the drive currently in use—in this case, drive C (represented by "C" in C:\>). The default drive is important because Windows 2000 automatically checks that drive for the appropriate program file when you issue a command. When working in a command line environment (whether MS-DOS or a

Command Prompt window under Windows 2000), **directory** is the term commonly used to refer to a folder. The **default directory**, represented by the backslash symbol (\ ) in C:\>, is the top-level folder of the drive. This top-level folder is called the **root directory** when working in a command line environment. It's also important to emphasize that the view you see within the Command Prompt window is typical of that found in a command line interface. In contrast to the Windows 2000 graphical user interface, the command line interface is a very simple user interface in which text is displayed in light grey against a black background.

2. While pressing and holding the **Alt** key, press and release the **Enter** key, and then release the **Alt** key. Windows 2000 switches to full-screen view. See Figure 1-10. Certain programs, such as graphics programs, work better in full-screen view than in windowed view, or you might prefer more space on the screen for working in a command line session under Windows 2000. However, if you want to use the Windows 2000 Clipboard to copy information from a DOS program to a Windows 2000 program, or vice versa, you have to work in the windowed view. (The **Clipboard** is an area of memory where Windows 2000 stores data that you want to copy or move.)

| Figure 1-10 | FULL-SCREEN VIEW |

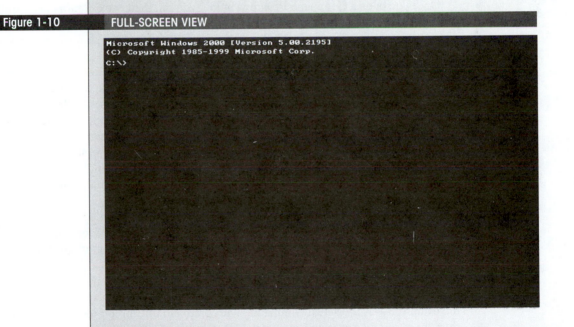

```
Microsoft Windows 2000 [Version 5.00.2195]
(C) Copyright 1985-1999 Microsoft Corp.
C:\>
```

3. Press **Alt+Enter** again to switch back to windowed view. The Alt+Enter shortcut key combination lets you quickly switch from a windowed view to a full-screen view, or vice versa.

4. Keep the Command Prompt window open for the next section.

| REFERENCE | WINDOW | | RW |

Opening a Command Line Session
- Click the Start button, point to Programs, point to Accessories, and then click Command Prompt.
- If you want to switch from windowed view to full-screen view (or vice versa), press and hold the Alt key, press and release the Enter key, and then release the Alt key.

After Windows 2000 opens a Command Prompt window, you are working in **MS-DOS mode**—a shell that emulates the MS-DOS operating environment using Windows 2000's MS-DOS subsystem. A **shell** is a program that acts as an intermediary between you and the underlying operating system. It provides an interface that allows you to issue commands or activate functions, and then translates your directives into more basic instructions the computer can carry out. In the MS-DOS command line subsystem, you are communicating with the Windows 2000 operating system underneath. You are not actually working with a version of DOS installed on and directly controlling your computer.

Using Windows 2000 Commands

Before introducing employees to some basic commands, Isabel first describes the two types of commands available for use in a Command Prompt window.

When you open a Command Prompt window, Windows 2000 opens and runs a program called Cmd.exe. The "exe" in the filename is a file extension that identifies the file as an "executable" program file. This type of program is called a **command interpreter**, **command processor**, or **shell**, because it is responsible for displaying the user interface, interpreting commands entered at the command prompt, and locating and loading the program for a specific command.

Once you open a Command Prompt window, you can then enter commands at the command prompt to perform specific operations. These commands used to be called DOS commands, but now they are called Windows 2000 commands. The commands fall into two groups: internal commands and external commands.

The program code for **internal commands** (also called built-in commands) is stored as a set of subprograms within the command interpreter program file, Cmd.exe. These subprograms are used for common types of operations, such as viewing information about files stored on a disk. When you open a command line session, Windows 2000 loads, or copies, Cmd.exe from disk into RAM. Then, Cmd.exe displays a command line user interface with a command prompt. Once Cmd.exe loads into memory, you can access the program code for any of the internal commands it contains. Since the operating system does not have to go back to disk to locate and load the program code for an internal command (it's already in memory), internal commands execute more quickly.

In contrast, the program code for **external commands** (also called utilities) must be located and loaded from disk. The program code for these commands resides in a specific file on disk in the System32 folder, which in turn is below your Windows directory (or folder). Depending on how Windows 2000 was installed on your computer, the Windows directory might be named WINNT, Windows, or perhaps have some other name. When you type an external command at the command prompt, you type the first part of the filename—the part before the file extension—as the actual command. The command interpreter locates the file on disk, and then loads the program into memory so that it can perform its intended function. Since the program code must be located and loaded from disk, external commands are slower.

Customizing the Command Prompt Window

In addition to customizing the Windows 2000 desktop, Isabel explains to you and the other workshop participants that you can also customize a Command Prompt window so the command line environment is easier to use and, at the same time, more interesting.

One simple way to customize the Command Prompt window is to change the title displayed on the title bar. To make this change, you use the TITLE command, which is an internal command. Like every other type of command, the TITLE command has a specific syntax.

Syntax refers to the proper format for entering a command, including how to spell the command, and whether the command uses required or optional parameters. A **parameter** is an item of data used with a command to change the way the command works. The TITLE command has the following syntax:

TITLE string

This command consists of two parts: the command itself (TITLE), and a parameter called a string. A **string** consists of a set of characters that are treated exactly as you enter them. For example, to change the title on the title bar from "Command Prompt" to "DOS Session," you would enter the following command:

TITLE DOS Session

In this example, "DOS Session" is a string that is used as the parameter for the TITLE command. When you enter a command, you can use uppercase, lowercase, or mixed case for the command itself. Windows 2000 will display the string in whatever case you prefer to use. This setting is not permanent. If you exit a Command Prompt window, and then open the Command Prompt window again later, Windows 2000 displays "Command Prompt" on the title bar. The TITLE command is found in Windows 2000 and Windows NT; Windows 95 and Windows 98 do not include this command.

Another way to customize the Command Prompt window is to change the background and foreground colors of the console with the use of the COLOR command—another internal command. The term **console** refers to the video display device—in this case, the monitor. The COLOR command is another command found in Windows 2000 and Windows NT. The syntax for this command is as follows:

COLOR *[attribute]*

After you enter the command, you specify an optional parameter called an **attribute** that determines the background color of the Command Prompt window and the foreground color of the text within this window. This command does not affect the desktop, only the Command Prompt window. Optional parameters are commonly indicated by including a reference to the parameter (in this example, "attribute") within square brackets. Therefore, you can enter the command with or without the optional parameter. If you enter the command COLOR without the optional parameter, Windows 2000 restores the console to the original colors used when you first opened the Command Prompt window. If you want to change the background and foreground colors in the Command Prompt window, you enter two hexadecimal digits (or values) for the attribute. A **hexadecimal digit** is a value in the hexadecimal, or base 16, numbering system. The values include 0-9 and A-F (for a total of 16 values). Figure 1-11 lists the hexadecimal digits for the background and foreground colors.

Figure 1-11	COLOR ATTRIBUTES			
hex digits				

0	Black		8	Gray
1	Blue		9	Light Blue
2	Green		A	Light Green
3	Aqua		B	Light Aqua
4	Red		C	Light Red
5	Purple		D	Light Purple
6	Yellow		E	Light Yellow
7	White		F	Bright White

corresponding color

For example, if you want to change the background color to blue and the foreground color to bright white, you would enter the following command:

COLOR 1F

Unlike the TITLE command, the COLOR command uses two parameters instead of one. When you next open a Command Prompt window, Windows 2000 reverts back to the original background color (black) and the original foreground color (light gray).

In the next set of steps, you are going to change the title in the title bar, and change the background and foreground colors of the Command Prompt window.

To customize the Command Prompt window:

1. At the command prompt, type **TITLE DOS Session** and then press **Enter**. The TITLE command changes the title on the title bar to "DOS Session," as shown in Figure 1-12, and then displays another command prompt so you can enter another command. The new title more clearly identifies what you are doing. If you make a typing mistake and notice it before you press the Enter key, you can use the Backspace key to correct the error. When you press the Enter key after entering a command at the command prompt, Windows 2000 locates and executes the instructions for the command. If you type a command and do not press Enter, nothing will happen.

   TROUBLE? If Windows 2000 informs you that the command you entered is not recognized as an internal or external command, operable program, or batch file, then you misspelled the command. Don't worry though; Windows 2000 displays another command prompt so you can try again. Just type the command again with the correct spelling and then press Enter.

Figure 1-12	CHANGING THE WINDOW TITLE

new title

command

```
DOS Session                                                    _ □ ×
Microsoft Windows 2000 [Version 5.00.2195]
(C) Copyright 1985-1999 Microsoft Corp.

C:\>TITLE DOS Session
C:\>
```

string

2. At the command prompt, type **COLOR 1F** (the number "1" followed by an upper-case "F") and then press **Enter**. Windows 2000 changes the background color to dark bright blue and the text color to bright white. See Figure 1-13.

   TROUBLE? If Windows 2000 displays Help information on the use of the Color command, you typed the lowercase letter "l" instead of the number "1". Press the Spacebar to continue (if necessary) and, at the next command prompt, repeat the step.

Figure 1-13	CHANGING THE BACKGROUND AND FOREGROUND COLORS

color attributes

command

```
DOS Session
Microsoft Windows 2000 [Version 5.00.2195]
(C) Copyright 1985-1999 Microsoft Corp.

C:\>TITLE DOS Session
C:\>COLOR 1F
C:\>
```

foreground color of text (bright white)

background color (dark blue)

3. Type **COLOR F0** (an "F" followed by a zero) and then press **Enter**. The Color command changes the background to bright white, and the foreground text to black. See Figure 1-14.

| Figure 1-14 | CHANGING THE BACKGROUND AND FOREGROUND COLORS |

changes background to bright white and foreground text to black

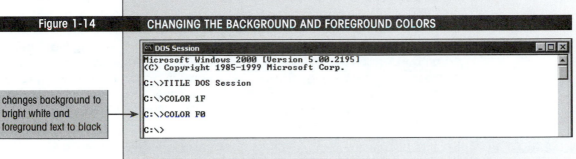

4. Keep the Command Prompt window open for the next section.

REFERENCE WINDOW **RW**

Customizing the Command Prompt Window
- To change the title on the Command Prompt window title bar, type TITLE, press the Spacebar, type the text you want to use for the title, and then press Enter.
- To change the background and foreground colors of the Command Prompt window, type COLOR, press the Spacebar, and type the color codes (or attributes) for the background and foreground colors.

In a Command Prompt window, the default screen colors are hard to read when demonstrating some programs and programming languages. By changing these colors, however, you can make your presentation easier to view.

Displaying the Windows 2000 Version

Isabel reminds you and the other staff members that, if you need to contact Microsoft technical support for assistance with troubleshooting a problem, one of the first questions the technical support representative will ask is what version of Windows you are using on your computer. You should therefore be able to check and verify the Windows version quickly so the technical support representative has an essential piece of information to help identify the source of the problem and find a solution to that problem.

Knowing the version of the operating system used on a computer is useful for several reasons. First, each operating system, and each version of an operating system, has different features and capabilities. If you attempt to perform a certain operation and experience difficulties, you should check the version of the operating system you are using so you can determine whether it contains the feature you want to use.

Second, if you are experiencing difficulties in using a program on your computer system, you should verify that the program is compatible with the specific version of the operating system installed on your computer. Likewise, when you purchase a new software product, the instructions for that new software product may indicate that the product is designed for a specific version of Windows. Before you install the software, you should check the Windows version on your computer to make sure the product will work properly.

If you are working in a Command Prompt window, you can quickly identify the version of Windows used on your computer using the Version (VER) command, which is an internal command.

To check the Windows version:

1. At the command prompt, type **VER** and then press **Enter**. Windows 2000 displays the version number of the operating system used on your computer. See Figure 1-15. This information should match what you see when you first open the Command Prompt window; however, that information may scroll off the screen as you continue to work, so you can always check the version using the Version command. Version 5.00.2195 is the original version of Windows 2000. Your version number may differ. You can also locate this same information by viewing properties of My Computer. Windows 2000 then lists the current version of the operating system on the General property sheet in the System Properties dialog box.

Figure 1-15	CHECKING THE WINDOWS VERSION

```
DOS Session                                          _ □ X
Microsoft Windows 2000 [Version 5.00.2195]
(C) Copyright 1985-1999 Microsoft Corp.

C:\>TITLE DOS Session

C:\>COLOR 1F

C:\>COLOR F0

C:\>VER                                              command

Microsoft Windows 2000 [Version 5.00.2195]          operating system and
C:\>_                                                version number
```

2. Keep the Command Prompt window open for the next section.

The Version command provides similar information under different versions of MS-DOS, Windows 95, Windows 98, and Windows NT Workstation 4.0.

Changing the Date and Time

Isabel next illustrates how to check and change the date and time quickly in a Command Prompt window. She emphasizes that the correct date and time are important because Windows 2000 records the date and time with the filename when you save a file. Then, for example, if you have two versions of a document stored in two different files, you can check the date and time saved to each file to determine which file contains the most recent version of that document. Therefore, you want to make sure that any files you create and save have the correct **date stamp** and **time stamp**. If you notice that the date or time is incorrect on your computer, you can use the DATE and TIME commands to change the date or time setting.

The DATE and TIME commands are internal commands, and their syntax is as follows:

DATE [/T | *date*]
TIME [/T | *time*]

The vertical bar (|) in this syntax diagram indicates that you can use one of the two optional parameters, but not both at the same time (they are mutually exclusive). A **Syntax diagram** is notation used in the Help system and computer reference manuals when you are looking up the options for using a command. The two optional parameters are the /T switch and the setting for either the date or the time.

For example, the syntax for the DATE command indicates that you can enter this command in one of three ways:

DATE
DATE /T
DATE *date*

If you just enter the command DATE, this program displays the current date and prompts you for a new date. If you enter the DATE command with the /T switch, this program displays the current date—it does not prompt you for a new date. A **switch** is an optional parameter that changes the way in which a command works.

If you enter the DATE command and include a specific date (such as 9-22-2003), this program will change the date. As shown, when you enter a specific date you use the general format *mm-dd-yy*. Type one or two digits for the month, a dash, one or two digits for the day, a dash, and the last two digits of the year. You can also use four digits for the year.

If you want to change the time setting on your computer, you can enter the command TIME, and wait for the command to prompt you; or you can enter TIME followed by a specific time in the format *hours:minutes:seconds.hundredths* A | P . The "A | P" means that you can specify A for "AM" or "P" for "PM", but not both at the same time.

In the next set of steps, you are going to look at different ways to use these commands.

To view and change the date setting on your computer:

1. Type **DATE /T** and then press **Enter**. On the next available line, the DATE command reports the date setting on your computer and also includes the day of the week. See Figure 1-16.

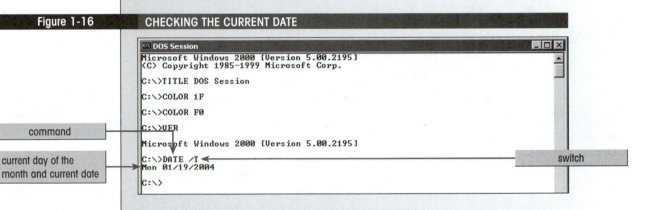

| Figure 1-16 | CHECKING THE CURRENT DATE |

Next, you will examine a variation of the DATE command that allows you to enter a specific date.

2. Press the **F3** key. Windows 2000 displays the previous command that you entered. See Figure 1-17. The F3 key is called the Repeat key, and you can use it to recall the previously entered command. You can also use the Up Arrow key ↑ to recall the previous command (you will examine the use of this key and others in more detail later).

TROUBLE? If F3 does not work, you may have pressed Enter twice after the last command you typed. In that case, you will have to type the DATE command again and then press Enter.

Figure 1-17   RECALLING THE PREVIOUS COMMAND

```
DOS Session                                                    _ □ ×
Microsoft Windows 2000 [Version 5.00.2195]
(C) Copyright 1985-1999 Microsoft Corp.

C:\>TITLE DOS Session

C:\>COLOR 1F

C:\>COLOR F0

C:\>VER

Microsoft Windows 2000 [Version 5.00.2195]

C:\>DATE /T
Mon 01/19/2004

C:\>DATE /T
```

command recalled with F3

press Backspace to delete this switch

3. Press the **Backspace** key *three* times to delete the /T switch and the space (see Figure 1-18), and then press **Enter**. Again, the DATE command displays the current date, with the day of the week. On the line after the one with the current date, the DATE command displays a prompt for you to enter a new date. See Figure 1-18. The DATE command also shows you the proper format for entering a date—namely, mm-dd-yy.

Figure 1-18   CHANGING THE DATE

```
DOS Session - DATE                                            _ □ ×
Microsoft Windows 2000 [Version 5.00.2195]
(C) Copyright 1985-1999 Microsoft Corp.

C:\>TITLE DOS Session

C:\>COLOR 1F

C:\>COLOR F0

C:\>VER

Microsoft Windows 2000 [Version 5.00.2195]

C:\>DATE /T
Mon 01/19/2004

C:\>DATE
The current date is: Mon 01/19/2004
Enter the new date: (mm-dd-yy)
```

edited command

current day with the month, day, and year

prompt to enter a new date

format for entering a new date

4. Type the date of your next birthday. For example, if your next birthday is September 22, 2004, type **9-22-04** and then press **Enter**. Windows 2000 displays a command prompt again. You have just recalled and edited a previously-entered command so you can use it in a different way. Notice that you do not type the day of the week. The operating system has a calendar that determines the day of the week from the date (for example, September 22, 2004 is a Wednesday).

TROUBLE? If you enter the date in the incorrect format, the DATE command will prompt you for the date again.

If you now open a program, and then create and save a file, Windows 2000 would record your birthday as the date the file was saved. That date would be incorrect. Let's change the date back to the current date.

5. Type **DATE**, press the **Spacebar**, type the current date in the format *mm-dd-yy*, and then press **Enter**. Even though it does not show you the change, the DATE command changed the date to the date you specified.

6. Type **TIME /T** and then press **Enter**. Windows 2000 displays the current time on the computer. See Figure 1-19. If the time were incorrect, you could use F3 to recall this command, delete the /T switch, and then enter the correct time.

| Figure 1-19 | CHECKING THE CURRENT TIME |

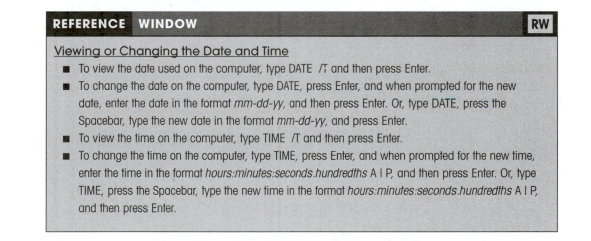

command

current time

7. Keep the Command Prompt window open for the next section.

| REFERENCE | WINDOW | RW |

Viewing or Changing the Date and Time

- To view the date used on the computer, type DATE /T and then press Enter.
- To change the date on the computer, type DATE, press Enter, and when prompted for the new date, enter the date in the format *mm-dd-yy*, and then press Enter. Or, type DATE, press the Spacebar, type the new date in the format *mm-dd-yy*, and press Enter.
- To view the time on the computer, type TIME /T and then press Enter.
- To change the time on the computer, type TIME, press Enter, and when prompted for the new time, enter the time in the format *hours:minutes:seconds.hundredths* A I P, and then press Enter. Or, type TIME, press the Spacebar, type the new time in the format *hours:minutes:seconds.hundredths* A I P, and then press Enter.

As noted earlier, if you know in advance what date you want to use, you can type the DATE command followed by the date. For example, if you want to change the date to July 9, 2003, you enter DATE 7-9-03. Windows 2000 will not prompt you for the date and will not show you the date change.

The DATE and TIME commands work in the same way under MS-DOS, Windows 95, Windows 98, and Windows NT Workstation 4.0; however, MS-DOS, Windows 95, and Windows 98 do not have the /T switch.

The date and time stamps are quite important in today's business world, where networked offices are located in different time zones, and the most recent versions of documents that people have worked on at multiple locations need to be determined.

Clearing the Screen

Isabel asks you and the other employees in her workshop to stop for a minute to examine the Command Prompt window. She comments that, by now, the Command Prompt window is cluttered with commands, messages, prompts, and your responses to the prompts, and that you are now entering commands at the bottom of the window.

To clear the window so you can work more easily, you use another internal command, the CLS command (for "Clear Screen").

To clear the window:

1. Type **CLS** and then press the **Enter** key. Windows 2000 clears the window and displays the command prompt and cursor in the upper-left corner of the window. See Figure 1-20. If you were working in full-screen mode, this command would clear the entire screen (not just a window).

| Figure 1-20 | OUTPUT CLEARED FROM WINDOW |

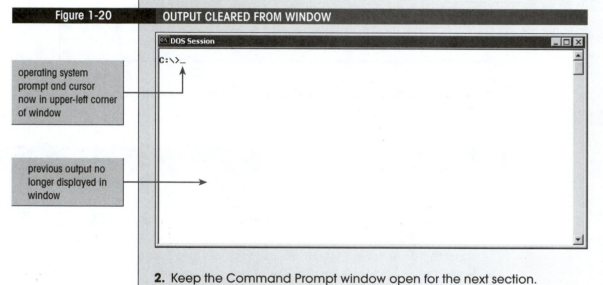

operating system prompt and cursor now in upper-left corner of window

previous output no longer displayed in window

2. Keep the Command Prompt window open for the next section.

The CLS command functions in the same way under MS-DOS, Windows 95, Windows 98, Windows NT Workstation 4.0, and Windows 2000.

Clearing the screen before issuing commands is a good habit to develop because it helps you to focus on one command operation at a time.

Formatting Diskettes

Isabel is now ready to show everyone how to format a diskette in a Command Prompt window.

Most diskettes sold currently are preformatted, and you can use them immediately, without formatting. If you purchase unformatted diskettes, you must format them before the operating system can store files on them. If you find you no longer need the files stored on a diskette, you can reformat the diskette, erasing whatever is stored on it so you can reuse the diskette. Even if you purchase preformatted diskettes, it is a good idea to reformat those diskettes on the computer that contains the operating system you intend to use with those diskettes, because they will last longer. Preformatted diskettes are formatted with an IBM-DOS or MS-DOS utility instead of Windows 2000. This means you might encounter difficulties if you use preformatted diskettes on a computer with Windows 2000, Windows 98, or Windows 95. Certain programs (like backup utilities) may not work with a diskette formatted using another operating system, the diskette may fail far earlier than you would typically expect (especially if you switch back and forth from a computer with Windows 2000 and one with DOS), or Windows 2000 may not be able to work with the diskette at all.

If you reformat preformatted disks, you should perform a full format, not a quick format, of the diskette. A **Quick Format** removes file entries from a diskette without checking it for defects. Also, if you are formatting a brand new (unformatted) diskette, you must perform a **Full Format**, which lays down new tracks and sectors and verifies the integrity of each sector on the diskette by performing a surface scan. When formatting a diskette, the operating system creates concentric recording bands, called **tracks**, around the inner circumference of the disk, as shown in Figure 1-21. Then, the formatting program subdivides each track into equal parts, called **sectors**. Although not all of them are shown in this diagram, there are 80 concentric tracks on a 3½-inch high-density diskette, and each track is divided into 18 sectors. Each sector in turn contains 512 bytes. A **byte** is the storage space required on a disk for one character. Assuming a single-spaced page contains approximately 3,500 bytes of data, then a sector stores approximately one-seventh of a page. If you create a one-page report, the operating system will use approximately seven sectors to record the contents of that document in a file on the diskette.

Figure 1-21	TRACKS AND SECTORS ON A FORMATTED 3½-INCH HIGH-DENSITY DISK

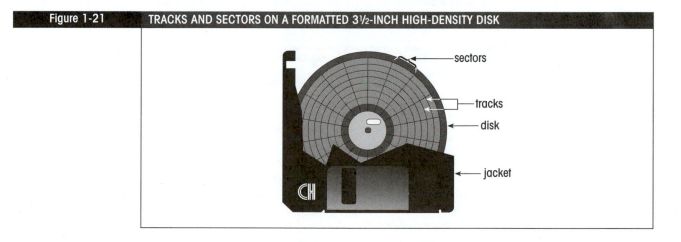

If you want to figure out the total storage capacity of a diskette, you can perform the following computation:

Number of sides formatted × Number of tracks per side × Number of sectors per track × Number of bytes per sector

2 sides × 80 tracks/side × 18 sectors/track × 512 bytes/sector = 1,474,560 bytes (or 1.44 MB)

During the **surface scan**, the operating system or Format utility records "dummy" data to each sector of the disk and reads that data back to verify that the sector supports read and write operations. If it encounters a problem reading or writing to a sector, it marks the cluster that contains that defective sector and does not store data in the defective sector. A **cluster**, or **allocation unit**, consists of one or more sectors of storage space on a disk, and the number of sectors per allocation unit or cluster varies with the type of disk. On a high-density diskette, an allocation unit is the same size as a sector.

2 × 80 × 18 × 512 bytes

To format a diskette, you use the FORMAT command. Although there are many different ways in which you can use this command, the basic syntax is as follows:

FORMAT *volume*

The **volume**, or drive name, is a required parameter or item of information. Therefore, you must specify the name of the disk drive that contains the diskette you want to format. If you use this syntax, you also must use a diskette that has the same storage capacity as the disk drive you are using. For example, if you want to format a diskette in a high-density disk drive, you would use a high-density diskette. If you want to format a double-density diskette (720 K) in a high-density drive, you must use the Format capacity switch (/F) and specify the number of kilobytes that the disk supports.

The FORMAT command is an external command, so Cmd.exe must locate the program instructions for this command in a file on the disk and then load the program into memory so you can use it.

To complete the next set of steps, you will need either a preformatted or an unformatted high-density diskette. If you use a formatted diskette with files, the FORMAT program will erase all the files from the diskette.

To format a diskette:

1. Insert a high-density diskette into drive A.

2. Type **FORMAT A:** and then press **Enter**. The FORMAT utility prompts you to insert a new diskette in drive A, and then press **Enter** when you are ready. See Figure 1-22.

Figure 1-22	PROMPT TO INSERT DISK TO FORMAT

command

```
DOS Session - FORMAT A:                                          _ □ ×

C:\>FORMAT A:          ←          required parameter
Insert new disk for drive A:                                    prompt to insert disk
and press ENTER when ready...          ←                        to format
```

3. Because you have already inserted a diskette, press **Enter**. The FORMAT utility identifies the type of file system used on the disk (always FAT for diskette), it shows you the format capacity (1.44 MB), and it shows the percentage complete. See Figure 1-23. The file system known as FAT is the same as the one used under MS-DOS. The **format capacity** is the storage capacity of the disk once formatted.

Figure 1-23	STATUS OF FORMAT OPERATION

```
DOS Session - FORMAT A:

                                                                type of filing system
                                                                on disk
C:\>FORMAT A:
Insert new disk for drive A:
and press ENTER when ready...
The type of the file system is FAT.
percentage of format      Verifying 1.44M          ←           format capacity of disk
complete                  35 percent completed.
```

After the format is complete, the FORMAT utility notes that it is initializing the File Allocation Table (FAT), which keeps track of space used on the disk, and then prompts you for a volume label. See Figure 1-24. The **volume label** is an electronic label assigned to the disk. You can use up to 11 characters, including spaces, for the volume label. Certain symbols, such as a period, are not allowed. If you attempt to use an invalid or unacceptable character, the FORMAT utility will inform you of this problem and will prompt you again for the volume label. For the volume label, you typically use a label that identifies the type of files you intend to store on the diskette. If you do not want to use a volume label (it is optional), you just press Enter.

Figure 1-24	PROMPT FOR VOLUME LABEL

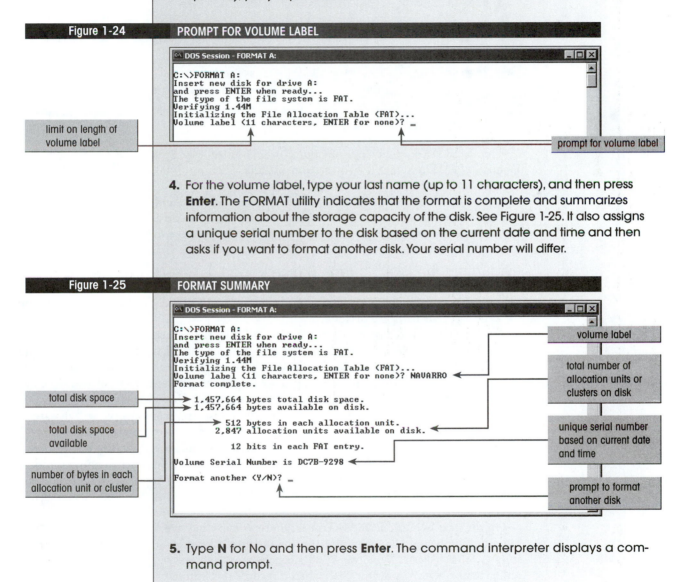

```
DOS Session - FORMAT A:                                    _ □ ×

C:\>FORMAT A:
Insert new disk for drive A:
and press ENTER when ready...
The type of the file system is FAT.
Verifying 1.44M
Initializing the File Allocation Table (FAT)...
Volume label (11 characters, ENTER for none)? _
```

limit on length of volume label

prompt for volume label

4. For the volume label, type your last name (up to 11 characters), and then press **Enter**. The FORMAT utility indicates that the format is complete and summarizes information about the storage capacity of the disk. See Figure 1-25. It also assigns a unique serial number to the disk based on the current date and time and then asks if you want to format another disk. Your serial number will differ.

Figure 1-25	FORMAT SUMMARY

```
DOS Session - FORMAT A:                                    _ □ ×

C:\>FORMAT A:
Insert new disk for drive A:
and press ENTER when ready...
The type of the file system is FAT.
Verifying 1.44M
Initializing the File Allocation Table (FAT)...
Volume label (11 characters, ENTER for none)? NAVARRO
Format complete.

    1,457,664 bytes total disk space.
    1,457,664 bytes available on disk.

        512 bytes in each allocation unit.
      2,847 allocation units available on disk.

         12 bits in each FAT entry.

Volume Serial Number is DC7B-9298

Format another (Y/N)? _
```

volume label

total number of allocation units or clusters on disk

unique serial number based on current date and time

prompt to format another disk

total disk space

total disk space available

number of bytes in each allocation unit or cluster

5. Type **N** for No and then press **Enter**. The command interpreter displays a command prompt.

During the formatting operation, the diskette spins in the disk drive unit at approximately 300 to 360 rpm's (revolutions per minute) and the drive light is on. You should *not* remove a diskette from a disk drive when the drive light is on. When the drive light is off, you can safely remove a diskette and insert another one.

REFERENCE WINDOW `RW`

Formatting a Diskette

- Click the Start button, point to Programs, point to Accessories, and click Command Prompt.
- Insert an unformatted or preformatted, but blank, diskette into drive A.
- Type FORMAT A: and then press Enter.
- When prompted for a volume label, type a label no longer than 11 characters, and press Enter; if you do not want to assign a volume label to the disk, just press Enter.
- When prompted as to whether you want to format another disk, type N if you do not need to format another disk. If you want to format a set of disks, type Y to repeat the process and format each disk.

The FORMAT command functions in a similar way in MS-DOS, Windows 95, Windows 98, Windows NT Workstation 4.0, and Windows 2000; however, Windows 2000 includes more switches.

It is a good idea to apply exterior labels to your diskettes, and write your name and the diskette's contents on them. This is especially important if you are working in a computer lab, because it's easy to forget to remove your diskette from the drive unit when you leave.

Evaluating the Disk Storage Space Report

Next, Isabel explains the information displayed by the FORMAT utility after it completes the process of formatting a diskette.

The first value listed shows the total amount of storage space on the diskette in bytes. The second value shows how much of this storage space is available for use, again, in bytes. Usually, these two values are identical and indicate that you can use all of the formatted storage space available on the diskette. If these values are different, you will also see a message that indicates the diskette contains a certain number of bytes in bad sectors. Although you can still use the rest of the storage space on the diskette, many people will discard the diskette rather than risk losing valuable data later. Diskettes are invariably certified to be error-free, and if you find that newly formatted diskettes contain bad sectors, you can return them for new ones. The disk drive unit may also be defective. If you format another diskette and if the FORMAT utility does not report any bad sectors for that diskette, the first diskette you formatted was probably defective. If subsequent diskettes you format also are reported to have bad sectors, you might need to have the disk drive replaced.

On the next line, the FORMAT program reports on the size of each allocation unit and the total number of allocation units on the diskette. Although a sector is the basic unit of storage on a diskette, Windows 2000 allocates storage space on a cluster-by-cluster basis rather than a sector-by-sector basis when it records the contents of a file to a disk.

Formatting a diskette is an important operation that ultimately determines how Windows 2000 interacts with the file system on the diskette, how it utilizes the storage space on the diskette, how it opens and retrieves files, and how it saves and writes files to the diskette.

Copying a Diskette

Isabel distributes an extra diskette to each of the individuals in the workshop. She explains that these diskettes contain files that you will use in upcoming sessions, and that each of you should make a copy of the diskette as a precautionary measure.

When you copy a diskette, the operating system makes a sector-by-sector copy of the original diskette, called the **source disk**, and records the exact information onto another diskette, called the **destination disk** or **target disk**. The source and destination disks must be the same size and same storage capacity. If your computer only has one floppy disk drive (which is the case on most computer systems today), you must use the same disk drive for both the source and destination disks, and copy from drive A to drive A. Even if your computer has two floppy disk drives—one for 3½-inch floppy disks and one for 5¼-inch floppy disks (found on much older computer systems)—you *cannot* use one drive for the source disk and the other drive for the destination disk. Likewise, you cannot perform a disk copy from drive C to drive A (or a Zip drive).

Since you typically use the same drive for both the source and destination disks, Windows 2000 asks you for the source disk first, then it copies the contents of the diskette. Next it asks you for the destination disk, and then copies the contents of the source disk onto the destination disk. The disk copy operation replaces any information already stored on the destination disk with the contents of the source disk. After the disk copy is complete, the source and destination disks are identical, except for their serial numbers. To protect your original diskette during the disk copy operation, write-protect it beforehand. When you **write-protect** a diskette, you prevent the operating system or any other program from recording data onto the diskette. Otherwise, if the destination disk is a preformatted diskette, and if you insert the diskettes in the wrong order, you end up with two blank diskettes! After the disk copy operation, you can remove the write-protection from the source disk. To write-protect a 3½-inch high-density disk, use your fingernail to move the plastic write-protect tab in the write-protect notch on the back of the disk so you can see through the write-protect opening. To remove write-protection, reverse this process and cover the rectangular opening in the write-protect notch.

To copy a diskette from the command prompt, use the DISKCOPY program. To familiarize you with how to examine Help information on a command, you will display Help for the DISKCOPY program in the next section.

Using the Help Switch

So that everyone will know how to find information on how to use various Windows 2000 commands, and therefore be able to work independently, Isabel next recommends that each of you view Help information on how to make a copy of a diskette with the DISKCOPY command.

You can use the **Help switch**, (/?), to display Help information for a specific command. The syntax for this switch is as follows:

[*command*] **/?**

You enter the command followed by /?. Windows 2000 extracts Help information from the command's program itself. The Help switch works with almost all commands.

To obtain Help information on the Diskcopy command:

1. Type **CLS** and then press **Enter**.

2. Type **DISKCOPY /?** and press **Enter**. Windows 2000 displays Help information on the DISKCOPY command. See Figure 1-26.

   TROUBLE? If Windows 2000 displays the message "Invalid parameter - \?," then type a backslash (\ ) rather than a slash (/). Repeat this step, but use the slash instead of the backslash for the switch.

Figure 1-26   **VIEWING HELP INFORMATION ON DISKCOPY**

The Help information reminds you that this command copies the contents of one diskette to another (floppy disk). As shown in the Help information for the Diskcopy command, the syntax is as follows:

DISKCOPY *drive 1: drive 2:* **[/V]**

As noted earlier, the brackets enclose optional parameters. *Drive 1:* is the drive that contains the source disk; *drive 2:* is the drive that contains the destination disk. If you do not specify the source and destination drives (they are optional parameters), then the DISKCOPY utility assumes you want to use the current drive as both the source and the destination. If you specify only *drive 1:*, the Diskcopy command assumes you want to use the same drive for the source and target disks. Because the Diskcopy command requires that both diskettes be the same size and the same storage capacity, you must use the same drive for both the source and target disks, and you *must* switch diskettes during the disk copy operation. If you have two drives of the same size *and* the same storage capacity, you can perform the disk copy using both drives. Insert your source diskette in one drive and your target diskette in the other drive. If you are performing a disk copy from a command prompt on drive C, you have to specify both drives. The Verify switch, /V, verifies that the data is copied correctly to the destination disk. The Help information also informs you that the disks must be the same type.

The Help switch (/?) is available in MS-DOS, Windows 95, Windows 98, Windows NT Workstation 4.0, and Windows 2000.

You are now ready to copy a diskette. To complete the next set of steps, you will need a copy of Data Disk #1 and your newly formatted diskette. Your instructor or technical support staff will provide you with a copy of this diskette, or instruct you how to copy the files for this disk from your computer network to a diskette. You can then use that diskette with the files for Data Disk #1 in these steps. If you have already made a copy of Data Disk #1 using a technique preferred by your instructor and technical support staff, then read, but do not keystroke, the following steps and examine the figures so you are familiar with the use of the procedure for copying a diskette.

Although you will not work with the files on Data Disk #1 until Tutorial 2, you can use that diskette for the following disk copy operation.

To make a copy of a diskette:

1. Make sure the source disk of Data Disk #1 is write-protected.

2. Insert Data Disk #1 into drive A. This is the source disk from which you will make a copy.

3. Type **DISKCOPY A: A:** and then press **Enter**. The DISKCOPY utility prompts you to insert the source disk in drive A (Figure 1-27), which you have already done.

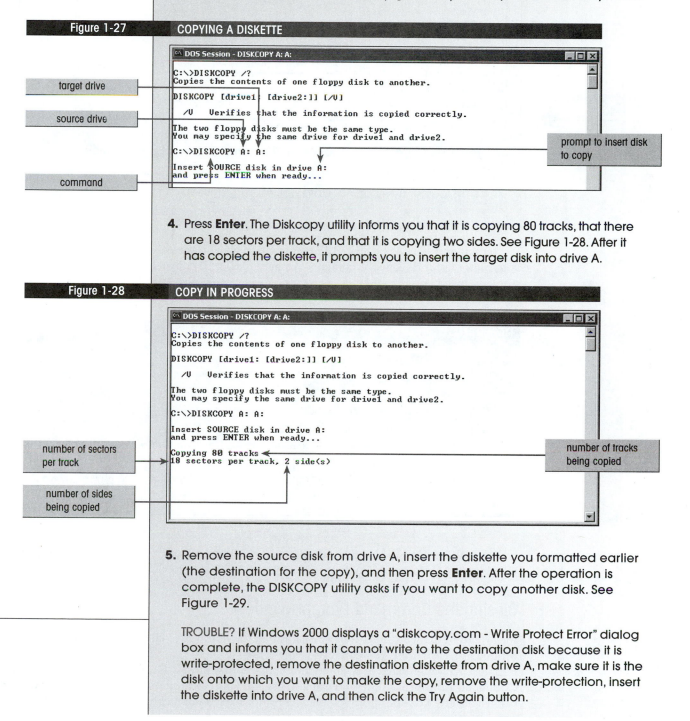

| Figure 1-27 | COPYING A DISKETTE |

4. Press **Enter**. The Diskcopy utility informs you that it is copying 80 tracks, that there are 18 sectors per track, and that it is copying two sides. See Figure 1-28. After it has copied the diskette, it prompts you to insert the target disk into drive A.

| Figure 1-28 | COPY IN PROGRESS |

5. Remove the source disk from drive A, insert the diskette you formatted earlier (the destination for the copy), and then press **Enter**. After the operation is complete, the DISKCOPY utility asks if you want to copy another disk. See Figure 1-29.

TROUBLE? If Windows 2000 displays a "diskcopy.com - Write Protect Error" dialog box and informs you that it cannot write to the destination disk because it is write-protected, remove the destination diskette from drive A, make sure it is the disk onto which you want to make the copy, remove the write-protection, insert the diskette into drive A, and then click the Try Again button.

Figure 1-29   PROMPT FOR TARGET DISK

```
DOS Session - DISKCOPY A: A:                                      _ □ ✕
C:\>DISKCOPY /?
Copies the contents of one floppy disk to another.

DISKCOPY [drive1: [drive2:]] [/V]

    /V   Verifies that the information is copied correctly.

The two floppy disks must be the same type.
You may specify the same drive for drive1 and drive2.

C:\>DISKCOPY A: A:

Insert SOURCE disk in drive A:
and press ENTER when ready...

Copying 80 tracks
18 sectors per track, 2 side(s)

Insert TARGET disk in drive A:        ◄───────    prompt for target disk
and press ENTER when ready...
Volume Serial Number is 506E-1D22

Copy another disk (Y/N)?  _
```

unique serial number for target disk

6. Type **N** for No, and then press **Enter**. The command interpreter displays a command prompt.

7. Remove your new copy of Data Disk #1 from drive A.

You can only use the DISKCOPY command to make copies of diskettes. As noted earlier, you cannot use it to copy the contents of a hard disk or to copy to a diskette with a different storage capacity or size.

REFERENCE WINDOW   **RW**

Copying a Diskette
- Click the Start button, point to Programs, point to Accessories, and then click Command Prompt.
- Write-protect the source disk, and then insert the source disk in drive A.
- At the command prompt, type DISKCOPY A: A: and then press Enter.
- When prompted to insert the source disk, press Enter.
- When prompted to insert the target disk, remove the source disk from drive A, insert the target disk, and then press Enter.
- When prompted as to whether you want to copy another diskette, type N and then press Enter if you are finished. If you want to make another copy of the same diskette, type Y and then press Enter.

The DISKCOPY command functions in a similar way in MS-DOS, Windows 95, Windows 98, Windows NT Workstation 4.0, and Windows 2000.

Closing the Command Prompt Window

At the end of the workshop, Isabel explains that the best way to close the Command Prompt window is to use the EXIT command.

The EXIT command is an internal command that closes the program that opened the Command Prompt window. You can also use the Close button on the right side of the title bar if you are working in a Command Prompt window (but obviously not in full-screen mode because there is no window). If you use the Close button to close the window, and if Windows 2000 displays an End Program dialog box and reports that it cannot end a program that is still active, you should click the Cancel button, close the program, and then type the EXIT command to close the Command Prompt window. You can also close the Command Prompt window by clicking the program menu icon on the left side of the title bar and then clicking Close.

Your instructor and technical support staff will explain the procedure for using the computers in your computer lab. Some computer labs require you to log off the computer you are using so the next person who uses that same computer is not logged on under your account (and therefore unable to access their class files). Other computer labs do not have a logon procedure, and therefore prefer that you not attempt to log off, restart, or shut down the computer. If you do not know what your computer lab procedures are, ask the technical support staff in your computer lab.

To close the Command Prompt window and log off your computer:

1. Type **EXIT** and then press **Enter**. Windows 2000 closes the Command Prompt window.

2. If your computer lab requires that you log off or restart the computer once you finish your work, click the **Start** button, click **Shut Down**, and if you do not see the Log off option in the "What do you want the computer to do?" list box in the Shut Down Windows dialog box, click the list arrow for this list box, click the **Log off** or **Restart** option, and then click **OK**.

You can also use the EXIT command to close an MS-DOS Prompt window in Windows 95, Windows 98, and Windows NT Workstation 4.0.

Before you return to your offices, Isabel emphasizes that operating system software is an indispensable component of a computer system. Although DOS was the predominant operating system software used on PCs until 1995, businesses and individuals now rely on the Windows 95, Windows NT Workstation 4.0, Windows 98, and Windows 2000 operating systems. Even so, DOS skills, concepts, features, and techniques are still important for understanding how Windows 2000 works and for evaluating and troubleshooting problems with a computer system.

Session 1.2 QUICK CHECK

1. The _____ is the drive that is currently in use, and that is identified in the command prompt.

2. When working in a command line environment, a(n) _____ is the term commonly used to refer to a folder.

3. The top-level folder is called the _____ when working in a command line environment.

4. Cmd.exe is an example of a type of program that is referred to as a(n) _____.

5. The program code, or routine, for _____ commands is stored within the program file Cmd.exe.

6. The program code for _____ commands resides in a specific file on disk.

7. _____ refers to the proper format for entering a command, including how to spell the command, and whether the command uses required or optional parameters.

8. A(n) _____ is an optional parameter that changes the way in which a command works.

9. A(n) _____ is an electronic label assigned to a disk.

10. In a Command Prompt window, you can use the _____ key to repeat or recall the previous command.

COMMAND REFERENCE

COMMAND	USE	BASIC SYNTAX	EXAMPLE
/?	Displays Help information on the use of an internal or external command	*command* /?	FORMAT /?
CLS	Clears the window or screen of previously displayed output	CLS	CLS
COLOR	Sets the background and foreground colors of a Command Prompt window	COLOR [*attribute*]	COLOR F0
DATE	Displays or changes the system date	DATE [/T I *date*]	DATE /T DATE 7-21-03
DISKCOPY	Copies the contents of a source disk to a destination disk	DISKCOPY *drive1: drive2:*	DISKCOPY A: A:
EXIT	Closes a Command Prompt window	EXIT	EXIT
FORMAT	Formats a disk for use with Windows 2000	FORMAT *volume*	FORMAT A:
TIME	Displays or sets the system time	TIME [/T I *time*]	TIME /T TIME 10:30 a TIME 4:30 p
TITLE	Displays a title on the title bar of the Command Prompt window	TITLE *string*	TITLE DOS Session
VER	Displays the Windows 2000 version	VER	VER

Items shown in italics and *not* enclosed within square brackets are required parameters. See Format command.

Items shown in italics and enclosed within square brackets are optional parameters. See Color command.

Items separated by a vertical bar (I) are mutually exclusive; you can use one or the other, but not both at the same time. See Date and Time commands.

REVIEW ASSIGNMENT

As part of its community outreach, SolarWinds participates in a student enrichment program with its local community college. Isabel and her staff hire students as interns so the students can gain valuable on-the-job experience that can be applied toward their degrees. During this next college session, Isabel hires Angelina Barrett, a student in the Computer Sciences department at the community college. Although Angelina is familiar with the basics of using Windows 2000, she is not familiar with working in a command line environment. Isabel asks you to work with Angelina to show her how to use basic internal and external Windows 2000 commands.

As you perform the following steps, record your answers to any questions so you can submit them to your instructor.

1. After you log on to your computer, open a Command Prompt window using the Start menu.

2. Change from a windowed view to a full-screen view. How did you perform this operation?

3. What is the default drive and directory (or folder) used by Windows 2000? How did you obtain this information?

4. What version of Windows 2000 is used on your computer? Use the Version command to verify that this is the correct version. What command did you use to perform this operation? Is this command an internal or external command?

5. Clear the screen. What command did you use?

6. At the command prompt, type COLOR 31 and then press Enter. What is the background color? What is the foreground color of the text?

7. At the command prompt, type COLOR 9F and then press Enter. What is the background color? What is the foreground color of the text? How does this combination of colors differ from the previous set of colors?

8. At the command prompt, type COLOR and then press Enter. What happens?

9. Clear the screen.

10. Type DATE /T and then press Enter. What is the current day of the week? What is the current date?

11. Type TIME /T and then press Enter. What is the current time?

12. Name two reasons why it is important to make sure that the date and time are set correctly on your computer.

13. Insert an unformatted, or blank, diskette into drive A. *Note*: You can use the same diskette you used in the tutorial.

14. Clear the screen, maximize the Command Prompt window, and display Help on the FORMAT command. What command did you use to display the Help information?

15. What does the /V:*label* switch do?

16. At the command prompt, type FORMAT A: /V: and immediately after /V:, type your last name (no more than 11 characters), and then press Enter. When prompted to insert the diskette, press Enter again. What format capacity is the Format utility using for the diskette? When prompted as to whether you want to format another diskette, type N (for No) and then press Enter.

17. Why didn't the FORMAT utility ask you for a volume label?

18. Use the Help switch to display Help information on the VOL command. What does this command do? What is the syntax of this command?

19. Type VOL A: and then press Enter. What information does Volume provide you?

20. Remove the diskette that you just formatted from drive A.

21. Obtain a copy of Data Disk #1, make sure this diskette is write-protected, and then insert it into drive A.

22. Display Help information on the DISKCOPY command. What does the /V switch do?

23. At the command prompt, type DISKCOPY A: A: /V and then press Enter. When prompted for the source disk, press Enter again. How many tracks is the DISKCOPY command copying? How many sectors are there per track? How many sides is it copying?

24. When prompted for the target disk, remove the copy of Data Disk #1 from drive A, insert the diskette you just formatted, and then press Enter. This step takes more time. What additional operation occurs during this phase?

25. When prompted as to whether you want to copy another diskette, type N (for No) and then press Enter. Remove your disk from drive A.

26. Type EXIT and then press Enter. What happens?

CASE PROBLEMS

Case 1. Customizing the Command Prompt Window at The Perfect Match The Perfect Match is an employment agency that specializes in temporary assignments for individuals with computer skills. One of their employees, Corey Tanner, recently decided to supplement his retirement income with part-time, temporary work. Many years ago, Corey worked on IBM PCs that used the MS-DOS operating system. Recently, he started a temporary assignment at the employment agency itself. While talking with one of the company's other employees, he learns that it is possible to customize the Command Prompt window with the COLOR command. Because he prefers to use a command line environment whenever possible, he decides to use part of his lunch break to experiment with the COLOR command. He asks you to show him how to use it.

As you perform the following steps, record your answers to any questions so you can submit them to your instructor.

1. Open a Command Prompt window and maximize the window.

2. Display Help information on the COLOR command.

3. What is the primary function of the COLOR command?

4. What is the syntax of the COLOR command? Does it use any optional or required parameters? Explain.

5. How many colors are available for the background and foreground colors?

6. Try the following combinations of background and foreground colors. Also, note the command that you used for each color combination.

   ■ Background = Blue, Foreground = Bright White
   ■ Background = Red, Foreground = Bright White
   ■ Background = Light Yellow, Foreground = Black
   ■ Background = Light Purple, Foreground = Bright White
   ■ Background = Light Aqua, Foreground = Black
   ■ Default background

7. Which of the above color combinations do you prefer, and why? Were there any other color combinations that you tried which you preferred over the ones in the previous step? What were they?

8. Restore the original background and foreground colors. How did you perform this operation?

9. Is there any way in which you might find this feature useful? Explain.

Case 2. *Formatting Diskettes at Fast Track Trainers* Fast Track Trainers provides contract training in the use of Microsoft Excel 2000 for its corporate customers in St. Paul, Minnesota. Samantha Kuehl, Fast Track Trainer's lead training specialist, works with you to prepare diskettes that contain copies of Excel 2000 files for employees to use during the hands-on workshops. To speed up the process of preparing these training diskettes, Samantha recommends you use the FORMAT and DISKCOPY commands in a Command Prompt window.

As you perform the following steps, record your answers to any questions so you can submit them to your instructor.

1. Open the Command Prompt window and then maximize the window.

2. Display Help information on the FORMAT command. Although there are five different approaches you can use for the syntax of the FORMAT command, which is the one required parameter for each of these approaches?

3. If Samantha wanted each of the student training diskettes to contain the volume label "Fast Track," would it be possible to add that volume label during the formatting process without being prompted for the information? If so, how would she specify that label when she used the FORMAT command?

4. If Samantha needed to format double-density diskettes that have a format capacity of 720K, what switch would she need to use with the FORMAT command? What command would she enter?

5. After returning from a workshop, what FORMAT switch could you use to reformat the diskettes quickly and erase the information contained on the diskettes? What command would you specify to perform this operation?

6. Perform a Quick Format of your diskette to test this use of the FORMAT command.

7. Are there any safety precautions you might want to keep in mind when using the FORMAT command? Explain.

8. Is there any way in which you might find this feature useful in your line of work? Explain.

Case 3. *Assigning Volume Labels at HiPerform Systems* HiPerform Systems is a small business that sells computer systems and hard disk drives, and also troubleshoots hard disk problems for its customers in Ipswich, Massachusetts. James Everett, the owner of HiPerform Systems, employs high-school students as technical support staff during the summer. As they customize or troubleshoot computers for their customers, they assign volume labels to newly-formatted hard disk drives or to drives that they restore. Because James Everett and his staff typically work in a command line environment as they are troubleshooting, restoring, and building systems, they use Windows 2000 commands for assigning labels to disks. As a way of thanking their customers for their business, they also provide them with a diskette that contains some useful command line utilities. James asks you to become more familiar with the use of the FORMAT, VOLUME, and LABEL commands so you can prepare these customer diskettes quickly.

As you perform the following steps, record your answers to any questions so you can submit them to your instructor.

1. Open the Command Prompt window, and maximize the window.

2. Display Help on the FORMAT command. What command did you enter?

3. Using this Help information, can you perform a Quick Format of a diskette and also assign a volume label to the diskette at the same time (without being prompted for it during the formatting operation)? If so, how would you perform this operation?

4. To test your answer to the previous question, perform a Quick Format on an unformatted or blank diskette and assign the volume label HPS to the disk. What command did you enter?

5. Display Help information on the VOL command. What does the Volume command do?

6. Using this Help information, check the volume label of the diskette you just formatted. What command did you enter? What volume label is assigned to the diskette?

7. Use the Volume command to view the label assigned to drive C. What command did you enter? What is the volume label (if any)?

8. Display Help information on the LABEL command. What does this command do?

9. Use the LABEL command to change the volume label on your disk to HiPerform. (*Note*: Make sure you do not change the volume label of drive C.) What command did you enter?

10. Use the Volume command to verify that the Label utility changed the volume name. Is the volume label different in any way from what you specified in the previous step? Explain.

11. Is there any way in which you might find these features useful in your line of work (or play)? Explain.

Case 4. *Changing the Time at Turing Enterprises* Melissa Turing operates a small independent business called Turing Enterprises that specializes in planning outings, camping adventures, whitewater rafting, hang gliding, travel tours, and other outdoor adventures for women in her local area. She uses her home computer for her customer mailing list, her schedule of events, business contacts, and the financial records for her business. She has observed that the time on her computer system gradually falls behind the actual time, and has to correct it periodically.

As you perform the following steps, record your answers to any questions so you can submit them to your instructor.

1. Open the Command Prompt window and then maximize the window.

2. Display Help information on the DATE command. What command can you enter to display the current date setting without displaying a prompt for a new date?

3. Check the current date on your computer. If the date were incorrect, how would you change it?

4. If you wanted to change the date on your computer to July 21, 2003, how would you do it?

5. Display Help information on the TIME command. What command can you enter to display the current time without displaying a prompt for a new time?

6. Check the current time on your computer. If the time were incorrect, how would you change it?

7. If you wanted to advance the time by 15 minutes from 9:00 am to 9:15 am to get an early start on keeping appointments, how would you do it?

8. If the time on your computer was set for 10:30 am, but it was actually 10:30 pm, how would you change the time?

9. Enter the commands TIME /T and TIME at the command prompt, and compare the differences. Why might you prefer to use the /T switch?

10. Is there any way in which you might find these features useful in your line of work (or play)? Explain.

QUICK | CHECK ANSWERS

Session 1.1

1. operating system
2. booting
3. utilities
4. command line, command prompt
5. dual-boot
6. full path
7. backward compatibility
8. virtual DOS machine *or* VDM
9. text mode
10. command

Session 1.2

1. current drive *or* default drive
2. directory
3. root directory
4. command interpreter
5. internal
6. external
7. syntax
8. switch
9. volume label
10. F3

DISPLAYING DIRECTORIES

Streamlining the Process for Locating Files at SolarWinds, Unlimited

OBJECTIVES

In this tutorial you will:

- Display a directory listing of filenames on the default drive and other drives

- Use switches with the Directory command to control scrolling, arrange files in alphabetical order, and produce a wide directory listing

- Display files by name, extension, size, and date and time

- Examine the use of long and short filenames

- Display files by attributes, date stamps, and short filenames

- Use wildcards to select groups of files

- Combine wildcards and switches

- Examine the Windows environment

- Specify default switches for the Directory command

SolarWinds Unlimited

One of your job responsibilities, as Isabel's assistant, is to keep an updated copy of all template files used by the staff to prepare documents. **Templates** are files that contain the general format, or layout, of a document, and may also contain data, such as text or formulas, commonly found in a specific type of document. In the case of SolarWinds Unlimited, these templates contain the company logo and specific document formats that provide consistency in preparing various types of documents for the company.

Although you are familiar with Windows, you have little experience with DOS. Because DOS skills are crucial to providing staff support, Isabel's first task is to show you how to work with the Directory command (DIR) under the Windows 2000 command prompt.

She points out that you might also need to use the command line environment to obtain information about files unavailable in the graphical user interface, such as type extensions for certain types of files.

In this section of the tutorial, you will examine the concept and use of the command history, and learn how to display files in a directory (or folder). You will use the most common switch options of the DIR command, including options for displaying an alphabetical list of filenames. You will also examine the component parts of a filename.

SESSION 2.1

In this session you will display directory listings on different drives, use switches with the Directory command to control scrolling, arrange files in alphabetical order, and produce a wide directory listing. You also will display files by name, extension, size, and date and time; examine the use of long and short filenames; and display files by attributes, date stamps, and short filenames.

Using the Command History

After showing you how to use the F3 function key to recall a command, Isabel explains that, although this key is useful, it allows you to recall only the last command you entered. When you open a Command Prompt window, however, the command processor automatically incorporates features of a program called DOSKEY to make it easier to recall and, if necessary, modify commands you've already entered. The command processor keeps track of the last 50 commands entered at the command prompt and stores them in an area of memory known as the **command history** (or **command stack**). You can recall commands from the command history and edit those commands. When the command history fills up, the command processor eliminates the oldest commands so it has room for the new commands you enter.

Using these features, you can recall commands stored in the command history. If you want to recall the previous command, press the Up Arrow key ↑. Each time you press ↑, you move back one step in the command history and retrieve and display the previous command. If you press the Down Arrow key ↓, you advance to the next command in the command history following the one currently displayed. You can also use the Page Up key to recall the oldest command in the command history and Page Down to recall the most recently issued command.

You can also edit the current command line so you do not need to enter it again from scratch, and you can recall and edit previously entered commands. Use the Left Arrow ← and Right Arrow → keys to move the cursor one character to the left or right on the command line so you can position the cursor at the point where you want to insert, edit, or replace text. Pressing the Home key will move the cursor to the beginning of the command line, and pressing the End key will move the cursor to the end of the command line.

By default, the command processor operates in **insert mode**. If you position the cursor anywhere on the command line and then start typing, it inserts the text you type. If you want to switch from insert mode to **overtype mode** so you can replace text by typing over the text, press the Insert key. After making changes, press the Insert key to switch back to insert mode. The Insert key is a **toggle key**—a key that alternates between two related uses each time you press it.

The F7 function key displays a list of commands from the command history in a pop-up box. You can then use the Up Arrow and Down Arrow keys to select the command you want. To execute the selected command, just press the Enter key.

Under MS-DOS, Windows 95, and Windows 98, one had to enter the command DOSKEY to access these features. In the Windows 2000 Command Prompt window, they are always available. Using DOSKEY, you can create macros that perform command operations. A **macro** is a user-defined program often used to automate routine procedures by storing commands for an operation or set of operations.

Displaying a Directory Listing

Isabel explains to you that the Directory (DIR) command is an internal command that displays information about files stored on disk, and that it is therefore an important tool for tracking the contents of a disk. You will rely on the Directory command, as well as other utilities that operate on files to maintain and update template files. Isabel provides you with a copy of a diskette containing the company's template files. She asks you to examine the files using the Directory command and become familiar with the contents of the disk.

Listing a Directory on the Default Drive

The Directory command shows you a directory listing of the drive you specify. If you do not specify a drive name, the Directory command will refer to the **default drive** shown in the command prompt and display the directory listing for that drive. Many Windows 2000 commands operate in the same way, using the default drive and directory if you don't specify otherwise.

To view the root directory of drive C:

1. Open the Command Prompt window.

2. Type **color f0** (an "F" followed by a zero) and then press **Enter**. The COLOR command changes the background of the window to bright white and the text to black. Note that you can type a command line in lowercase when convenient. From now on, all instructions steps will be in lower-case.

   TROUBLE? If you see help text for the COLOR command beginning with "Sets the default console foreground and background colors," you may have typed the letter "o" instead of a zero (0). Press a key to view the remainder of the Help display, if necessary. Then, retype the command in this step.

3. Type **dir** and then press **Enter**. The Directory command displays a **directory listing** containing information on the subdirectories and files in the root directory on drive C. See Figure 2-1. A **directory**, or folder, acts as a container for files and other directories. The **root directory** is the top-level folder on drive C. When drive C was originally formatted, the operating system or a formatting utility created the first directory on that drive—the top-level folder, or root directory—as the primary container for the drive's files and directories. Because you did not specify a drive, DIR assumes you want to view a directory listing of the current drive (drive C) and the current directory (the root directory). On the computer used in this figure, it appears as though there are no files in the root directory of drive C— only subdirectories of the root directory. A subdirectory (also known as a subfolder) is a directory that is contained within, and subordinate to, another directory. After you examine a directory listing of your diskette in the next section, you'll examine the parts of a directory listing in more detail. Because different systems are configured differently and contain different types of installed software, your directory listing for the root directory will differ from that shown in the figure and might appear in alphabetical order.

Figure 2-1   DIRECTORY LISTING OF DRIVE C ROOT DIRECTORY

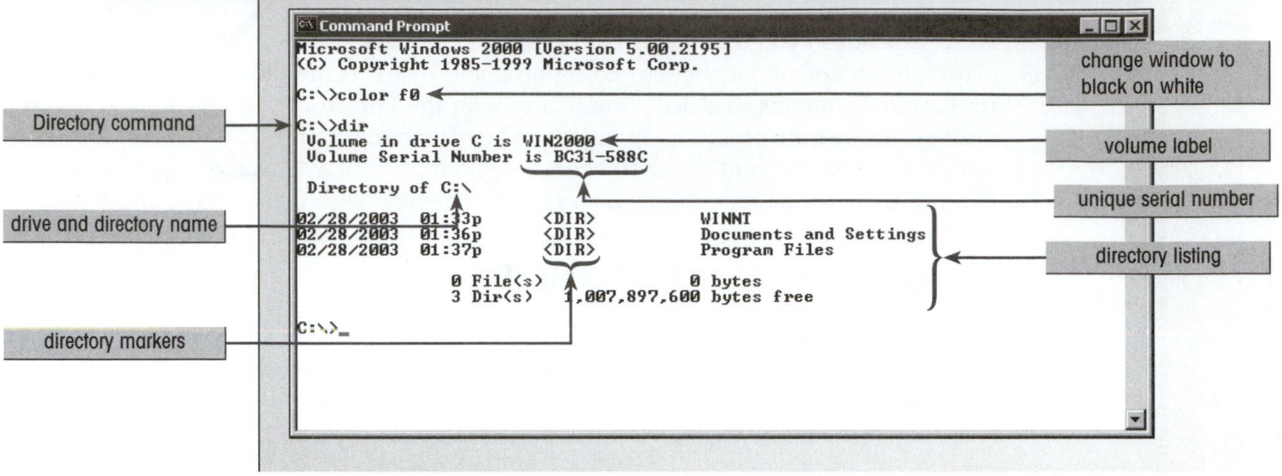

```
Command Prompt                                                    _ □ ×
Microsoft Windows 2000 [Version 5.00.2195]
(C) Copyright 1985-1999 Microsoft Corp.

C:\>color f0

C:\>dir
 Volume in drive C is WIN2000
 Volume Serial Number is BC31-588C

 Directory of C:\

02/28/2003  01:33p    <DIR>          WINNT
02/28/2003  01:36p    <DIR>          Documents and Settings
02/28/2003  01:37p    <DIR>          Program Files
               0 File(s)              0 bytes
               3 Dir(s)   1,007,897,600 bytes free

C:\>_
```

Directory command

drive and directory name

directory markers

change window to black on white

volume label

unique serial number

directory listing

REFERENCE WINDOW   RW

Listing a Directory on the Default Drive
■ Click the Start button, point to Programs, point to Accessories, and then click Command Prompt.
■ In the Command Prompt window, type DIR and then press Enter.

   If your directory listing contains more directory and file names than the Directory command can list in the window, Windows 2000 adjusts the window view through a process called **scrolling**. By default, the Command Prompt window displays only 25 lines at one time. Once Windows 2000 scrolls through the first part of the directory listing, a partial directory remains in the window. DIR lists the files in **disk order**—the order in which the system keeps track of files.

Listing a Directory on Another Drive

   If you want to view the contents of a directory on another drive, you must specify the name of the drive when you use the Directory command. The syntax is as follows:

   DIR [*drive name*]

   As noted in Tutorial 1, the square brackets indicate that the drive name is an optional parameter. In the next set of steps, you are going to examine the Data Disk you created in Tutorial 1. If you reused that disk and erased its contents, you will need to make another copy of Data Disk #1. If necessary, refer to the instructions in Tutorial 1.

To view a directory listing of the drive that contains your diskette:

1. Insert your copy of Data Disk #1 into drive A.

2. Type **dir**, press **Spacebar**, type **a:** (the name of the drive), and then press **Enter**. Make sure you leave a space between the DIR command and the drive name. Also, remember to type the colon (**:**) after the drive letter. The Directory command displays a directory listing of your Data Disk. See Figure 2-2.

TROUBLE? If Windows displays "'DIRA:' is not recognized as an internal or external command, operable program or batch file," you did not include a space between **DIR** and **A:**. Retype the command, making sure to include the space.

TROUBLE? If you see the heading "Directory of C:\," and the message "File Not Found," you did not type the colon (**:**) after the drive letter A. In this case, the Directory command assumed you wanted to view information on a file named "A". The Directory command needs the colon to distinguish a drive letter from a file name. Press ↑ to recall the command, and then add the colon to the end of the line.

| Figure 2-2 | PARTIAL VIEW OF A DIRECTORY LISTING |

file times
file dates
file sizes
filenames and extensions

```
Command Prompt
02/27/2002  08:53p          34,304 3 Year Sales Projection.xls
11/20/2003  08:55a          25,088 Projected Growth Memo.doc
08/08/2003  04:12p          20,480 Proposal.doc
03/27/2003  11:19a          22,028 Sales.wk4
10/31/2003  03:33p          14,848 Savings Plan.xls
09/23/2003  01:12p          14,848 Loan Payment Analysis.xls
09/23/2003  01:12p          31,232 Fonts.xls
06/26/2003  10:24a          53,248 Hardware.ppt
06/26/2003  09:30a          52,736 Application Software.ppt
06/26/2003  10:40a          42,496 Software.ppt
06/26/2003  10:55a          41,984 Using the Mouse.ppt
08/08/2003  03:22p          26,624 Formatting Features.xls
07/22/2003  01:32p          20,992 Format Code Colors.xls
07/09/2003  09:42a          49,152 Addressing Cells.xls
10/16/2003  10:31a          84,534 Colors of the Rainbow.bmp
10/16/2003  09:52a          84,446 Color Palette.bmp
10/16/2003  10:15a          17,910 Palette #1.bmp
10/16/2003  10:21a          17,910 Palette #2.bmp
01/24/2003  08:45a          18,944 Balance Sheet.xls
01/02/2003  03:43p          26,624 Sales Projections.xls
04/09/2003  02:12p          21,504 Employees.xls
              41 File(s)  1,248,070 bytes
               0 Dir(s)     207,872 bytes free
C:\>_
```

partial directory
number of files on the diskette
storage space used by files
available storage

REFERENCE WINDOW **RW**

Listing a Directory on Another Drive
- Open a Command Prompt window, if necessary.
- In the Command Prompt window, type DIR, press the Spacebar, type the drive name, and then press Enter.

When you specify a drive name as part of a command, you are instructing the command to use that drive instead of the default drive. For some commands, such as the Directory command, the drive name is an optional parameter; for other commands, such as the Format command, it is a required parameter.

Changing the Default Drive

If you intend to perform many different operations from the same drive, it is easier to change the default drive to that drive. To change drives, specify the new drive by entering a command that identifies the device name of the drive.

To change the default drive:

1. Type **a:** and then press **Enter**. Windows 2000 updates the command prompt to show you the current drive. Drive A is now the default drive.

2. Type **dir** and then press **Enter**. The DIR command displays a directory listing of your diskette, but you did not need to specify the drive name this time. Instead, DIR uses the current drive specified in the command prompt.

REFERENCE WINDOW   **RW**

Changing the Default Drive
- Open a Command Prompt window, if necessary.
- In the Command Prompt window, type the name of the drive (with the colon), and then press Enter.

If you need to refer to the current drive in a command, you do not need to type the drive name. This feature simplifies the process of entering commands.

Parts of a Directory Listing

By default, the Directory command's directory listing contains five columns of information. If you're already familiar with MS-DOS, you'll find that Windows 2000 provides a new layout.

- **File date** The first column shows a date for each file. See Figure 2-2. By default, the Directory command displays the date the file was last modified. For example, "Sales Projections.xls", the next to last file, was last saved on 01/02/2003. Each time you save a file to disk, Windows 2000 records the current date with the filename. (*Note*: Data Disk files may display a future date if you are using this book soon after its publication.)

- **File time** The second column shows the time for each file, again set for the time when the file was last modified. For example, "Sales Projections.xls" was last saved at 3:43 p.m. Windows 2000 also records the time with the filename when you save a file to disk. When you create a new file, Windows 2000 separately records the file's creation date and time. It also records the date a file was most recently accessed.

- **Directory marker** The third column identifies subdirectories (or subfolders) within the current directory by displaying the directory marker <DIR>. Earlier, when you viewed a directory of drive C (shown in Figure 2-1), the Directory command identified subdirectories with the use of this directory marker. You'll work with directories in Tutorial 4. If your diskette contains no directories, you'll see an empty column.

- **File size** The fourth column lists the size of each file in bytes (or characters). For example, "Sales Projections.xls" is 26,624 bytes in size. A **byte** is the amount of storage space one character requires on disk. When it displays file sizes, DIR uses commas to offset every three places to the left of the decimal point. DIR does not display the size of directories.

■ **Long filename** The fifth column shows long filenames for files created under windows, or short filenames given to files created under MS-DOS or by the Windows operating system. Like Windows 95, Windows 98, and Windows NT Workstation 4.0, Windows 2000 supports the use and display of long filenames up to 255 characters in length. The Directory command displays file extensions, even if Windows 2000 does not display them in My Computer, Windows Explorer, or in the Open and Save As dialog boxes. A filename typically has two parts—the main part of the filename, and a file extension separated by the last period (.) in the filename (in UNIX, long filenames may contain multiple periods). The **file extension** identifies the type of information in a file. Although file extensions usually are three characters in length, they can be shorter (such as "ra") or longer (such as "html"). Windows programs typically assign extensions to their data files automatically, so you rarely have to include a file extension with a filename. By default, Windows 2000 does not display file extensions in My Computer, Windows Explorer, Open, or Save As, but displays a file type icon determined by the hidden extension. See Figures 2-3 and 2-4 for a list of common extensions used for data and program files. Although it is possible for a directory or folder to have a file extension, the vast majority of directory or folder names do not have a file extension.

Figure 2-3	FILE EXTENSIONS, PART 1		
FILE EXTENSION	**FILE TYPE**	**FILE EXTENSION**	**FILE TYPE**
386	Virtual Device Driver (Windows 3.x)	DER	Security Certificate
ACA & ACF	Microsoft Agent Character File (HTTP)	DIR	Macromedia Director Movie
ACG	Microsoft Agent Preview File	DLL	Dynamic Link Library (Application Extension)
ACS	Microsoft Agent Character File	DOC	Microsoft Word
ACW	Microsoft Accessibility Wizard	DOCHTML	Microsoft Word HTML Document
AIF, AIFC, & AIFF	Audio Interchange File Format	DOS	DOS Configuration File
AIFC	AIF Compressed	DOT	Microsoft Word Template
ANI	Animated Cursor	DOTHTML	Microsoft Word HTML Template
ART	ART Image	DQY	ODBC Query File
ASC	ASCII (DOS, DOS Text, Text, or Print File)	DRV	Device Driver
ASF	Active Streaming Format File	DUN	Dial-Up Networking
ASX	Active Streaming Format Metafile	EML	EMail (Outlook Express Mail Message)
AU	Audio (Sound Clip)	EPS	Encapsulated Postscript
AVI	Audio Video Interleaved	EXE	Executable (Application)
BAK	Backup	FAV	Outlook Bar Shortcuts
BAT	Batch (User-Defined Program)	FMT	Format (Lotus 1-2-3, dBASE)
BKF	Microsoft Backup File	FND	Saved Search
BIN	Binary	FON	Font File

Figure 2-3	FILE EXTENSIONS, PART 1, CONTINUED		
FILE EXTENSION	**FILE TYPE**	**FILE EXTENSION**	**FILE TYPE**
BMP	Windows Bitmap Graphics	GIF	Graphics Interchange Format
CAB	Cabinet (Compressed Program)	GRA	Microsoft Graph 2000 Chart
CAT	Security Catalog	GRP	Group (Microsoft Program Group)
CCC	Microsoft Chat Conversation	HLP	Help
CDA	CD Audio Track	HT	HyperTerminal
CDF	Channel Definition File	HTM & HTML	Hypertext Markup Language
CER	Security Certificate	HTT	HyperText Template
CFG	Configuration	ICO	Icon
CHK	Check Disk & Recovered File Fragments	IDX	Index (Database)
CHM	Compiled HTML	III	Intel IPhone Compatible
CIL	Clip Gallery Download Package	INF	Setup Information
CLP	Clipboard Clip	INI	Initialization (Configuration Settings)
CNF	SpeedDial Conferencing	INS	Internet Communication Settings
CNT	Contents (Help)	IQY	Microsoft Excel Web Query File
COM	Command (DOS Program)	ISP	Internet Communication Settings (Internet Signup)
COV	Fax Coverpage File	ITS	Internet Document Set
CPD & CPE	Cover Page Editor Document (FAX)	IVF	Indeo Video File
CPI	Code Page Information	JPG, JPEG, JPE	Joint Photographic Experts Group
CPL	Control Panel Extension	JFIF	JPEG File Interchange Format
CRL	Certificate Revocation List	JS	JScript Script File
CRT	Security Certificate	JSE	Jscript Encoded Script File
CSS	Cascading Style Sheet	KBD	Keyboard
CSV	Comma Separated Values (Text)	LEX	Lexicon
CUR	Cursor (Static)	LNK	Link (Shortcut)
DAT	Database	LOG	Log
DBF	Database (dBASE)	LSF	Streaming Audio/Video
DCX	DCX Image Document	LSX	Streaming Audio/Video Shortcut
DIB	Windows Device Independent Bitmap	LWV	Microsoft Linguistically Enhanced Sound
DIF	Data Interchange Format		

| Figure 2-4 | FILE EXTENSIONS, PART 2 | | |

FILE EXTENSION	FILE TYPE	FILE EXTENSION	FILE TYPE
M1V	Movie Clip	SND	AU Format Sound
MDA	Microsoft Access Add-In	SPC	PKCS #7 Certificates
MDB	Microsoft Access Database	SST	Microsoft Serialized Certificate Store
MDW	Microsoft Access Workgroup Information	STL	Certificate Trust List
MHT & MHTML	Microsoft MHTML	SYS	System
MID & MIDI	Musical Instrument Device Interface (Sound)	TGA	Targa (Graphics)
MOV	Quick Time Movie	TIF & TIFF	Tagged Image File Format (Graphics)
MP2 & MP2V	Movie Clip	TMP	Temporary File
MPA	Movie Clip	TTC	TrueType Collection Font
MPEG or MPE	Moving Pictures Experts Group	TTF	TrueType Font
MPV2	Movie Clip	TXT	Text
MSC	Microsoft Common Console Document	UDL	Microsoft Data Link
MSG	Message (Outlook Express Item)	ULS	Internet Location Service
MSI	Microsoft Installer (Windows Installer Package)	URL	Uniform Resource Locator (Internet Shortcut)
MSP	Microsoft Patch (Windows Installer Patch)	VBE	VBScript Encoded Script File
NFO	MSInfo.Document (System Information)	VBS	VBScript Script File
NLU	Norton AntiVirus LiveUpdate	VCF	vCard File
NMW	NetMeeting Whiteboard	VIR	Virus Infected File
NWS	Outlook Express News Message	WAB	Address Book File
OFT	Outlook Item Template	VXD	Virtual Device Driver
OQY	Microsoft Excel OLAP Query File	WAV	Wave Sound
OSS	Office Search	WAX	Windows Media Audio Shortcut
OTF	OpenType Font	WB1	Quattro Pro for Windows 5.0
P12	Personal Information Exchange	WBK	Microsoft Word Backup Document
P7B & P7R	PKCS #7 Certificates	WDB	Microsoft Works Database
P7C	Digital ID File	WHT	Microsoft NetMeeting Old Whiteboard
P7S	PKCS #7 Signature	WIF	WIF Image Document
PBK	Dial-Up Phonebook	WIZ	Microsoft Word Wizard
PCD	Photo CD Image	WK1, WK3, WK4	Lotus 1-2-3
PCX	Picture Exchange (PC Paintbrush Graphics)	WKS	Lotus 1-2-3 & MS Works Spreadsheets
PDF	Portable Document Format (Acrobat)	WLG	Dr. Watson Log File

Figure 2-4	FILE EXTENSIONS, PART 2, CONTINUED		
FILE EXTENSION	**FILE TYPE**	**FILE EXTENSION**	**FILE TYPE**
PFM	Type 1 Font	WM	Streaming Audio/Video
PFX	Personal Information Exchange	WMA	Windows Media Audio
PIF	Program Information File (DOS Shortcut)	WMF	Windows Metafiles
PMA, PMC, PML, PMR, & PMW	Performance Monitor File	WMV	Windows Media Audio/Video
PNG	Portable Network Graphics	WPD	WordPerfect Document
PPT	Microsoft PowerPoint Presentation	WPS	Microsoft Works Word Processing
PRF	PICSRules File	WQ1, WQ2	Quattro Pro
PRN	DOS Print File	WRI	Windows 3.x Write
PSS	System Configuration Utility Backup (for System Files)	WSF	Windows Script File
PWL	Password List	WSH	Windows Script Host Settings File
QDS	Directory Query	WVX	Windows Media Audio/Video Shortcut
QIC	Backup File for MS Backup Quarter Inch Cartridge	XBM	X Bitmap
QT	Quick Time (Video Clip)	XLA	Microsoft Excel Add-In
RA, RAM, & RM	Real Audio, or RealMedia File (Sound)	XLB	Microsoft Excel Worksheet
RAT	Rating System File	XLC	Microsoft Excel Chart
REG	Registration	XLD	Microsoft Excel DialogSheet
RLE	Run Length Encoded (Compressed Bitmap)	XLK	Microsoft Excel Backup File
RMI	MIDI Sequence	XLM	Microsoft Excel 4.0 Macro
RQY	Microsoft Excel OLE DB Query	XLS	Microsoft Excel Worksheet
RTF	Rich Text Format (Formatted)	XLSHTML	Microsoft Excel HTML Document
SAM	Ami & AmiPro	XLT	Microsoft Excel Template
SCP	Dial-Up Networking Script	XLTHTML	Microsoft Excel HTML Template
SCR	Screen Saver	XLV	Microsoft Excel VBA Module
SCT	Windows Script Component	XLW	Microsoft Excel Workspace
SET	Settings (File Set for Microsoft Backup)	XNK	Exchange Shortcut
SHB	Shortcut into a Document	XSL	XSL Stylesheet
SHS	Scrap	ZAP	Software Installation Settings
SLK	SLK Data Import Format	ZIP	Zip (Compressed)

Below the directory listing, the Directory command shows the total number of files and the total disk storage space used by those files. This disk has a total of 41 files, which use 1,248,070 bytes of space. A total of 207,872 free bytes of space remain on the diskette. If your diskette has bad, or defective, sectors, the total space left on your disk will be less.

Displaying Help on DIR Command Switches

So you can gain necessary skills for troubleshooting problems within the command line environment, Isabel suggests you become familiar with the different ways in which you can use the Directory command to view information about files on a diskette. Because there are many different switches available for this command, you can use the Help switch to find out which ones meet your needs in a given situation.

To view Help information on the DIR command:

1. At the command prompt, type **dir /?** and then press **Enter**. Windows 2000 displays the first window of Help information on this internal command. See Figure 2-5. At the top of the window, the Help information tells you that this command displays a list of files and subdirectories in a directory. It follows this information with the syntax of the command and then a list of DIR command line switches. You will examine the most commonly used switches in this section of the tutorial, and more advanced switches in the second half of the tutorial.

Figure 2-5	DIRECTORY COMMAND HELP DISPLAY, PART 1

directory Help switch

partial Help display

pause prompt

2. Press the **Spacebar**. Information on other switches appears in the remaining Help text. See Figure 2-6.

Figure 2-6	DIRECTORY COMMAND HELP DISPLAY, PART 2

partial Help display

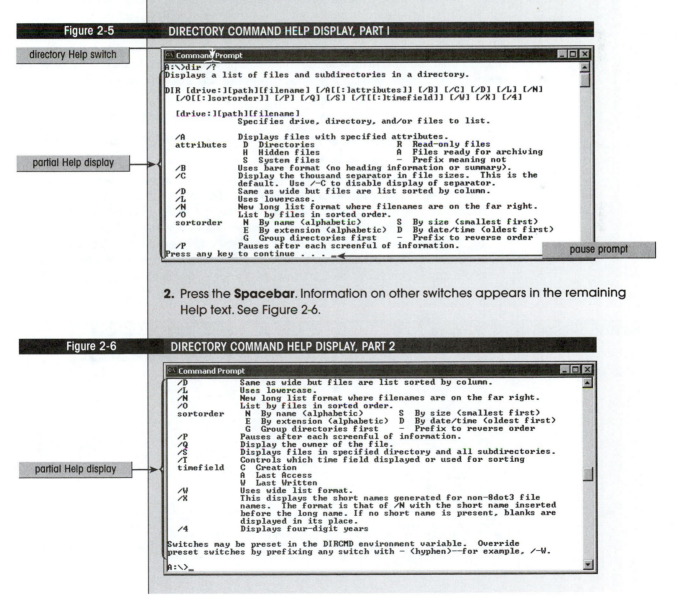

REFERENCE WINDOW   **RW**

Displaying Help on Directory Command Switches
- Open a Command Prompt window, if necessary.
- In the Command Prompt window, type DIR /? and then press Enter.
- Press the Spacebar to view the remaining Help text, and then return to the command prompt.

The Help switch provides valuable information about the variety of switches you can use with the DIR command. You'll find it especially useful when you need a quick reminder about how to use particular switches.

Pausing a Directory Listing

If the directory listing you are viewing with the Directory command contains information on more files than the Directory command can display in the window, Windows 2000 will scroll the directory listing. If you want to control this scrolling, you can use one of the Directory command's switches. The **Pause switch (/P)** modifies the Directory command so DIR displays a directory listing one full window or screen at a time, pausing to give you a chance to read the information in the window. The Pause switch is also referred to as the Page switch, because it outputs pages one window or screen at a time.

Let's try the Pause switch.

To view a directory listing one full window at a time:

1. Type **dir /p** and then press **Enter**. DIR displays the first full window, which contains part of the directory listing. See Figure 2-7. At the top of the window, the DIR command displays the volume label. If you did not assign a volume name to the diskette when you formatted it, DIR will tell you that the volume in the drive has no label. In this figure, DIR also shows the serial number assigned to the diskette. On the third line, DIR informs you that you are seeing a directory listing for a specific disk drive. At the bottom of this window, DIR displays a prompt to press any key to continue. Certain keys do not work, such as Caps Lock, Shift, Ctrl, Alt, Scroll Lock, Pause/Break, and Print Screen.

Figure 2-7   DIR PAUSES AFTER DISPLAYING THE FIRST SCREEN OF THE DIRECTORY LISTING

```
Command Prompt - dir /p                                          _ □ ×
Volume in drive A has no label.
Volume Serial Number is F065-B557

Directory of A:\

11/05/2003  04:22p          24,064 File0000.chk
11/05/2003  02:35p          10,258 ~WRC0070.tmp
09/05/2003  02:25p          13,824 Commission on Sales.xls
03/21/2003  08:08a          15,872 Client Invoices.xls
11/17/2003  04:41p          15,872 Weekly Worklog.xls
10/29/2003  10:30a          74,024 Invoice Form.wk4
05/07/2003  09:48a          15,872 Software Quotes.xls
05/30/2003  11:22a          22,016 Andre's Employee Payroll.xls
07/01/2003  08:31p          15,360 Daily Sales.xls
01/23/2003  09:21a          78,848 2002 Sales Summary #2.xls
04/18/2003  01:33p          16,896 Advertising Income.xls
01/08/2003  02:06p          24,064 Break Even Analysis.xls
01/23/2003  08:16a          41,472 2002 Sales Summary #1.xls
01/10/2003  10:54a          22,016 Data Systems Budget.xls
01/16/2003  10:46a          20,992 Five Year Growth Plan.xls
01/15/2003  02:21p          17,408 Five Year Plan Template.xls
03/28/2003  04:41p          22,528 Product List.xls
01/03/2003  12:02p          27,648 Product Sales Projection.xls
10/22/2003  01:52p          23,040 Regional Sales Projections.xls
Press any key to continue . . .
```

partial directory

pause prompt

2. Press a key, such as the **Spacebar** or any other key to continue. DIR displays the remainder of the directory listing. See Figure 2-8.

Figure 2-8   **DIR DISPLAYS THE NEXT, AND LAST, SCREEN OF THE DIRECTORY LISTING**

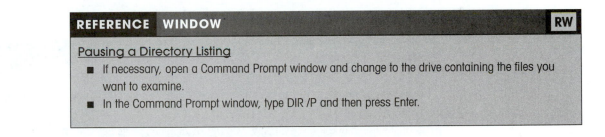

partial directory

```
Command Prompt                                                    _ □ ×
02/27/2002  08:53p              34,304 3 Year Sales Projection.xls
11/20/2003  08:55a              25,088 Projected Growth Memo.doc
08/08/2003  04:12p              20,480 Proposal.doc
03/27/2003  11:19a              22,028 Sales.wk4
10/31/2003  03:33p              14,848 Savings Plan.xls
09/23/2003  01:12p              14,848 Loan Payment Analysis.xls
09/23/2003  01:12p              31,232 Fonts.xls
06/26/2003  10:24a              53,248 Hardware.ppt
06/26/2003  09:30a              52,736 Application Software.ppt
06/26/2003  10:40a              42,496 Software.ppt
06/26/2003  10:55a              41,984 Using the Mouse.ppt
08/08/2003  03:22p              26,624 Formatting Features.xls
07/22/2003  01:32p              20,992 Format Code Colors.xls
07/09/2003  09:42a              49,152 Addressing Cells.xls
10/16/2003  10:31a              84,534 Colors of the Rainbow.bmp
10/16/2003  09:52a              84,446 Color Palette.bmp
10/16/2003  10:15a              17,910 Palette #1.bmp
10/16/2003  10:21a              17,910 Palette #2.bmp
01/24/2003  08:45a              18,944 Balance Sheet.xls
01/02/2003  03:43p              26,624 Sales Projections.xls
04/09/2003  02:12p              21,504 Employees.xls
              41 File(s)      1,248,070 bytes
               0 Dir(s)         207,872 bytes free

A:\>
```

REFERENCE WINDOW   **RW**

Pausing a Directory Listing
- If necessary, open a Command Prompt window and change to the drive containing the files you want to examine.
- In the Command Prompt window, type DIR /P and then press Enter.

The Pause (or Page) switch is the most commonly used switch for the DIR command, because directories often contain more files than will fit in the available window space. You can use this switch for the Directory command in all versions of Windows and DOS.

Viewing a Wide Directory Listing

If you want to view more filenames within the available window, you can use another command line switch. The **Wide switch (/W)** displays filenames in columns across the width of the window, and thus enables you to view more filenames at once. Although this switch displays the full filename with a period separating the main part of the filename from the file extension, it does not show the file size, date, and time. The number of columns the Wide switch displays depends on the length of the longest filenames. If the directory folder contains a very long filename, the switch will be unable to display the names side by side and you will still just see them in a single column.

Let's view a directory listing using the Wide switch. Remember that you can recall the last command you entered. Then you can **edit**, or modify, the command so it uses a different switch.

To view a wide directory listing:

1. Type **cls** and then press **Enter** to clear the window of the last directory listing.

2. Press the ↑ until you recall "dir /p." Press **Backspace** until you delete the "p." Then type **w** (the command should read "dir /w"). Now press **Enter**. DIR produces a directory listing that includes all of the files on your diskette in the window. See Figure 2-9.

Figure 2-9	**DIR DISPLAYS A WIDE DIRECTORY LISTING IN MULTIPLE COLUMNS**

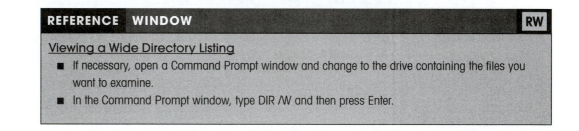

first column

second column

partial wide directory

```
Command Prompt
File0000.chk                      ~WRC0070.tmp
Commission on Sales.xls           Client Invoices.xls
Weekly Worklog.xls                Invoice Form.wk4
Software Quotes.xls               Andre's Employee Payroll.xls
Daily Sales.xls                   2002 Sales Summary #2.xls
Advertising Income.xls            Break Even Analysis.xls
2002 Sales Summary #1.xls         Data Systems Budget.xls
Five Year Growth Plan.xls         Five Year Plan Template.xls
Product List.xls                  Product Sales Projection.xls
Regional Sales Projections.xls    Sales Projection Models.xls
3 Year Sales Projection.xls       Projected Growth Memo.doc
Proposal.doc                      Sales.wk4
Savings Plan.xls                  Loan Payment Analysis.xls
Fonts.xls                         Hardware.ppt
Application Software.ppt          Software.ppt
Using the Mouse.ppt               Formatting Features.xls
Format Code Colors.xls            Addressing Cells.xls
Colors of the Rainbow.bmp         Color Palette.bmp
Palette #1.bmp                    Palette #2.bmp
Balance Sheet.xls                 Sales Projections.xls
Employees.xls
            41 File(s)      1,248,070 bytes
             0 Dir(s)         207,872 bytes free
A:\>_
```

REFERENCE	WINDOW	RW

Viewing a Wide Directory Listing

■ If necessary, open a Command Prompt window and change to the drive containing the files you want to examine.

■ In the Command Prompt window, type DIR /W and then press Enter.

You can also use the **Down** switch (**/D**) to view filenames in columns. It works just like the /W switch, except that the /D switch arranges filenames vertically instead of horizontally. When the /W switch displays filenames, it displays each filename in sequence "across," meaning on the same line as the previous name (in disk order, unless you specify sorting). When /W reaches the right side of the window, it displays the next name at the beginning of the following line on the left side. The /D switch, on the other hand, displays the next filename "down" instead of "across"—it puts the next name below the previous one in the same column and produces the same number of columns the /W switch would. By default, both /W and /D display filenames in disk order.

You'll find the **/D** switch of DIR in Windows 2000 and Windows NT, but not Windows 98 or Windows 95. You can use the /W switch in all versions of Windows and DOS.

Sorting Directory Listings

Next, you want to verify that the diskette includes a certain file containing a template for a balance sheet. Because DIR does not always display the directory listing in an order that makes it easy to find a file, you can use the **Order switch** (**/O**) to display filenames in alphabetical order. You can also combine this switch with the Pause switch to view one full window at a time.

To display the directory listing in alphabetical order by file-name, one full window at a time:

1. Type **dir /p /o** (making sure you type the letter "o" and not a zero for the Order switch) and then press **Enter**. DIR displays the first full window of filenames in alphabetical order. See Figure 2-10. The ninth file, "**Balance Sheet.xls**," is the one you need. Note that the title bar displays your command during execution, until it finishes and another command prompt appears.

   TROUBLE? If Windows 2000 displays the error message "Invalid switch - "0"," you may have typed the numeral zero (0) instead of the letter o. Recall the command, and change the zero to the letter o.

Figure 2-10	DIR DISPLAYS THE DIRECTORY LISTING IN ALPHABETICAL ORDER BY FILENAME

command displayed during execution

file containing balance sheet

alphabetical directory listing

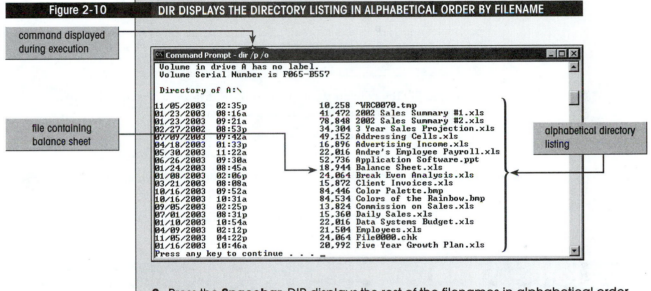

2. Press the **Spacebar**. DIR displays the rest of the filenames in alphabetical order. Windows 2000 then displays the command prompt.

3. Close the Command Prompt window.

You'll find the Order switch in all versions of Windows and all versions of DOS after DOS 5.0.

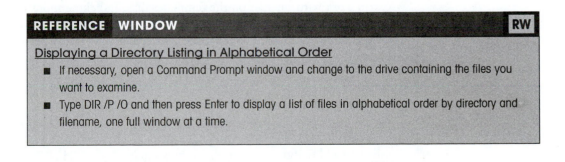

REFERENCE WINDOW **RW**

Displaying a Directory Listing in Alphabetical Order
- If necessary, open a Command Prompt window and change to the drive containing the files you want to examine.
- Type DIR /P /O and then press Enter to display a list of files in alphabetical order by directory and filename, one full window at a time.

The Page, Wide, and Order switches are the most commonly used and handiest switches for the Directory command.

Now that you have used the DIR command and some of its most basic switches, in the next session you will learn additional ways in which to use the DIR command.

Session 2.1 QUICK CHECK

1. Windows 2000 keeps track of the last 50 commands you enter at the command prompt in an area of memory known as the _____.

2. To alternate between inserting and replacing text as you type, use the _____ key.

3. If you do not specify a drive name, the Directory command will refer to the _____ drive shown in the Command Prompt window and display the directory listing for that drive.

4. If your directory listing contains more directory and file names than the Directory command can list in the window, Windows 2000 adjusts the window view through a process called _____.

5. By default, DIR lists the files in _____ —which is the order in which the system keeps track of the files.

6. The _____ identifies the type of information in a file.

7. To modify the Directory command so DIR displays a directory listing one full window at a time, use the _____ switch.

8. To display filenames in columns across the window, and therefore enable you to view more filenames at once, use the _____ switch.

9. What alternative to the above switch can you use, which arranges filenames vertically instead of horizontally?

10. To display filenames in alphabetical order, use the _____ switch.

SESSION 2.2

In this session you will use advanced DIR command line switches, such as adding sort order parameters to the /order switch. You will specify file characteristics normally concealed from view, including five file attributes and short filenames, as well as switches that change the appearance of the DIR display. You will use wildcards with switches, examine the Windows environment, and specify default switches for the Directory command.

Using Advanced Command Line Switches

As you work with the files on the templates disk, Isabel mentions to you that the Directory command has more advanced switches that are helpful in certain situations. Furthermore, some of the switches used with the Directory command have additional parameters that further enhance their usefulness.

Using Sort Order Parameters

You can use sort order parameters with the Order switch to view a directory listing in order by filename, file extension, size, and date and time. The sort order parameters are one-character codes you add to the Order switch, as shown in Figure 2-11. For example, if you want to sort a directory listing by file size, you would use the Size (**S**) sort order parameter in one of two ways:

DIR /O:S
DIR /OS

Although the syntax for the Directory command indicates that you should use a colon after the Order switch and before the sort order parameter, this command still works properly if you do not include the colon.

Figure 2-11	SORT ORDER PARAMETERS FOR THE ORDER SWITCH
SORT ORDER PARAMETERS	**DISPLAYS FILENAMES IN ORDER BY**
/OE or /O:E	File extension only
/OEN or /O:EN	File extension, then by main part of filename
/OD or /O:D	File date and time
/OS or /O:S	File size
/ON or /O:N	Main part of filename only
/O or /ONE or /O:NE	By main part of filename and then by file extension

You can also reverse the sort order by placing a minus sign (-) in front of the sort order parameter. For example, if you wanted to display filenames in reverse order by file size, you would use the Sort order parameter in one of the following two ways:

DIR /O:-S
DIR /O-S

Isabel recommends you try several of these sort order parameters so you become familiar with their use. So you know what types of files are contained on this templates disk, use the **Extension** (**E**) sort order parameter with the Order switch. You can also combine this switch with the Page switch to control scrolling in the Command Prompt window.

You can also combine sort order parameters with the Order switch. For example, if you want to display filenames in order by file extension first, then by filename, use the following command:

DIR /OEN

In the above command, /OEN means "in order, by extension, then by name."

To view a directory listing in alphabetical order by file extension:

1. Make sure your copy of Data Disk #1 is in drive A, open a Command Prompt window, change the foreground and background colors if necessary, change to drive A, and then clear the window.

2. Type **dir /p /oe** and then press **Enter**. The Directory command displays filenames in order by file extension, and pauses after the first full window. See Figure 2-12. The first four files have the same file extension, "bmp," which indicates they are bitmap image files produced with a graphics program like Paint. The next file has the file extension "chk," which means it is a Recovered File Fragment created by the Check Disk (CHKDSK) utility program, and then the next two files have the file extension "doc," which stands for "Document." Microsoft Word adds the file extension "doc" to files that you create in it, so these are Word files. Even though the filenames are arranged in order by file extension, note that files with the same file extension are not arranged alphabetically by the main part of the filename. For example, the Directory command lists "Palette #2.bmp" before "Palette #1.bmp."

Figure 2-12   DIRECTORY LISTING IN ALPHABETICAL ORDER BY FILE EXTENSION

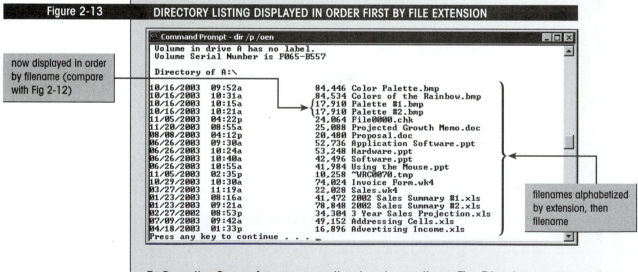

file extension

filenames in alphabetical order by file extension

Files with the "tmp" file extension are temporary files; files with the "wk4" file extension are Lotus 1-2-3 spreadsheet files; and files with the "xls" extension are Microsoft Excel spreadsheet files.

3. Press the **Spacebar**, or any other key, to continue. The Directory command displays the remainder of the directory listing sorted by file extension.

4. Type **dir /p /oen** and then press **Enter**. The Directory command now lists the filenames in order first by file extension, then in order next by the main part of the filename. See Figure 2-13. Note that "Palette #1.bmp" is now listed before "Palette #2.bmp."

Figure 2-13   DIRECTORY LISTING DISPLAYED IN ORDER FIRST BY FILE EXTENSION

now displayed in order by filename (compare with Fig 2-12)

filenames alphabetized by extension, then filename

5. Press the **Spacebar**, or any other key, to continue. The Directory command displays the remainder of the directory listing sorted by file extension and then the main part of the filename.

Displaying a Directory Listing in Alphabetical Order by File Extension
- If necessary, open a Command Prompt window and change to the drive containing the files you want to examine.
- Type DIR /P /OE and then press Enter to display a list of files in alphabetical order by file extension, one full window at a time.
- Type DIR /P /OEN and then press the Enter key to display a list of files in alphabetical order by file extension first, then by the main part of the filename second, one full window at a time.

If you need to locate important files you created or modified on a certain date, you can do so quickly by using the **Date (D)** sort order parameter. When you use this sort order parameter, the Directory command lists the files in order by date, from the file with the oldest date to the most recently created file. Because you more often than not will need to locate files on which you have recently worked, you can reverse this order by placing a minus sign in front of the Date sort order parameter. DIR then lists the files in reverse order by date, with the most recently created files listed first.

To view a directory listing by file date from the most recent date:

1. Type **dir /p /o-d** and then press **Enter**. Make sure you do not include a blank space between the /o and -d. The Directory command displays filenames in order from the most recent file dates to the oldest file date. See Figure 2-14.

Figure 2-14	DIRECTORY LISTING IN REVERSE ORDER BY FILE DATE AND TIME

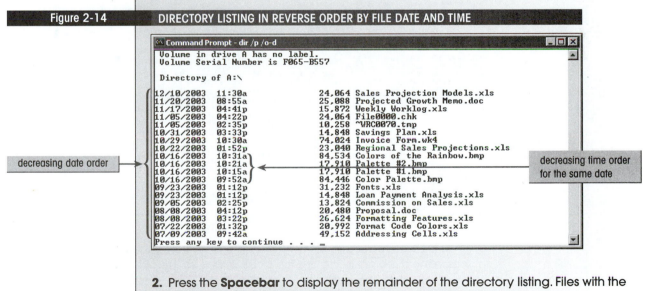

2. Press the **Spacebar** to display the remainder of the directory listing. Files with the oldest file dates are listed last in the directory listing.

REFERENCE   WINDOW   **RW**

Displaying a Directory Listing in Order by File Date
- If necessary, open a Command Prompt window and change to the drive containing the files you want to examine.
- Type DIR /P /OD and then press Enter to display files in order by file date (from the oldest file to the most recent file), one full window at a time.
- Type DIR /P /O-D and then press the Enter key to display files in reverse order by file date (from the most recent file to the oldest file), one full window at a time.

You can use the Directory command to check file sizes periodically to determine how efficiently you are using storage space on a disk. If you use the **Size (S)** sort order parameter, the Directory command will list files from the smallest to the largest, or you can use the minus sign to reverse the order and list files from the largest to the smallest. Because large files have the greatest impact on the availability of disk space, you are most likely to list those files first.

To view a directory listing in reverse order by file size:

1. Type **dir /p /o-s** and then press **Enter**. DIR displays the first full window of directory information. The files are listed in reverse order by file size, starting with the largest file on the diskette. See Figure 2-15.

Figure 2-15	DIRECTORY LISTING IN REVERSE ORDER BY FILE SIZE

```
Command Prompt - dir /p /o-s                                    _ □ ×
Volume in drive A has no label.
Volume Serial Number is F065-B557

Directory of A:\

10/16/2003   10:31a          84,534 Colors of the Rainbow.bmp
10/16/2003   09:52a          84,446 Color Palette.bmp
01/23/2003   09:21a          78,848 2002 Sales Summary #2.xls
10/29/2003   10:30a          74,024 Invoice Form.wk4
06/26/2003   10:24a          53,248 Hardware.ppt
06/26/2003   09:30a          52,736 Application Software.ppt
07/09/2003   09:42a          49,152 Addressing Cells.xls
06/26/2003   10:40a          42,496 Software.ppt
06/26/2003   10:55a          41,984 Using the Mouse.ppt
01/23/2003   08:16a          41,472 2002 Sales Summary #1.xls
02/27/2002   08:53p          34,304 3 Year Sales Projection.xls
09/23/2003   01:12p          31,232 Fonts.xls
01/03/2003   12:02p          27,648 Product Sales Projection.xls
08/08/2003   03:22p          26,624 Formatting Features.xls
01/02/2003   03:43p          26,624 Sales Projections.xls
11/20/2003   08:55a          25,088 Projected Growth Memo.doc
01/08/2003   02:06p          24,064 Break Even Analysis.xls
12/10/2003   11:30a          24,064 Sales Projection Models.xls
11/05/2003   04:22p          24,064 File0000.chk
Press any key to continue . . . _
```

decreasing order by size

2. Press the **Spacebar** to display the remainder of the directory listing. The last files in the directory listing are the smallest files on the diskette.

REFERENCE **WINDOW**   **RW**

<u>Displaying a Directory Listing in Order by File Size</u>

- If necessary, open a Command Prompt window and change to the drive containing the files you want to examine.
- Type DIR /P /OS and then press Enter to display files in order by file size (from the smallest to the largest file), one full window at a time.
- Type DIR /P /O-S and then press Enter to display files in reverse order by file size (from the largest to the smallest file), one full window at a time.

By using this last option, you can quickly locate the largest files in the first window and decide whether to archive these files. When you **archive** a file, you copy a file you no longer use (but want to keep) from your hard disk to some type of storage medium, such as a recordable CD, DVD, tape, Zip disk or perhaps even a diskette, so you still have a copy of the file, but it is not taking up valuable storage space on your hard disk.

Displaying Short Filenames

As noted earlier, if you use programs designed for Windows 2000, Windows 98, Windows NT Workstation 4.0, or Windows 95, you can use long filenames with up to 255 characters to more clearly identify the contents and purpose of a file. You can also include special symbols or characters, such as the ampersand (&), pound sign (#), dollar sign ($), percent symbol (%), apostrophes (' or '), as well as opening and closing parentheses and spaces. You can also assign long filenames to folders so you can clearly identify the types of files stored within those folders.

If you assign a long filename to a folder or file, all of these versions of Windows also automatically create a short filename for the file to provide compatibility with older programs designed to run under DOS and Windows 3.x (such as Windows 3.1 and 3.11). A **short filename** is an MS-DOS filename (also called an **MS-DOS-Readable filename** or an **alias**) that follows the rules and conventions for 8.3 filenames (that is, names that allow 8 characters and then a 3-character extension). These types of filenames are also referred to as 8dot3 filenames.

When Windows 2000 creates a short filename, it uses the first six characters of the long filename, and then follows this with a tilde (~), a unique number (starting with 1), a period, and the first three (or fewer) characters of the file extension (the characters that follow the last period in the filename). Windows 2000 strips out characters that MS-DOS cannot read as well as spaces and any extra periods, and it displays all short filenames in uppercase (the default for DOS). If you use a filename that follows the 8.3 filenaming convention for DOS and Windows 3.x programs and also use all uppercase characters, then the long filename and alias are the same. Windows 98 and Windows 95 use this same approach.

For example, if you have a directory folder named "Cressler Graphics, Inc.", Windows 2000 will assign this folder the short name CRESSL~1 (assuming there is no other file with the same name) with no file type extension, because the long filename has none (the usual case with directory folder names). Note that mixed case and lowercase (which Windows 2000 recognizes) are converted to uppercase (the default for the DOS operating system). If another file in the same folder had already been assigned the short filename CRESSL~1, Windows 2000 would use an **algorithm**, or formula, to increment the number until a unique filename is found. Windows 2000 would then check to see if another folder (or file if the file has no file extension, such as some Windows 2000 system files) used the short filename CRESSL~2. If not, it would use this short filename for the "Cressler Graphics, Inc." folder.

If there are five or more files that would end up with short filenames where the first six characters are the same, Windows 2000 and Windows NT 4.0 uses a different approach than Windows 98 or Windows 95 for creating a short filename. They use the first two characters of the long filename, and then they mathematically generate the next four characters of the filename. Next, they add a tilde (~) followed by the number 1 (or if necessary, a unique number to avoid a duplicate filename).

In a My Computer or Windows Explorer window, you might see a folder, shortcut, and file with the same name; however, the file extension (if present) differs. Folders usually do not have file extensions. Shortcuts have the file extension "lnk" (for link) or, in the case of shortcuts to DOS programs, "pif" (for Program Information File). Files usually have a file extension that associates the file with a program.

The short filename is important for DOS programs and Windows 3.x programs used under Windows 2000 (as well as Windows 98, Windows NT Workstation 4.0, and Windows 95) because those programs do not recognize long filenames for folders and files. Instead, these programs can recognize only the short filename for folders and files. If you open a program designed for a version of Windows after Windows 3.x, such as Microsoft Word 2000, and then attempt to open a file, you will see only the long filenames in the Open and Save As dialog boxes. If you open a DOS program or a Windows 3.x program (such as an earlier version of Microsoft Word), and then attempt to open a file, you will see only the short filenames in the Open and Save As dialog boxes. This can make it difficult to know which folder or file to open or which file to replace.

To illustrate these two different ways of displaying filenames, examine the next two figures. Figure 2-16 shows an Open dialog box for Microsoft Word 2000—a program that recognizes long filenames. Note that you can see long filenames for folders and files. Also note that the long filenames "2002 Sales Summary #1.xls" and "2002 Sales Summary #2.xls," and the long filenames "Five Year Growth Plan.xls" and "Five Year Plan Template.xls," are similar.

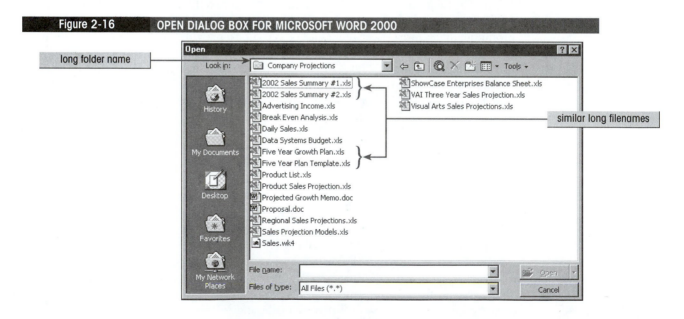

Figure 2-16   **OPEN DIALOG BOX FOR MICROSOFT WORD 2000**

Figure 2-17 shows an Open dialog box for Collage Complete—a Windows 3.1 program used to create the figures in this book. Notice that you can see only the short filenames for folders and files. 2002SA~1.XLS and 2002SA~2.XLS are the short filenames for "2002 Sales Summary #1.xls" and "2002 Sales Summary #2.xls." The "1" and the "2" after the tildes in the short filenames bear no relationship to the "1" and "2" after the pound signs (#) in the original long filenames. If you had created the file "2002 Sales Summary #2.xls" first, its short filename would be 2002SA~1.XLS, and the short filename for "2002 Sales Summary #1.xls" would be 2002SA~2.XLS. Likewise, FIVEYE~1.XLS and FIVEYE~2.XLS are the short filenames for the files "Five Year Growth Plan.xls" and "Five Year Plan Template.xls," but there is no way to tell which is which from these short filenames.

Figure 2-17	OPEN DIALOG BOX FROM A WINDOWS 3.1 APPLICATION

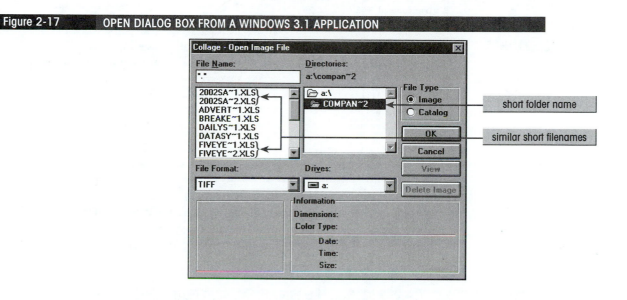

Under Windows 2000 and Windows NT 4.0, you can use the **/X** switch of the Directory command to see short filenames for both files and directories (Tutorial 4 covers directories). This feature might prove useful if you want to know the short filename for a directory or file before you switch to a Windows 3.1 or DOS program and then use the short filename.

To view short filenames in a directory listing:

1. Type **dir /p /o /x** and then press **Enter**. The directory listing now contains the short filename along with each long filename. See Figure 2-18. Note that the short filenames for "2002 Sales Summary #1.xls" and "2002 Sales Summary #2.xls" are similar (2002SA~1.XLS and 2002SA~2.XLS), and note that all short filenames are in uppercase. The operating system assigns the numbers in short filenames without regard to any numbering in the long filenames. For example, "2002 Sales Summary #2.xls" has the short name 2002SA~1.xls because it happened to receive its short filename first during a copy operation, before "2002 Sales Summary #1.xls."

   TROUBLE? If your directory listing includes blank lines or lines containing just a few characters, then a long filename on the preceding line was too long to fit on one line, and it wrapped around to the next line.

Figure 2-18 DIRECTORY LISTING WITH SHORT AND LONG FILENAMES

short filenames

similar short filenames

long filenames

```
Command Prompt - dir /p /o /x
 Volume in drive A has no label.
 Volume Serial Number is F065-B557

 Directory of A:\

11/05/2003  02:35p              10,258 ~WRC0070.TMP  ~WRC0070.tmp
01/23/2003  08:16a              41,472 2002SA~2.XLS  2002 Sales Summary #1.xls
01/23/2003  09:21a              78,848 2002SA~1.XLS  2002 Sales Summary #2.xls
02/27/2002  08:53p              34,304 3YEARS~1.XLS  3 Year Sales Projection.x
ls
07/09/2003  09:42a              49,152 ADDRES~1.XLS  Addressing Cells.xls
04/18/2003  01:33p              16,896 ADVERT~1.XLS  Advertising Income.xls
05/30/2003  11:22a              22,016 ANDRE'~1.XLS  Andre's Employee Payroll.
xls
06/26/2003  09:30a              52,736 APPLIC~1.PPT  Application Software.ppt
01/24/2003  08:45a              18,944 BALANC~1.XLS  Balance Sheet.xls
01/08/2003  02:06p              24,064 BREAKE~1.XLS  Break Even Analysis.xls
03/21/2003  08:08a              15,872 CLIENT~1.XLS  Client Invoices.xls
10/16/2003  09:52a              84,446 COLORP~1.BMP  Color Palette.bmp
10/16/2003  10:31a              84,534 COLORS~1.BMP  Colors of the Rainbow.bmp
09/05/2003  02:25p              13,824 COMMIS~1.XLS  Commission on Sales.xls
Press any key to continue . . .
```

2. Press the **Spacebar** to display the next part of the directory listing. See Figure 2-19. Note that a long filename—like Fonts.xls, which also meets the guidelines for naming files under MS-DOS (8.3 characters)—has identical long and short filename (except the short filename is in uppercase).

Figure 2-19 DIRECTORY LISTING WITH SHORT AND LONG FILENAMES

similar short and long filenames

```
Command Prompt - dir /p /o /x
01/10/2003  10:54a              22,016 DATASY~1.XLS  Data Systems Budget.xls
04/09/2003  02:12p              21,504 EMPLOY~1.XLS  Employees.xls
11/05/2003  04:22p              24,064 FILE0000.CHK  File0000.chk
01/16/2003  10:46a              20,992 FIVEYE~1.XLS  Five Year Growth Plan.xls
01/15/2003  02:21p              17,408 FIVEYE~2.XLS  Five Year Plan Template.x
ls
09/23/2003  01:12p              31,232 FONTS.XLS     Fonts.xls
07/22/2003  01:32p              20,992 FORMAT~2.XLS  Format Code Colors.xls
08/08/2003  03:22p              26,624 FORMAT~1.XLS  Formatting Features.xls
06/26/2003  10:24a              53,248 HARDWARE.PPT  Hardware.ppt
10/29/2003  10:30a              74,024 INVOIC~1.WK4  Invoice Form.wk4
09/23/2003  01:12p              14,848 LOANPA~1.XLS  Loan Payment Analysis.xls
10/16/2003  10:15a              17,910 PALETT~1.BMP  Palette #1.bmp
10/16/2003  10:21a              17,910 PALETT~2.BMP  Palette #2.bmp
03/28/2003  04:41p              22,528 PRODUC~1.XLS  Product List.xls
01/03/2003  12:02p              27,648 PRODUC~2.XLS  Product Sales Projection.
xls
11/20/2003  08:55a              25,088 PROJEC~1.DOC  Projected Growth Memo.doc
08/08/2003  04:12p              20,480 PROPOSAL.DOC  Proposal.doc
10/22/2003  01:52p              23,040 REGION~1.XLS  Regional Sales Projection
s.xls
Press any key to continue . . .
```

3. Press the **Spacebar** as many times as necessary to view the remainder of the directory listing, until you see the command prompt.

REFERENCE WINDOW RW

Displaying Short Filenames in a Directory Listing

- If necessary, open a Command Prompt window and change to the drive containing the files you want to examine.
- Type DIR /P /O /X and then press Enter to display a list of files in alphabetical order by long and short filenames, one full window at a time.

Understanding how Windows 2000 works with long and short filenames is important if you work with DOS, Windows 3.x, and programs for later versions of Windows on the same or different computer systems. You will need to know how long and short filenames work if you provide support to clients who might have a variety of software configurations on their computers, if you troubleshoot problems, or if you set up, configure, and customize computers for other users. When using DOS and Windows 3.x programs, think carefully about how you name files and adopt a convention or approach that makes it easy to locate files by their short filenames. For example, instead of using long filenames like "Five Year Growth Plan.xls" (with the short filename FIVEYE~1.XLS) and "Five Year Plan Template.xls" (with the short filename FIVEYE~2.XLS), you could use the long filenames "Five Year Growth Plan.xls" (with the short filename FIVEYE~1.XLS) and "Template for a Five Year Plan.xls" (with the short filename TEMPLA~1.XLS). Then you could easily tell these files apart in a Windows 3.x program from their short filenames.

In the Command Prompt window, the DIR command in Windows 98 and Windows 95 uses a different approach from Windows 2000 (and Windows NT 4.0) to display short filenames. The Windows 95/98 DIR command has no /X switch, but always lists the short filename and type extension at the beginning of each line and then displays the long filename at the end of the line, like the DIR command in Windows NT 4.0 and Windows 2000. Again, Windows 95 and 98 do not support long filenames when you boot to "Command prompt only" or "Safe mode command prompt only" from their Startup Menu; the DIR command then shows only short filenames.

Displaying a Directory using File Attributes

The Directory command contains an Attribute (/A) switch for displaying files with specific file attributes. An **attribute** is a setting consisting of a bit turned on or off by the operating system, and defines a particular characteristic of the file. Files with the **System** (**S**) attribute are operating system files. Files with the **Hidden** (**H**) attribute on are not displayed in directory listings. System files typically have both the System and Hidden attribute turned on to protect the files. You can open files with the **Read-Only** (**R**) attribute on, but you cannot save any changes to the file under the same filename (you have to use a different filename). At the command prompt, you cannot delete files with the Read-Only attribute on (although you can in My Computer and Windows Explorer). Each time you create a new file, or open, modify, and save an existing file, Windows 2000 turns on the **Archive** (**A**) attribute of the file to indicate that it has not been backed up by any standard backup utility. A backup utility can turn off the Archive attribute when it backs up a file. Later, if you make changes to the file, the operating system will turn on its Archive attribute again, so you can back up only newly changed files with your backup utility. Files with their **Directory** (**D**) attribute turned on are directories. As in UNIX, and other operating systems a directory folder is actually a specialized type of file, which the operating system treats differently from regular files.

If you need to troubleshoot a problem or check certain files to make sure they have a certain attribute turned on, you can use the Attribute switch (/A) with one of the attribute parameters described above.

To view files with a specific attribute turned on:

1. Type **c:** and then press **Enter**. Windows 2000 changes the default drive to drive C—as shown by the command prompt.

2. Type **cls** and then press **Enter** to clear the window.

3. Type **dir /o /p** and then press **Enter**. The Directory command displays the contents of the root directory of drive C in alphabetical order (one full window or screen at a time if there are more directories and files than will fit within the window or screen). On the computer used for Figure 2-20, the directory listing shows that the root directory contains only subdirectories (and no files). On this computer, the figure shows three subdirectories of the root directory.

Figure 2-20	DIR DISPLAYS THE ROOT DIRECTORY OF DRIVE C

directory command with Order and Pause switches

```
Command Prompt                                                    _ □ ×

C:\>dir /o /p
 Volume in drive C is WIN2000
 Volume Serial Number is BC31-588C

 Directory of C:\

02/28/2003  01:36p    <DIR>          Documents and Settings
02/28/2003  01:37p    <DIR>          Program Files
02/28/2003  01:33p    <DIR>          WINNT

               0 File(s)              0 bytes
               3 Dir(s)    1,007,897,600 bytes free

C:\>_
```

regular directory listng

4. View the remainder of the directory listing and display the command prompt (if necessary), clear the window, type **dir /o /p /as** and then press **Enter**. In the computer used for Figure 2-21, the Directory command now displays a list of ten files and four subdirectories. Your display may differ. For example, the "Recycled" directory was not displayed in the previous directory listing. This directory is where Windows 2000 stores items you delete and send to the Recycle Bin. All of the files and directories are normally hidden from view because they have their System attribute turned on. In fact, their Hidden attribute is also turned on. When a directory listing contains both directories and files, the Order switch lists directories in alphabetical order first, and files in alphabetical order next.

Figure 2-21	ONLY FILES AND DIRECTORIES WITH THE SYSTEM ATTRIBUTE TURNED ON

Attribute switch for system files

```
Command Prompt                                                    _ □ ×

C:\>dir /o /p /as
 Volume in drive C is WIN2000
 Volume Serial Number is BC31-588C

 Directory of C:\

05/17/2003  06:04p    <DIR>          cmdcons
04/21/2003  11:09a    <DIR>          Recycled
06/17/2003  09:04p    <DIR>          RECYCLER
06/16/2003  10:13a    <DIR>          System Volume Information
12/07/1999  12:00p          148,992  arcldr.exe
12/07/1999  12:00p          162,816  arcsetup.exe
05/17/2003  06:05p              268  boot.ini
04/16/2003  10:51p              512  bootsect.dos
12/07/1999  05:00a          229,264  cmldr
04/16/2003  11:47p                0  IO.SYS
04/16/2003  11:47p                0  MSDOS.SYS
12/07/1999  05:00a           34,468  NTDETECT.COM
12/07/1999  05:00a          214,416  ntldr
07/03/2003  08:47a      100,663,296  pagefile.sys
              10 File(s)    101,454,032 bytes
               4 Dir(s)   1,009,269,248 bytes free

C:\>_
```

directories and files with the System attribute only

Ntldr (which stands for NT Loader) is the operating system file that boots your computer. NTDetect.com is the operating system file that, during booting, checks the hardware components installed on your computer so Windows 2000 can properly configure your computer system. Boot.ini is an operating system file containing boot settings. Pagefile.sys, the largest of all the files, is an operating system file referred to as a **paging file**, or **swap file**. When Windows 2000 needs more RAM than is installed on your computer in order to support programs, it sets aside storage space on the hard disk as supplemental RAM. That storage space is the paging file. If Windows 2000 needs more memory, it will temporarily write parts of memory you are not currently using to the paging file on disk, so it can load other program code and documents. On the computer in Figure 2-22, Windows 2000 set aside 96 MB of hard disk storage space for the paging file. (Note that there are 1,024 bytes in each kilobyte, and 1,024 kilobytes in each megabyte.) The combination of RAM plus the paging file constitutes what is called **virtual memory**.

5. View the remainder of the directory listing and display the command prompt (if necessary), clear the window, type **dir /o /p /ah** and then press **Enter**. In the computer in Figure 2-22, the Directory command now displays a list of twelve files and four directories with their Hidden attribute on. Your display may differ. The additional two files not shown in the previous directory listing figure are Config.sys and Autoexec.bat—the MS-DOS startup configuration files. You can use the scroll bar to view the output of the previous command.

Figure 2-22	FILES AND SUBDIRECTORIES WITH THE HIDDEN ATTRIBUTE ONLY

Attribute switch for hidden files

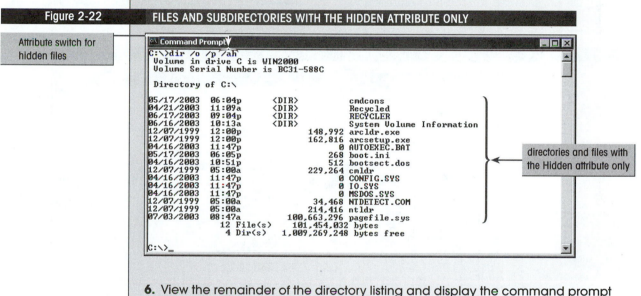

directories and files with the Hidden attribute only

6. View the remainder of the directory listing and display the command prompt (if necessary), clear the window, type **dir /o /p /ar** and then press **Enter**. The Directory command now displays a list of files with their Read-Only attribute turned on. Your display may differ from Figure 2-23. This directory listing also contains one directory—Program Files—which contains all or the majority of the installed software (other than the operating System) on your computer.

Figure 2-23   FILES AND SUBDIRECTORIES WITH THE READ-ONLY ATTRIBUTE ONLY

Attribute switch for
read-only files

```
Command Prompt
C:\>dir /o /p /ar
 Volume in drive C is WIN2000
 Volume Serial Number is BC31-588C

 Directory of C:\

05/17/2003  06:04p    <DIR>          cmdcons
06/16/2003  12:02p    <DIR>          Program Files
12/07/1999  12:00p           148,992 arcldr.exe
12/07/1999  12:00p           162,816 arcsetup.exe
05/17/2003  06:05p               268 boot.ini
12/07/1999  05:00a           229,264 cmldr
04/16/2003  11:47p                 0 IO.SYS
04/16/2003  11:47p                 0 MSDOS.SYS
12/07/1999  05:00a            34,468 NTDETECT.COM
12/07/1999  05:00a           214,416 ntldr
               8 File(s)        790,224 bytes
               2 Dir(s)   1,009,269,248 bytes free

C:\>
```

directories and files
with the Read-only
attribute only

7. View the remainder of the directory listing and display the command prompt (if necessary), type **dir /o /p /a** and then press **Enter**. If you use the Attribute (/A) switch without attribute parameters, the Directory command displays all files—no matter which attributes are turned on or off. Again, your display may differ from Figure 2-24. You can think of /A as specifying "all files."

Figure 2-24   ALL FILES AND SUBDIRECTORIES REGARDLESS OF ATTRIBUTES

```
Command Prompt - dir /o /p /a
 Volume in drive C is WIN2000
 Volume Serial Number is BC31-588C

 Directory of C:\

05/17/2003  06:04p    <DIR>          cmdcons
06/19/2003  09:28p    <DIR>          Documents and Settings
06/16/2003  12:02p    <DIR>          Program Files
04/21/2003  11:09a    <DIR>          Recycled
06/17/2003  09:04p    <DIR>          RECYCLER
06/16/2003  10:13a    <DIR>          System Volume Information
06/20/2003  01:50p    <DIR>          WINNT
12/07/1999  12:00p           148,992 arcldr.exe
12/07/1999  12:00p           162,816 arcsetup.exe
04/16/2003  11:47p                 0 AUTOEXEC.BAT
05/17/2003  06:05p               268 boot.ini
04/16/2003  10:51p               512 bootsect.dos
12/07/1999  05:00a           229,264 cmldr
04/16/2003  11:47p                 0 CONFIG.SYS
04/16/2003  11:47p                 0 IO.SYS
04/16/2003  11:47p                 0 MSDOS.SYS
12/07/1999  05:00a            34,468 NTDETECT.COM
12/07/1999  05:00a           214,416 ntldr
07/03/2003  08:47a       100,663,296 pagefile.sys
Press any key to continue . . . _
```

all directories and files
listed using /A switch

8. View the remainder of the directory listing and display the command prompt (if necessary), type **dir /o /p /ad** and then press **Enter**. The directory listing now contains only directories—no matter what other attributes are on or off for the directories. No files are listed. Again, your display may differ from Figure 2-25. You can use this switch whenever you want to see just the names of subdirectories of a directory quickly.

Figure 2-25	DIR DISPLAYS ONLY SUBDIRECTORIES

Attribute switch for directories only

```
Command Prompt                                              _ □ ×

C:\>dir /o /p /ad
 Volume in drive C is WIN2000
 Volume Serial Number is BC31-588C

 Directory of C:\

05/17/2003  06:04p    <DIR>        cmdcons
06/19/2003  09:28p    <DIR>        Documents and Settings
06/16/2003  12:02p    <DIR>        Program Files
04/21/2003  11:09a    <DIR>        Recycled
06/17/2003  09:04p    <DIR>        RECYCLER
06/16/2003  10:13a    <DIR>        System Volume Information
06/20/2003  01:50p    <DIR>        WINNT
               0 File(s)           0 bytes
               7 Dir(s)   1,009,037,824 bytes free

C:\>_
```

only directories listed

9. If necessary, view the remainder of the directory listing and display the command prompt.

REFERENCE   WINDOW   **RW**

Displaying a Directory Listing by File Attribute

- If necessary, open a Command Prompt window and change to the drive containing the files you want to examine.
- Type DIR /P /O /AS and then press Enter to display a list of files with the System attribute turned on in alphabetical order by filename, one full window at a time.
- Type DIR /P /O /AH and then press Enter to display a list of files with the Hidden attribute turned on in alphabetical order by filename, one full window at a time.
- Type DIR /P /O /AR and then press Enter to display a list of files with the Read-Only attribute turned on in alphabetical order by filename, one full window at a time.
- Type DIR /P /O /A and then press Enter to display a list of all files (no matter which attribute is on or off for each file) in alphabetical order by filename, one full window at a time.
- Type DIR /P /O /AD and then press Enter to display a list of directories with the Directory attribute turned on in alphabetical order by name, one full window at a time.

The Attribute switch and the same attribute parameters are available when working at the command prompt in Windows 98, Windows NT, Windows 95, and MS-DOS, and are invaluable when you need to check attributes of system and configuration files. Although you can select and view files based on their attributes using My Computer or Windows Explorer, the DIR command makes it easier and more straightforward.

Using Wildcards

Isabel informs you that employees will frequently ask about the availability of certain types of files on the templates disk. Until you are more familiar with the disk, Isabel tells you that you can quickly search for files using wildcards with the Directory command. This skill will also improve your proficiency when troubleshooting in a Command Prompt window.

Wildcards simplify the process of selecting files with similar filenames or similar file extensions. A **wildcard** is a symbol that substitutes for one or more characters in a filename. There are two wildcard characters—the question mark and the asterisk. The **question**

mark (?) substitutes for a single character in a filename, whereas the **asterisk** (*) typically substitutes for one or more characters. You can use wildcards with any command that operates on files. In the case of the Directory command, you can use wildcards to select and display information on a set of files within a directory, rather than display information about all the files. You can also combine wildcards with switches to improve the results of your selections. The advantage of using wildcards is that you can quickly and efficiently perform operations at the command prompt.

Using the Asterisk Wildcard

Carlos Escobar, SolarWinds' new financial analyst, asks you if there are any Microsoft Excel files on the templates disk containing sales projections, so that he can create financial forecasts for the coming year.

Because files produced with Microsoft Excel have the file extension "xls," you can use the following command with the asterisk wildcard to display a list of spreadsheets:

DIR *.XLS /O /P

The "*.XLS" in the command is called a **file specification**, and it provides information about the type of files you want to select and display in a directory listing. The asterisk instructs the Directory command to display all files regardless of the main part of the filename. The "XLS" instructs the Directory command to display only files with "xls" as the file extension (case does not matter).

To select files with the same file extension:

1. Make sure your Data Disk is in drive A, type **a:** and then press **Enter** to change to drive A.

2. Type **dir *.xls /o /p** and then press **Enter**. The Directory command displays the names of files with the "xls" file extension in alphabetical order by filename, and then pauses after the first full window. See Figure 2-26. As you can see, the asterisk substitutes for any combination of characters in the main part of the filename. The one feature all these files have in common is the "xls" file extension.

| Figure 2-26 | ASTERISK WILDCARD SELECTS FILES WITH THE SAME FILE EXTENSION |

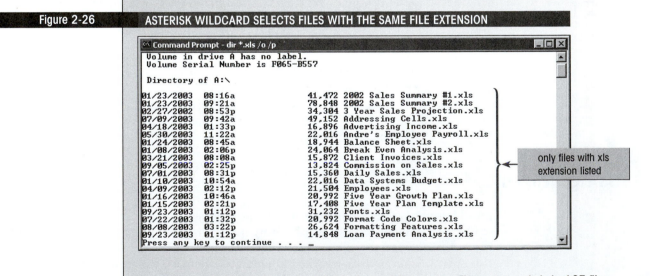

3. Display the next (and last) full window of filenames. There are a total of 27 files out of the 41 files on the disk that contain "xls" as the file extension.

You would like to narrow down the selection even more for Carlos. You notice a file in the directory listing with Projection at the end of the main part of the filename, and decide to list only Excel files with the word "Projection" in their names.

To use a file specification that narrows the selection:

1. Clear the window, type **dir *projection.xls /o /p** and then press **Enter**. The Directory command lists two files that are sales projections. See Figure 2-27. Notice that both filenames have the word "Projection" at the end of the main part of the filename. The asterisk wildcard selected all filenames that had any combination of characters before the word "Projection." Case does not make a difference in the file specification.

Figure 2-27	DIRECTORY OF FILENAMES THAT END WITH THE WORD "PROJECTION"

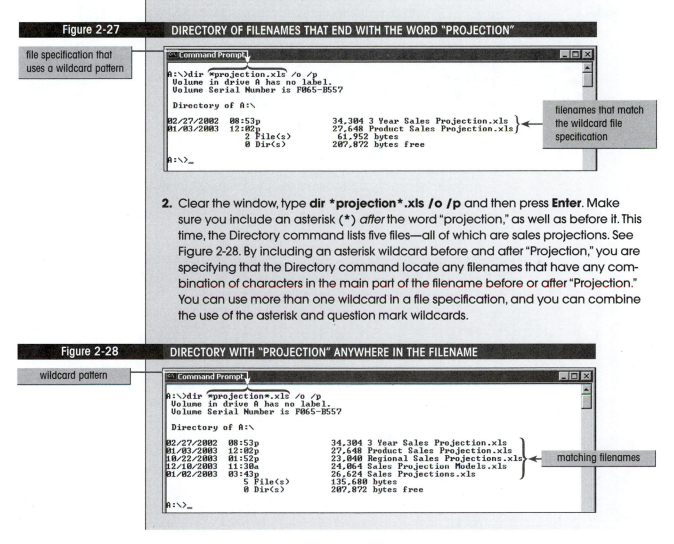

file specification that uses a wildcard pattern

filenames that match the wildcard file specification

2. Clear the window, type **dir *projection*.xls /o /p** and then press **Enter**. Make sure you include an asterisk (*****) *after* the word "projection," as well as before it. This time, the Directory command lists five files—all of which are sales projections. See Figure 2-28. By including an asterisk wildcard before and after "Projection," you are specifying that the Directory command locate any filenames that have any combination of characters in the main part of the filename before or after "Projection." You can use more than one wildcard in a file specification, and you can combine the use of the asterisk and question mark wildcards.

Figure 2-28	DIRECTORY WITH "PROJECTION" ANYWHERE IN THE FILENAME

wildcard pattern

matching filenames

Note the flexibility and power in using more than one wildcard character in a file specification. Of the three selections you tested, the last one is the most useful because it includes all the files that might work for Carlos.

Another common use of the asterisk wildcard is to select all filenames that begin with a certain character or combination of characters. You could, for example, look for all files that begin with "Sales" in the main part of the filename, and that contain any file extension.

To select files with "Sales" at the beginning of the filename:

1. Clear the window.

2. Type **dir sales*.* /o** and then press **Enter**. The Directory command locates three files that contain "Sales" at the beginning of the filename. See Figure 2-29. Two of the files have the "xls" file extension, while the other has a "wk4" file extension (a Lotus 1-2-3 Release 5 for Windows file). Because you included an asterisk wildcard for the file extension, the Directory command accepted any combination of characters for the file extension.

Figure 2-29	DIRECTORY OF ALL FILENAMES BEGINNING WITH THE WORD "SALES"

wildcard pattern

```
A:\>dir sales*.* /o
 Volume in drive A has no label.
 Volume Serial Number is F065-B557

 Directory of A:\

12/10/2003  11:30a            24,064 Sales Projection Models.xls
01/02/2003  03:43p            26,624 Sales Projections.xls
03/27/2003  11:19a            22,028 Sales.wk4
               3 File(s)          72,716 bytes
               0 Dir(s)       207,872 bytes free

A:\>_
```

matching filenames

The file specification DIR SALES* would have also worked exactly the same way. If you don't specify a file extension, the Directory command includes files with any, or no, file extension.

REFERENCE WINDOW   RW

Using the Asterisk Wildcard in a File Specification

- If necessary, open a Command Prompt window and change to the drive containing the files you want to examine.
- Type DIR, press the Spacebar, type * (an asterisk), type . (a period), type a file extension, press the Spacebar, type /P /O, and then press the Enter key to display a list of files with a specific file extension in alphabetical order by filename, one full window at a time.
- Type DIR, press the Spacebar, type the file specification with one or more asterisks to substitute for one or more characters in the filename, press the Spacebar, type /P /O, and then press Enter to display a list of files with filenames that differ by one or more characters in the filename, in alphabetical order one full window at a time.
- Type DIR, press the Spacebar, type the first character or initial characters in the filename, type * (an asterisk), press the Spacebar, type /P /O, and then press Enter to display a list of files that have the same first character or initial characters at the beginning of the filename, in alphabetical order by filename one full window at a time.

Another common use of this wildcard is to display all files starting with a certain letter of the alphabet. For example, if you enter the command DIR S*, the Directory command will list all files that start with the letter "S." This feature is useful if you recall only the first few letters or words of the filename.

Using the Question Mark Wildcard

One of SolarWinds' in-house trainers asks you for a copy of the PowerPoint presentation files on computer hardware and software for an upcoming training session for new staff members.

One common use of the question mark wildcard is to select a group of files with filenames that are identical except for one character. For example, assume you have a set of files containing quarterly sales summaries for 2002 and 2003, as follows:

2002 First Quarter Sales Summary.xls	2003 First Quarter Sales Summary.xls
2002 Second Quarter Sales Summary.xls	2003 Second Quarter Sales Summary.xls
2002 Third Quarter Sales Summary.xls	2003 Third Quarter Sales Summary.xls
2002 Fourth Quarter Sales Summary.xls	2003 Fourth Quarter Sales Summary.xls

You want to locate the sales summaries for the fourth quarter of these two years so you can analyze the company's performance from one year to the next. The only difference between the two filenames is the character at the fourth position of the main part of the filename. To view a directory listing of just these files, substitute the question mark wildcard for the fourth character, as follows:

DIR 200? Fourth Quarterly Sales Summary.xls

The question mark wildcard in this file specification substitutes for the fourth character in the filename, and this file specification would select "2002 Fourth Quarter Sales Summary.xls" and "2003 Fourth Quarter Sales Summary.xls." To save typing, you could also use the following abbreviated file specification where you combine the two types of wildcards: **DIR 200? Fo***

You can use the question mark wildcard and a similar strategy to locate the PowerPoint presentations on computer hardware and software on your disk. The filenames of these files are Hardware.ppt and Software.ppt. Not only is the extension the same, but the last four characters of the main part of the filename are the same. The first four characters are the only ones that vary.

To select the PowerPoint files on computer hardware and software:

1. Clear the window, type **dir ????ware.ppt /o** and then press **Enter**. The Directory command displays the two files you wanted to find. See Figure 2-30. Notice that both files have exactly the same number of characters in the main part of the filename (plus the same file extension). After trying this command, see if "DIR *WARE.PPT /O" also works.

Figure 2-30	USING QUESTION MARK WILDCARDS TO SELECT SIMILAR FILENAMES

wildcard pattern

```
Command Prompt                                                    _ □ ×
A:\>dir ????ware.ppt /o
 Volume in drive A has no label.
 Volume Serial Number is F065-B557

 Directory of A:\

06/26/2003  10:24a                 53,248 Hardware.ppt
06/26/2003  10:40a                 42,496 Software.ppt
               2 File(s)           95,744 bytes
               0 Dir(s)           207,872 bytes free

A:\>_
```

matching filenames

2. Clear the window, type **dir *ware.ppt /o** and then press **Enter**. The Directory command displays one additional file—one you might or might not need, but note that changing the wildcard specification did produce different results. See Figure 2-31. Note that while the question mark wildcard showed filenames with letters replacing the question marks in a one-for-one substitution, the asterisk wildcard allows any number of letters to substitute for the asterisk.

| Figure 2-31 | USING AN ASTERISK WILDCARD TO SELECT SIMILAR FILENAMES |

wildcard pattern

```
A:\>dir *ware.ppt /o
 Volume in drive A has no label.
 Volume Serial Number is F065-D557

 Directory of A:\

06/26/2003  09:30a            52,736 Application Software.ppt
06/26/2003  10:24a            53,248 Hardware.ppt
06/26/2003  10:40a            42,496 Software.ppt
               3 File(s)     148,480 bytes
               0 Dir(s)      207,872 bytes free

A:\>_
```

matching filenames

This particular use of wildcards with the DIR command is invaluable if you need to locate a small group of files within a directory that contains hundreds of files.

REFERENCE WINDOW   RW

Using the Question Mark Wildcard in a File Specification
- If necessary, open a Command Prompt window and change to the drive containing the files you want to examine.
- Type DIR, press the Spacebar, type the filename and substitute the question mark wildcard for one or more specific characters in the filename that might differ in the filenames on disk, press the Spacebar, type /P /O, and then press Enter to display a list of files with filenames that differ by one or more characters in a specific position of the filename, in alphabetical order one full window at a time.

The use of wildcards provides a powerful tool for selecting groups of files based on their file extensions, or some other set of characters within the filenames that distinguishes them from other files on the disk.

Using the Windows Environment

After working with the Directory command and its switches, you realize that you always use the Sort Order and Page switches. You ask Isabel if there is any way to specify these switches as default switches for the Directory command so you do not need to type them each time. Isabel tells you that you need to create an environment variable for the Directory command and specify these switches as the setting for that variable.

Windows 2000 and other programs store important settings in a small area of memory called the **Windows environment** (formerly known as the DOS environment). Windows 2000, and the other programs you use, will check the Windows environment for specific settings. The settings in the Windows environment are assigned to environment variables. An **environment variable** is a symbolic name associated with a specific setting. For example, you can create an environment variable by the name of DIRCMD, and then assign switches to this environment variable. When you use the Directory command, it will automatically check the Windows environment and use the switches as default settings.

To assign a setting to an environment variable, use the SET command, which is an internal command. Its syntax is as follows:

SET *variable = string*

Variable is the name of the environment variable, and *string* is the setting you want to assign to the environment variable. For example, if you want to store the Pause and Order switches in the Windows environment for use with the Directory command, enter the following command:

SET DIRCMD=/P /O

Now, whenever you enter "DIR" at the command prompt, the Directory command will execute your command as though you had entered "DIR /P /O." Later, if you prefer to use another setting, you can repeat this command and specify new switches.

When you assign a setting to the DIRCMD environment variable, you must not leave a blank space between DIRCMD and the equal sign. If you include a space, Windows 2000 does not use the new setting when you enter the DIR command.

If you want to view the contents of the Windows environment, type SET and then press Enter.

To examine the Windows environment and then specify default switches for the Directory command:

1. Click the **Maximize** button 🔲 to maximize the Command Prompt window, and then clear the window.

2. Type **set** and then press **Enter**. The Setting command displays the environment variables in the Windows environment, and the settings assigned to these variables. See Figure 2-32. Notice that the USERNAME variable identifies the user currently logged on the computer. On the computer in Figure 2-32, there is no DIRCMD environment variable. Your Windows environment will differ.

Figure 2-32	SETTINGS IN THE WINDOWS ENVIRONMENT (YOURS MAY DIFFER)

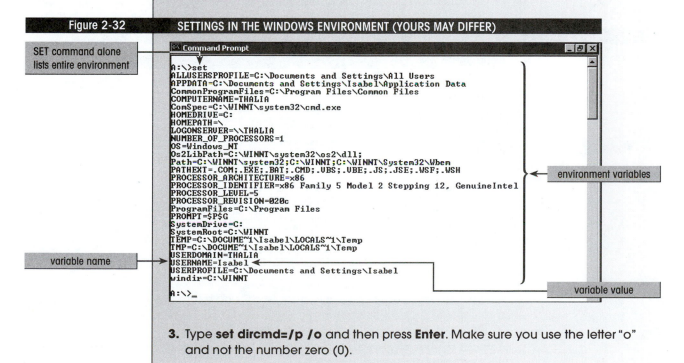

3. Type **set dircmd=/p /o** and then press **Enter**. Make sure you use the letter "o" and not the number zero (0).

4. Clear the window.

5. Type **set** and then press **Enter**. Notice that the DIRCMD environment variable you defined is now stored in the Windows environment along with the settings you assigned for this variable. See Figure 2-33.

Figure 2-33   **DIRCMD ENVIRONMENT VARIABLE IN WINDOWS ENVIRONMENT**

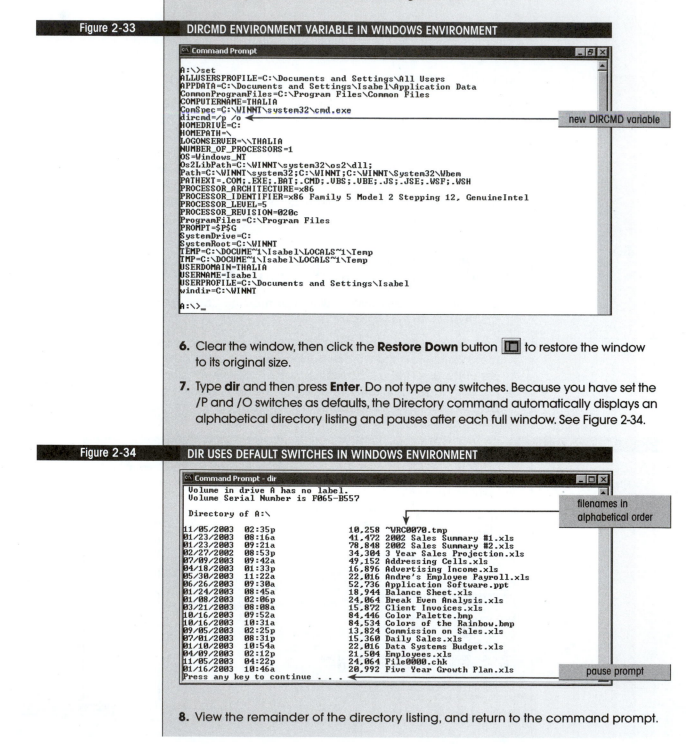

6. Clear the window, then click the **Restore Down** button to restore the window to its original size.

7. Type **dir** and then press **Enter**. Do not type any switches. Because you have set the /P and /O switches as defaults, the Directory command automatically displays an alphabetical directory listing and pauses after each full window. See Figure 2-34.

Figure 2-34   **DIR USES DEFAULT SWITCHES IN WINDOWS ENVIRONMENT**

8. View the remainder of the directory listing, and return to the command prompt.

You can temporarily override these settings by entering the Directory command with a different switch.

To display filenames in order by size, overriding a default setting:

1. Type **dir /o-s** and then press **Enter**. The Directory command displays the file-names in reverse order by file size. See Figure 2-35. Because you changed the parameter associated with the Order switch, the Directory command overrides the default setting for the Order switch in the Windows environment. As you can tell, however, the Directory command still uses the Pause switch.

Figure 2-35	OVERRIDING ONE OF THE SWITCHES IN THE WINDOWS ENVIRONMENT

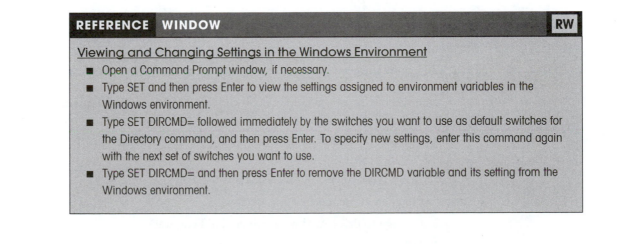

reverse order by file size

2. View the remainder of the directory listing, and return to the command prompt.

3. Close the Command Prompt window.

This setting stays in the Windows environment and remains in effect until you specify a new setting, remove this setting, or exit the Command Prompt window. To specify a new setting, enter "SET DIRCMD=" with a list of the new switches you now want to use. To remove this setting from the temporary Windows environment in your Command Prompt window, type "SET DIRCMD=" without any settings, and then press Enter.

REFERENCE WINDOW   **RW**

Viewing and Changing Settings in the Windows Environment

- Open a Command Prompt window, if necessary.
- Type SET and then press Enter to view the settings assigned to environment variables in the Windows environment.
- Type SET DIRCMD= followed immediately by the switches you want to use as default switches for the Directory command, and then press Enter. To specify new settings, enter this command again with the next set of switches you want to use.
- Type SET DIRCMD= and then press Enter to remove the DIRCMD variable and its setting from the Windows environment.

This timesaving tool streamlines and simplifies the use of the Directory command—the most commonly used command.

Isabel is pleased with the progress you have made in such a short time. When working in a Command Prompt window, you now can quickly provide the information needed by other staff members and also provide copies of the template files employees need to be productive and meet their deadlines.

Session 2.2 QUICK CHECK

1. A(n) _____ allows only 8 characters and then a 3-character extension.

2. A(n) _____ is a setting consisting of a bit that is turned on or off by the operating system, and defines a particular characteristic of the file.

3. _____, the largest of all the files in the root directory folder, is an operating system file referred to as a paging file, or swap file.

4. A(n) _____ is a symbol that substitutes for one or more characters in a filename.

5. A(n)_____ provides information about the type of files you want to select and display in a directory listing.

6. An environment _____ is a symbolic name associated with a specific setting.

7. What character do you use to reverse a sort order parameter when you use the Order switch?

8. What command would you enter at the command prompt to display filenames in alphabetical order by file extension only?

9. What command would you use to view the contents of the Windows environment?

10. What command would you enter to make DIR default to displaying filenames in order by name, one full window at a time?

For the Tutorial 2 Command Reference table, go to page 93.

REVIEW ASSIGNMENT

To handle the ever-increasing workload during the busiest months of the year, Isabel hires another part-time assistant to help with computer support. She wants all staff members to be comfortable in both Windows 2000 and the command prompt environments, so she asks you to show the techniques and tricks you have learned to the new employee, Langston Ellis.

As you complete each step, write down the commands you use, as well as the answer to any questions so you can submit them to your instructor.

1. Insert your copy of Data Disk #1 into drive A.

2. Open a Command Prompt window.

3. Change to drive A. What command did you use?

4. What is the current default drive now?

5. Display a directory listing of the default drive. What command did you use?

6. Display a directory listing of drive C. What command did you use?

7. Change to drive C. What command did you use?

8. From drive C, display a directory listing of the Data Disk in drive A in alphabetical order by filename, and pause the directory listing after each full window. What command did you use?

9. From drive C, display a wide directory listing of drive A in alphabetical order by filename. What command did you use? Describe how the Directory command lists the files in the Command Prompt window.

10. From drive C, display a directory listing of drive A so files are listed first in alphabetical order by file extension, then by file size (for each type of file extension), pausing the directory listing after each full window. What command did you use? What are the names of the first four files in the directory listing?

11. From drive C, display a directory listing of drive A, and show short filenames for files with the "ppt" file extension in alphabetical order. What command did you use? What are the short and long filenames of the files the Directory command lists?

12. From drive C, display a directory listing of the system files on drive C. What command did you use? What filenames did the Directory command list?

13. From drive C, display a directory listing of all the "doc" files on drive A. What command did you use? What filenames did the Directory command list?

14. Use the SET command to assign to the DIRCMD variable switches that (a) arrange filenames in alphabetical order, (b) display short filenames as well as long filenames, and (c) pause a directory listing after each full window. What command did you use?

15. Display a directory listing of the root directory of drive C, displaying directories only, and with short filenames. What command did you use? What is the short filename for the Program Files directory (or folder)? And for the Documents and Settings directory (or folder)? What is the name of your Windows directory (or folder)? Does it have a short filename? If not, what would be the short filename of this directory (or folder)?

16. Close the Command Prompt window.

CASE PROBLEMS

Case 1. Classifying Files at Steppingstone Development Services Steppingstone Development Services is a non-profit organization that provides in-house training and job development services. The employees at Steppingstone use a combination of DOS, Windows 3.1, and Windows 2000 software. Office manager Angela Pinelli has received a diskette from a branch office. Before her staff makes changes to the files on the disk, she wants to document the entire contents of the disk.

Angela needs to prioritize the order in which her office will work on files, so she asks you to document the long and short filenames on the disk. She also asks you to organize the information on the reports using different switches, and then record the results.

As you complete each step, write down the commands you use so you can submit them to your instructor.

1. Open a Command Prompt window.

2. Insert your copy of Data Disk #1 into drive A, and make it the current default drive. What command did you use to change from drive C to drive A?

3. List the diskette files on screen without using any switches. Did you have to specify the drive? Explain.

4. What type of order did the Directory command use to list the files? Explain.

5. Perform each of the operations below, and indicate the DIR command you used to list both long and short filenames.

   - List files by file extension
   - List files in date order
   - List files in order by file size
   - List all filenames containing the word "Employee" in alphabetical order by filename
   - List all filenames containing the word "Plan" in alphabetical order by filename

6. Which of these types of directory listings would you find useful in your field of specialty?

Case 2. Creating Files at Fast Track Trainers Samantha Kuehl, Fast Track Trainer's lead training specialist, needs a set of files for an upcoming employee workshop on working with files in a Command Prompt window. She asks you to prepare a set of files that illustrates the advantages and disadvantages of using different types of filenames. She suggests that you examine the files on one of the other training diskettes to see if you can adapt any of them for this new workshop.

As you perform the following steps, record your answers to any questions so you can submit them to your instructor.

1. After examining one of the training diskettes used for an earlier training session, you notice a set of files on the disk named Project1.doc, Project2.doc, Project3.doc, Project4.doc, and Project5.doc. When discussing the Directory command, what feature(s), if any, could Samantha demonstrate with the use of these files? Are there any features that she could not demonstrate? Explain.

2. You notice that the same diskette contains 12 simple text files with the "txt" file extension. What feature(s), if any, could Samantha demonstrate with the use of these files?

3. Another training diskette contains a set of files named "First Quarter Sales Summary.xls," "Second Quarter Sales Summary.xls," "Third Quarter Sales Summary.xls," and "Fourth Quarter Sales Summary.xls." What feature(s), if any, could Samantha demonstrate with the use of these files?

4. You also notice a set of graphics files approximately 10 times larger than the average file size of the remaining files on the same disk. What feature(s), if any, could Samantha demonstrate with the use of these files?

5. An older training diskette contains a set of files named QTR1_INC.WK3, QTR2_INC.WK3, QTR3_INC.WK3, and QTR4_INC.WK3. What feature(s), if any, could Samantha demonstrate with the use of these files?

6. If you need to create files with five different versions of your resume, what types of filenames would you choose for those files? Consider factors such as the advantages and disadvantages of long filenames vs. short filenames, the difficulty or ease of locating all these files, and the difficulty or ease of identifying how one file differs from all the others.

Case 3. Using Wildcards to Locate Files at Northbay Computers   Northbay Computers sells and rents computer equipment and supplies for homeowners and businesses. Jonathan Baum, a recent high school graduate, has just been hired to provide training, troubleshooting support, and general assistance to customers. Although Jonathan has a strong background with Windows 2000, he has now discovered that DOS skills are an important part of troubleshooting systems. One common complaint of customers is that they are unable to locate important files they need to complete a project. Although you know how to locate files using the Windows 2000 Search Assistant, he asks you to show him how to improve his skills with the use of wildcards at the command line.

As you complete each step, write down the commands you use, as well as the answer to any questions, so you can submit them to your instructor.

1. Insert your copy of Data Disk #1 into drive A.

2. Open a Command Prompt window.

3. Change the default drive to drive A.

4. Display an alphabetical directory listing of all files with the "bmp" file extension. What command did you use? What files does the Directory command find when you try this command?

5. Display an alphabetical directory listing of all files with "D" as the first character in the filename. What command did you use? What files does the Directory command find when you try this command?

6. Display an alphabetical directory listing of all files with "Software" at the beginning of the filename. What command did you use? What files does the Directory command find when you try this command?

7. Display an alphabetical directory listing of all files with "Plan" anywhere in the main part of the filename. What command did you use? What files does the Directory command find when you try this command?

8. Display an alphabetical directory listing of all files with "Fi" as the first two characters of the filename, any character as the third character of the filename, "e" as the fourth character of the filename, any characters in the remainder of the filename, and any file extension. What command did you use? What files does the Directory command find when you try this command?

9. Display a directory listing of all files with the "xls" file extension in order from the smallest file to the largest file, and pause the directory listing after each full window. What command did you use? What is the first file in the directory listing, and what is the file size for this file? What is the last file in the directory listing, and what is the file size for this file?

10. Display a directory listing of all files with the "xls" file extension in order by file date, and pause the directory listing after each full window. What command did you use? What is the first file in the directory listing, and what is the file date of this file? What is the last file in the directory listing, and what is the file date of this file?

Case 4. Customizing the Windows Environment at Townsend & Sumner Publishing

Townsend & Sumner Publishing is a San Francisco-based firm that contracts with corporate clients to produce employee training manuals on the use of specialized client software. To produce these manuals, Townsend & Sumner's staff must work with many different types of Windows and DOS programs, and compile information, graphics, concept art, and illustrations from many different files. Mike Lyman, who supervises the production of these manuals, keeps track of and provides other staff members with the files they require for these projects. He asks you to help him customize the Windows environment so he can quickly locate files.

As you complete each step, write down the commands you use as well as the answer to any questions so you can submit them to your instructor.

1. Insert your copy of Data Disk #1 into drive A.

2. Open a Command Prompt window, and then maximize the Command Prompt window.

3. Display the variables in the Windows environment. What command did you use? How are the variables organized in the Windows environment? Locate the *SystemDrive* environment variable. What is the setting assigned to this variable?

4. Create a DIRCMD environment variable, and assign switches to the variable that:

   ■ Pause the directory listing after every full window

   ■ Display a list of all files—no matter what type of attribute(s) each file is assigned

   ■ Display filenames in alphabetical order by file extension and then by the main part of the filename

5. What command did you enter to assign these settings to the DIRCMD variable?

6. Check the Windows environment to make sure the setting is assigned to the DIRCMD variable. What command did you use? What setting does the Windows environment show for this variable?

7. Display a directory listing of the files on the Data Disk in drive A. What are the names of the first four files in the directory listing? What do these files have in common?

8. Override the Order switch in the Windows environment and display the directory listing in reverse order by file date so the most recent file is listed first and the oldest file is listed last. What command did you enter? What is the first file in the directory listing, and what is its file date? What is the last file in the directory listing, and what is its file date?

9. Exit the Command Prompt window.

10. Open and maximize the Command Prompt window again, and then display the settings in the Windows environment. Is the DIRCMD variable still listed? Why or why not?

11. Close the Command Prompt window.

QUICK | CHECK ANSWERS

Session 2.1

1. command history or command stack
2. Insert
3. default
4. scrolling
5. disk order
6. file extension
7. /P
8. /W
9. /D
10. /O

Session 2.2

1. short filename
2. attribute
3. Pagefile.sys
4. wildcard
5. file specification
6. variable
7. minus sign (-)
8. DIR /OE
9. SET
10. DIR /O /P or DIR /P /O

COMMAND REFERENCE			
COMMAND	**USE**	**BASIC SYNTAX**	**EXAMPLE**
drive name	Changes the default drive	*drive name*	A: C:
DIR	Displays a list of files and subdirectories within a directory	DIR [*drive*]	dir dir a:
DIR [*file specification*]	Displays a directory listing of a single file or a group of files	DIR [*file specification*]	dir Sales.wk4 dir "Product List.xls"
DIR /?	Displays Help information on the DIR command	DIR /?	dir /?
DIR /A	Displays a directory listing of files that have the same file attribute. The file attributes include: D Directory H Hidden S System R Read-only A Archive	DIR /A*attribute*	dir /a dir /as
DIR /O	Displays a directory listing in alphabetical order by filename	DIR /O	dir /o

COMMAND REFERENCE (CONTINUED)

COMMAND	USE	BASIC SYNTAX	EXAMPLE
DIR /O<sort order>	Displays a directory listing in order using a sort order parameter. The sort order parameters include: D File date and time S File size E File extension N Main part of filename	DIR O:<sort order parameter> DIR /O<sort order parameter>	dir /o:s dir /os
DIR /O-<sort order>	Displays a directory listing in *reverse* order using a sort order parameter. The sort order parameters include: D File date and time S File size E File extension N Main part of filename	DIR /O:-<sort order parameter> DIR /O-<sort order parameter>	dir /o:-s dir /o-s dir /oen
DIR /P	Pauses the display of a directory listing	DIR /P	dir /p
DIR /W	Displays filenames in a directory listing in columns across the width of the screen	DIR /W	dir /w
DIR /X	Displays a directory listing with short filenames as well as long filenames	DIR /X	dir /x
SET	Displays, sets, or removes environment variables from the Windows environment	SET	set set dircmd=/p /o
SET DIRCMD	Assigns default switches to the DIRCMD environment variable in the Windows environment for use with the DIR command	SET DIRCMD=[*switches*]	set set dircmd=/p /o
SET DIRCMD=	Removes settings for the DIRCMD environment variable from the Windows environment	SET DIRCMD=	set dircmd=

WILDCARDS

*	Used in a file specification to represent one or more characters		dir *.xls dir sales*.* dir *projection*.xls dir *.*
?	Used in a file specification to represent a single character		dir ????ware.ppt

Items shown in italics and *not* enclosed within square brackets are required parameters

Items shown in italics and enclosed within square brackets are optional parameters

OBJECTIVES

In this tutorial you will:

- Understand the importance and features of ASCII text files

- Redirect the output of a command to an ASCII text file

- View the contents of an ASCII text file

- Pipe output to the MORE filter

- Redirect input from an ASCII text file on disk

- Sort and search the content within an ASCII text file

- Append output to an ASCII text file

- Redirect command output to the printer

- Copy, rename, and delete files

WORKING WITH FILES

Using File Commands, Redirection, Piping, and Filters at SolarWinds, Inc.

CASE

SolarWinds Unlimited

As you work with Isabel to provide staff support, you discover that the Command Prompt window supports all of the types of file operations that you typically perform in the Windows 2000 graphical user interface. Not only are these operations faster, but in some cases, you can perform certain types of file operations (such as renaming groups of files) in the Command Prompt window that are not possible from the Windows graphical user interface. Because one of your job responsibilities is to develop and provide the necessary template files needed by the staff, you realize that a better understanding of file operations within the Windows 2000 command line operating environment will improve your productivity and efficiency.

SESSION 3.1

In this session, you will examine the use and importance of ASCII text files, and then you will create and view the contents of ASCII text files. You will use the output redirection operator to store the output of a command in an ASCII text file. You will use the pipe operator to use the output of a command as the input for another command and combine the pipe operator with the MORE filter to page the output of a command. You will use the input redirection operator to write the contents of an ASCII text file to the window, the SORT filter to sort the contents of an ASCII text file, and the FIND filter to locate information within an ASCII text file. Finally, you will use the append output redirection operator to add the output of a command to the end of an existing ASCII text file.

Working with ASCII Text Files

At the weekly meeting of the support staff, Isabel explains to you that most of the configuration and initialization files used by the Windows 2000 operating system are ASCII text files, so it's important that you and other support staff be familiar with these types of files. Furthermore, she notes that ASCII text files are commonly used with other operating systems, such as UNIX.

An **ASCII text file** is a simple file format in which data is stored as text, and therefore it is often referred to as a text file. The name ASCII stands for **A**merican **S**tandard **C**ode for **I**nformation Interchange. This file format is so common and so important that applications like the ones included in Microsoft Office recognize this standard coding format for storing information in a file and adapt their software packages to use, or support, this file format. It is also common practice to refer to ASCII text files as text files, print files, DOS files, or DOS text files.

In contrast, files produced by word processing software and other types of application software store formatting codes for special features (such as fonts, boldface, and underlining), so that you must use that software application when you work on a file created with that application. You can, however, use word processing applications to open and work with ASCII text files. Furthermore, many of these word processing applications can automatically convert ASCII text files into the file format typically used by that application, or vice versa.

The original standard ASCII coding scheme uses 7 bits to represent all uppercase and lowercase letters of the alphabet, the numeric digits 0 through 9, punctuation symbols, and special control codes. Each ASCII character is assigned a numerical code, called the **ASCII code** or **ASCII value**, such as ASCII 65 for the uppercase letter "A," ASCII 97 for the lowercase letter "a," and ASCII 13 for Ctrl+M. By using 7 bits to encode characters and symbols, these values range from 0 (zero) to 127, for a total of 128 codes. **Control codes** are codes for the use of the Ctrl key with another key. For example, when you press the Tab key to indent a line while creating an ASCII text file, you insert a tab code, Ctrl+I (or ASCII 9). At the end of each line in an ASCII text file, there is an ASCII code for a carriage return, Ctrl+M (ASCII 13); a line feed, Ctrl+J (ASCII 10); or both. Some ASCII text files contain a form feed code, Ctrl+L (ASCII 12), to indicate a page break and the start of a new page. In all versions of Windows and DOS, ASCII text files use a special type of code—an **end-of-file (EOF) code**—Ctrl+Z (ASCII 26), as the last character to mark the end of a text-only file (UNIX text files use Ctrl+D or ASCII 4).

The **extended ASCII** code has values that range from 0 (zero) to 255 because it uses 8 bits to encode characters. The 128 additional codes include values for foreign-language characters or symbols, graphics characters, and scientific characters.

You can produce an ASCII control code or character by pressing and holding the Alt key while you type the ASCII value *on the numeric keypad only*. For example, if you press and hold down the Alt key while you type 65 (or 065) using the numeric keypad in a Command Prompt window, the command interpreter will display the character "A." Figure 3-1 contains examples of ASCII characters and codes for both the original and extended ASCII character sets. In some cases, application programs redefine these codes.

Figure 3-1	EXAMPLES OF ASCII CHARACTERS AND CODES

ASCII CODE	KEY, OR KEY COMBINATION
009	Ctrl+I (Control code for tab)
010	Ctrl+J (Control code for line feed)
012	Ctrl+L (Control code for page break)
013	Ctrl+M (Control code for carriage return)
026	Ctrl+Z (EOF, or end-of-file, code)
027	Esc key
032	Spacebar
047	/
048	0
049	1
050	2
058	:
059	;
065	A
066	B
067	C
092	\
097	a
098	b
099	c
126	~ (Tilde symbol)
156	£ (British pound sterling)
201	╔ (Box drawing character)
229	σ (Sigma symbol)
246	÷ (Division symbol)

All versions of Windows also support the **ANSI (American National Standards Institute)** character set, which supports characters from different languages. The first 128 characters in the ANSI character set are identical to the first 128 characters in the ASCII character set. The next 128 characters, however, differ for each supported language.

Another important character set, and file format, is **Unicode**. This file format uses 16 bits (or two bytes) to encode characters, so it can represent 65,536 characters and symbols. Unicode can therefore represent all the symbols in all written languages in the world. Unicode has assigned approximately 39,000 of the total possible 65,536 characters, numbers, and symbols (21,000 of these are used to represent Chinese ideographs).

Using Redirection to Create an ASCII Text File

Isabel asks you to produce a list of the files stored on the templates disk so that you have a record of the template files currently used by the staff. She notes that you can create the list by redirecting the output of the Directory command to a file on disk.

When you work in a command line environment, the operating system expects input from the keyboard (called the **standard input device**), and directs or sends output to the screen (the **standard output device**). You can change the destination for the output. For example, you can instruct the operating system to send the output to a printer or a file on diskette. To send output to a device other than the standard output device, you **redirect**, or change the destination of that output with the output redirection operator. The **output redirection operator** is the greater than symbol (>). If you want to redirect output to a file, specify the name of the file you want to create following the output redirection operator. For example, if you want to redirect output to a printer, specify the name of your printer port.

The general syntax for redirecting output to a file on disk is as follows:

> [*command*] > *filename*

If *filename* specifies a file that already exists, the above redirection will overwrite the file, and you will lose its previous contents. If you want to add to an existing file instead, see the section "Appending Output to an ASCII Text File" later in this tutorial.

If you want to redirect output to a printer, use the following syntax:

> [*command*] > *printer port*

Before you use the output redirection operator, you want to set up your Command Prompt window and make sure the file name you want to assign to the new file is not already in use.

To set up your computer:

1. Open a Command Prompt window.

2. Type **color f0** (an "f" followed by a zero) and then press **Enter**. The COLOR command changes the background color to white, and the foreground color for text to black.

TROUBLE? If Windows 2000 displays Help information on the use of the COLOR command and does not change the background and foreground colors, then you typed the letter "O" rather than a zero (0). Press the Spacebar to view the next Help screen, and then enter the command again, but use a zero (0) rather than the letter "O."

3. Insert your copy of Data Disk #1 into drive A, and then change the default drive to drive A.

TROUBLE? If you no longer have your copy of Data Disk #1, make a new copy of this diskette.

4. Clear the window, type **dir /o** and then press **Enter**. This diskette contains 41 files that use 1,248,070 bytes of storage space. See Figure 3-2. Notice the directory listing has no file named "Templates.txt" — the filename you will use for the redirected output of the Directory command in the next set of steps.

TROUBLE? If the operating system informs you that "0" is an invalid switch, then you typed the numeral zero (0) rather than the letter "o" for the Order switch. Repeat the command, and use the letter "o" rather than a zero (0) for the Order switch.

Figure 3-2   **DISPLAYING A DIRECTORY IN ORDER BY FILENAME**

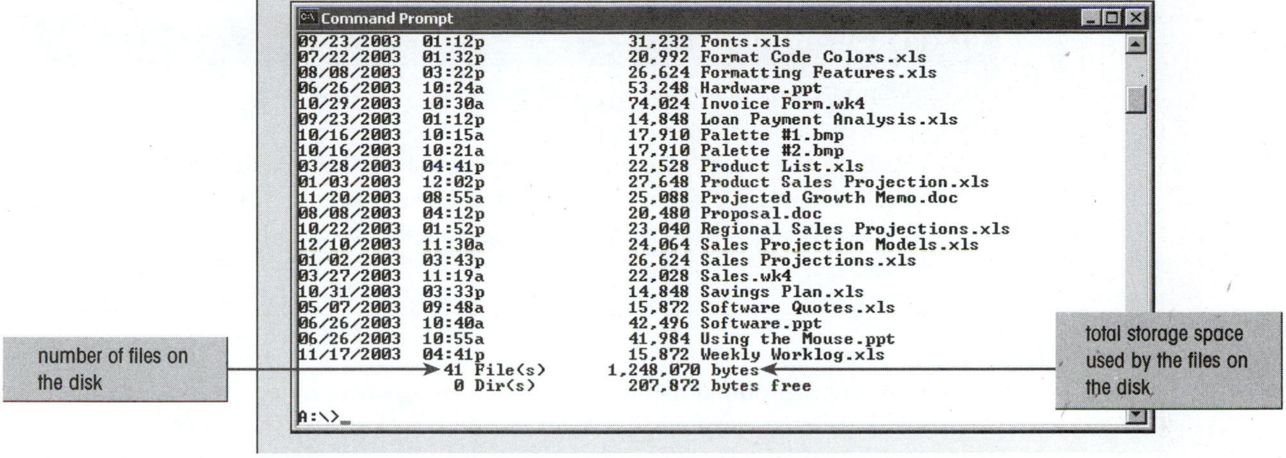

number of files on the disk

total storage space used by the files on the disk.

Now you're ready to create an ASCII text file that contains a list of the files on your Data Disk.

To Create an ASCII text File:

1. Type **dir /o > Templates.txt** and then press **Enter**. This command redirects output to a file on your disk. Notice that the Directory command did not display a directory listing in the window.

2. Type (or recall) **dir /o** and then press **Enter**. There is now a new file by the name of Templates.txt. See Figure 3-3. You created this ASCII text file in the last step when you redirected output to a file rather than to the window. Note that the file is 2,736 bytes in size (less than a page in length). Because ASCII text files do not contain formatting or very much text, they are generally small files that require relatively little storage space on disk. The date and time on your Templates.txt file will differ.

Figure 3-3   **VIEWING AN UPDATED DIRECTORY WITH A NEW ASCII FILE**

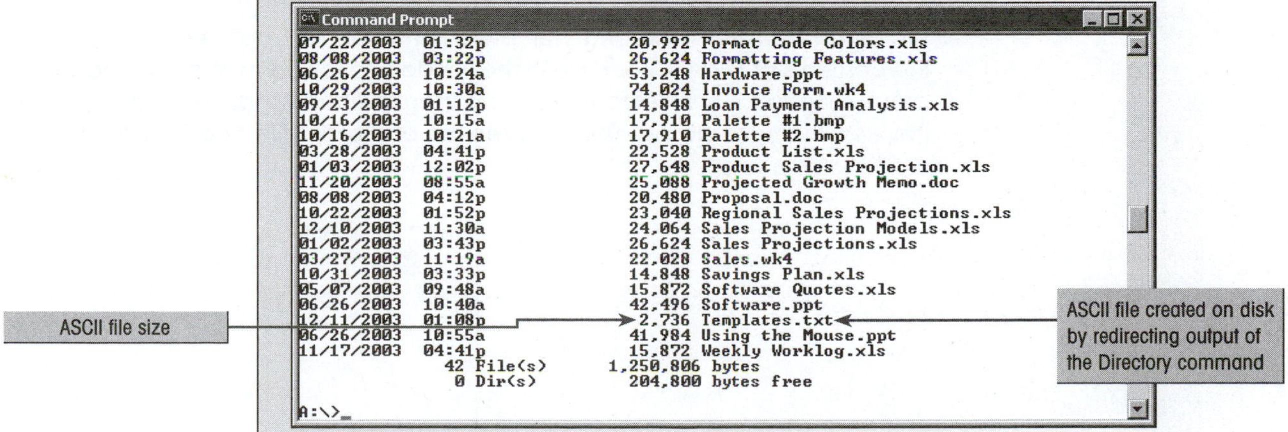

ASCII file size

ASCII file created on disk by redirecting output of the Directory command

The output redirection operator is very useful. You have to be careful, however, when redirecting output to a file on disk. As noted earlier, if you specify the filename of an existing file on disk, the operating system will overwrite the existing file without warning you. That's why you should always display a directory listing first to make sure that the filename that you intend to use for the redirected output does not already exist.

REFERENCE WINDOW **RW**

Redirecting Output of a Directory Listing to a File on Disk
- Open a Command Prompt window.
- Change the default drive to the drive that contains the files you want to examine.
- Type DIR followed by a space and any file specification and switches that you want to use, press the Spacebar, type > (the output redirection operator), press the Spacebar, and type the name of the file that will store the output, and then press Enter.

You can redirect output to a file on disk the same way in other versions of Windows, as well as with different versions of MS-DOS (and UNIX, which introduced redirection). In Windows 95 and later versions of Windows, including Windows 2000, you must put quotation marks around filenames containing spaces.

Viewing the Contents of an ASCII Text File

You can use the TYPE command—another internal command—to display the contents of an ASCII text file in a window or on the screen. The general syntax of the TYPE command is as follows:

TYPE *filename*

The filename is a required parameter.

One advantage of the TYPE command is that you do not need to start a program and then open a file to view its contents. You cannot, however, use the TYPE command to view the contents of a program file or a file produced by an application such as Microsoft Word. If you do, the TYPE command attempts to interpret the file's formatting codes as ASCII characters and therefore will display symbols or blanks in the window or on the screen.

To view the contents of the Templates.txt file:

1. Type **type templates.txt** and then press **Enter**. The TYPE command displays the contents of this ASCII text file in the window, followed by the command prompt. Because the file contains more than 25 lines, Windows 2000 adjusts the view in the window so you only see the end of the file. See Figure 3-4.

| Figure 3-4 | VIEWING THE CONTENTS OF AN ASCII FILE |

partial contents of the ASCII file

```
07/22/2003   01:32p          20,992 Format Code Colors.xls
08/08/2003   03:22p          26,624 Formatting Features.xls
06/26/2003   10:24a          53,248 Hardware.ppt
10/29/2003   10:30a          74,024 Invoice Form.wk4
09/23/2003   01:12p          14,848 Loan Payment Analysis.xls
10/16/2003   10:15a          17,910 Palette #1.bmp
10/16/2003   10:21a          17,910 Palette #2.bmp
03/28/2003   04:41p          22,528 Product List.xls
01/03/2003   12:02p          27,648 Product Sales Projection.xls
11/20/2003   08:55a          25,088 Projected Growth Memo.doc
08/08/2003   04:12p          20,480 Proposal.doc
10/22/2003   01:52p          23,040 Regional Sales Projections.xls
12/10/2003   11:30a          24,064 Sales Projection Models.xls
01/02/2003   03:43p          26,624 Sales Projections.xls
03/27/2003   11:19a          22,028 Sales.wk4
10/31/2003   03:33p          14,848 Savings Plan.xls
05/07/2003   09:48a          15,872 Software Quotes.xls
06/26/2003   10:40a          42,496 Software.ppt
12/11/2003   01:08p               0 Templates.txt
06/26/2003   10:55a          41,984 Using the Mouse.ppt
11/17/2003   04:41p          15,872 Weekly Worklog.xls
               42 File(s)     1,248,070 bytes
                0 Dir(s)        200,704 bytes free
A:\>_
```

note file size

The output that you see in the window appears as if you had used the Directory command to display the contents of the disk, scrolling down without pausing after the window fills. How can you verify that you used the TYPE command with a text file instead of the DIR command? Note that this directory listing includes an entry for the Templates.txt file at a size of zero (0) bytes. The previous directory listing did not include this entry. When you gave the command to redirect the output of DIR to the Templates.txt file, you immediately created that file on the diskette, and therefore the directory listing included it. However, the file size remained zero while your command was still redirecting its output to the file. If you use the DIR command now, this new filename entry will not show a zero length.

2. Clear the window.

Bear in mind that the directory listing you displayed above is not a current listing of your files. Instead, the TYPE command displayed the contents of the Templates.txt file—the "snapshot" you took of the directory listing at one specific point in time. As you change the contents of a directory—adding, changing, or deleting files—you can create any number of such snapshot files. In sections to come, you will use other commands to rearrange and display parts of this file.

Windows 2000 uses ASCII text files for many purposes, particularly configuration and log files. So that you become familiar with some of these files, Isabel suggests you look at Boot.ini on the hard drive, an important configuration file that displays a menu from which you can pick the operating system or Windows 2000 component you want to use to boot your computer.

To view the contents of the Boot.ini configuration file:

1. If necessary, clear the Command Prompt window.

2. Type **type c:\boot.ini** and then press **Enter**. The TYPE command displays the contents of this configuration file, as shown in Figure 3-5. On the computer used for this figure, there are two options for booting the computer—using Microsoft Windows 2000 Professional or using Microsoft Windows 2000 Recovery Console. Your options might differ.

Figure 3-5 **DISPLAYING AN ASCII TEXT CONFIGURATION FILE**

contents of ASCII text configuration file boot.ini

command to display boot.ini configuration file on drive C

The TYPE command works in the same basic way in other versions of Windows, and different versions of MS-DOS. Again, beginning with Windows 95, you must put quotation marks around filenames containing spaces. Also, under Windows 2000 and Windows NT 4.0, the TYPE command can display the contents of multiple files.

Piping Output to the MORE Filter

After you ask Isabel whether there is a way to control scrolling of the output of a command like the TYPE command that does not have a Pause, or Page switch. Isabel explains that you can pipe the output of the TYPE command to the MORE filter, and thereby control scrolling.

As noted, the TYPE command does not have a Pause switch, and ASCII text files often contain more than 25 lines of text. To display only one screen or window at a time and avoid automatic scrolling, you must send the output of the TYPE command to the MORE filter. A **filter** is a command that can modify the output of another command. The **MORE filter** (or command) is an external command that displays a screen or window of output, pauses, and then displays a "--More--" prompt which permits you to continue when you are ready.

To combine the use of the MORE filter with another command, use the pipe operator, which is usually located on the backslash (\) key and appears as either a solid vertical line or as a vertical line divided into two parts. The **pipe operator** (|) redirects the output produced by one command so that the output then becomes the input for another command. For example, the following command will display the output of an ASCII text file one screen or window at a time:

TYPE Templates.txt | MORE

The first command, TYPE, produces the output, and the operating system redirects the output so that it becomes the input for the MORE filter. The MORE command then displays the output of the TYPE command one screen or window at a time. The redirection of the output of one command so that it becomes the input for another command is called **piping**, and the entire command line is called a **pipeline**. The general syntax for piping output to the MORE filter is as follows:

[command] | **MORE**

> *To display the contents of the Templates.txt file one screen or window at a time:*
>
> **1.** Type (or recall) **type templates.txt**, press the **Spacebar**, type **| more** and then press **Enter**. The MORE filter displays the first part of this ASCII text file. See Figure 3-6. Notice that the output is identical to what you would expect with the Directory command and Pause switch. The "-- More --" prompt at the end of the directory listing tips you off to the fact that this is not a directory listing produced with the DIR command.

| Figure 3-6 | PIPING OUTPUT WITH THE MORE FILTER |

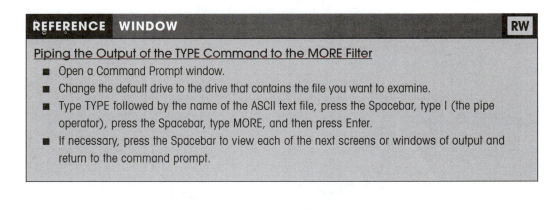

piped output

More prompt

2. Press the **Spacebar**. The MORE filter displays the next part of this ASCII text file.

3. Press the **Spacebar**. The MORE filter displays the remainder of the file, and then you see the command prompt.

You can use the pipe operator and the MORE filter with any other command that produces more than a full screen or window of output so that you can view all the information generated by the command.

REFERENCE   WINDOW   **RW**

Piping the Output of the TYPE Command to the MORE Filter

- Open a Command Prompt window.
- Change the default drive to the drive that contains the file you want to examine.
- Type TYPE followed by the name of the ASCII text file, press the Spacebar, type | (the pipe operator), press the Spacebar, type MORE, and then press Enter.
- If necessary, press the Spacebar to view each of the next screens or windows of output and return to the command prompt.

You can use the TYPE command, the pipe operator, and the MORE filter to view the contents of Readme files included with software packages. When software manufacturers release a software product, they often include Readme files with the latest information on the use of the product—information that is not included in the manual or the software product's Help system. These files are ASCII text files with names such as Readme, Read.me, Readme.doc, or Readme.1st, and they are copied to your hard disk when you install the software. You can then examine these files for important information that you might need to configure the software product so that it works with the hardware components of your computer system. These Readme files might also contain troubleshooting information.

You can pipe output to the MORE filter in the same way in other versions of Windows, as well as in different versions of MS-DOS and UNIX. Remember that when using operating systems that support long filenames, you must put quotation marks around filenames containing spaces.

Redirecting Input Using an ASCII Text File

Isabel explains that you can perform the same type of operation using a different technique. You can redirect the input to the MORE filter directly without using the TYPE command and the pipe operator.

As noted earlier, the operating system assumes that input will come from the standard input device — the keyboard. However, input can come from a file instead. To redirect input from a file, use the **input redirection operator** (<). The general syntax for redirecting input from a file to the MORE filter is as follows:

MORE < *filename*

When you perform this type of redirection, the MORE filter pages the output one screen at a time.

To redirect input from a file on disk to the MORE filter:

1. Clear the window, type **more < templates.txt** and then press **Enter.** The operating system redirects input from the Templates.txt file on disk to the MORE filter, and the MORE filter displays one screen or window at a time. See Figure 3-7. Your view of this file is identical to the one produced by piping output of the TYPE command to the MORE filter. Note, however, that the title bar shows the MORE command name, because, unlike the previous command's display, this screen output is not piped.

Figure 3-7   REDIRECTING INPUT TO THE MORE FILTER

```
Command Prompt - MORE                                              _ □ X
 Volume in drive A has no label.
 Volume Serial Number is 1CBD-C548

 Directory of A:\

11/05/2003   02:35p              10,258  ~VRC0070.tmp
01/23/2003   08:16a              41,472  2002 Sales Summary #1.xls
01/23/2003   09:21a              78,848  2002 Sales Summary #2.xls
02/27/2002   08:53p              34,304  3 Year Sales Projection.xls
07/09/2003   09:42a              49,152  Addressing Cells.xls
04/18/2003   01:33p              16,896  Advertising Income.xls
05/30/2003   11:22a              22,016  Andre's Employee Payroll.xls
06/26/2003   09:30a              52,736  Application Software.ppt
01/24/2003   08:45a              18,944  Balance Sheet.xls
01/08/2003   02:06p              24,064  Break Even Analysis.xls
03/21/2003   08:08a              15,872  Client Invoices.xls
10/16/2003   09:52a              84,446  Color Palette.bmp
10/16/2003   10:31a              84,534  Colors of the Rainbow.bmp
09/05/2003   02:25p              13,824  Commission on Sales.xls
07/01/2003   08:31p              15,360  Daily Sales.xls
01/10/2003   10:54a              22,016  Data Systems Budget.xls
04/09/2003   02:12p              21,504  Employees.xls
11/05/2003   04:22p              24,064  File0000.chk
01/16/2003   10:46a                      Growth Plan.xls
-- More --                               -More- prompt
```

redirected page input • *-More- prompt*

2. Press and hold down the **Ctrl** key, press and release **C**, and then release the **Ctrl** key. Ctrl+C interrupts the command, displays ^C (the Ctrl key is represented by the ^ character) on the next line, and then returns you to the command prompt. See Figure 3-8.

Figure 3-8   **CANCELING A COMMAND**

command output
interrupted and canceled
with Ctrl+C

```
Command Prompt                                                    _ □ ✕
 Volume Serial Number is F065-B557

 Directory of A:\

11/05/2003  02:35p              10,258 ~WRC0070.tmp
01/23/2003  08:16a              41,472 2002 Sales Summary #1.xls
01/23/2003  09:21a              78,848 2002 Sales Summary #2.xls
02/27/2002  08:53p              34,304 3 Year Sales Projection.xls
07/09/2003  09:42a              49,152 Addressing Cells.xls
04/18/2003  01:33p              16,896 Advertising Income.xls
05/30/2003  11:22a              22,016 Andre's Employee Payroll.xls
06/26/2003  09:30a              52,736 Application Software.ppt
01/24/2003  08:45a              18,944 Balance Sheet.xls
01/08/2003  02:06p              24,064 Break Even Analysis.xls
03/21/2003  08:08a              15,872 Client Invoices.xls
10/16/2003  09:52a              84,446 Color Palette.bmp
10/16/2003  10:31a              84,534 Colors of the Rainbow.bmp
09/05/2003  02:25p              13,824 Commission on Sales.xls
07/01/2003  08:31p              15,360 Daily Sales.xls
01/10/2003  10:54a              22,016 Data Systems Budget.xls
04/09/2003  02:12p              21,504 Employees.xls
11/05/2003  04:22p              24,064 File0000.chk
01/16/2003  10:46a              20,992 Five Year Growth Plan.xls
^C
A:\>_
```

If a command produces more output than you expected, you can interrupt (and cancel) the command with Ctrl+C.

REFERENCE WINDOW   **RW**

Redirecting Input from an ASCII Text File to the MORE Filter
- Open a Command Prompt window.
- Change the default drive to the drive that contains the file you want to examine.
- Type MORE, press the Spacebar, type < (the input redirection operator), press the Spacebar, type the name of the ASCII text file, and then press Enter.
- Press Spacebar to view each of the next screens or windows of output and return to the command prompt, or if you want to interrupt the output of the command, press and then release Ctrl+C.

You can use this technique of redirecting input to the MORE filter for configuration and initialization files so that you can examine the contents of the files one screen or window at a time. **Initialization files** are files like Boot.ini that contain the file extension "ini," and that contain settings used by the operating system and other programs.

In all versions of Windows, MS-DOS, and UNIX, you can use the MORE filter by redirecting input from a file as above. In general, you redirect input the same way in these operating systems. As noted before, you must put quotation marks around filenames containing spaces for those operating systems that support long filenames.

Viewing Other Kinds of Files

Isabel tells you that in Windows 2000, you can also use the MORE command like the TYPE command, specifying the filename directly without redirecting input. For example, you could have typed "more templates.txt" in the previous section, without the "<" input redirection symbol. This reproduces the way the MORE command works in UNIX. To use the MORE filter this way in Windows NT 4.0, you must use the /E (Extended features) switch.

Although the TYPE and MORE commands are designed for ASCII text files, you can use them with other kinds of files when you need to get an idea of a file's contents, regardless of its format. Files with the "chk" extension provide a good example. The Check Disk utility, creates these files, which contain recovered file fragments resulting from disk errors. They are **binary files**, which can contain any kind of data, rather than just ASCII text, so you will usually see strange characters when you display them with the TYPE command or MORE filter. Isabel suggests you use both commands to examine such a file named File0000.chk on your diskette.

To view a recovered file fragment in File0000.chk:

1. Clear the Command Prompt window, type **type file0000.chk**, and then press **Enter**. In this particular file, you see only a short string of characters as in Figure 3-9, because the TYPE command encounters an End-of-File code (EOF, Ctrl-Z, or ASCII 26) a short way into the file. This code can appear anywhere in binary files, which do not use the EOF code to denote the actual end of the file. However, the TYPE command always stops when it encounters an EOF code.

Figure 3-9	USING THE TYPE COMMAND ON A BINARY FILE

command to display
recovered file fragment

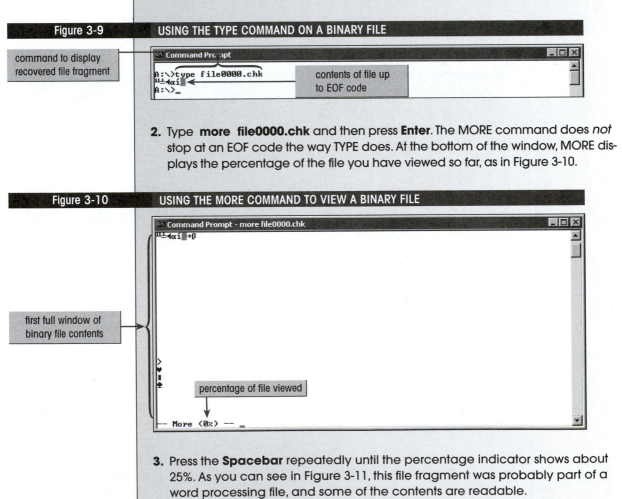

contents of file up
to EOF code

2. Type **more file0000.chk** and then press **Enter**. The MORE command does *not* stop at an EOF code the way TYPE does. At the bottom of the window, MORE displays the percentage of the file you have viewed so far, as in Figure 3-10.

Figure 3-10	USING THE MORE COMMAND TO VIEW A BINARY FILE

first full window of
binary file contents

percentage of file viewed

3. Press the **Spacebar** repeatedly until the percentage indicator shows about 25%. As you can see in Figure 3-11, this file fragment was probably part of a word processing file, and some of the contents are readable.

Figure 3-11	USING MORE TO VIEW READABLE BINARY FILE CONTENTS

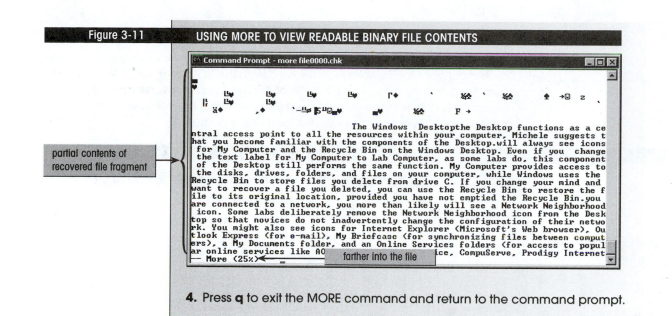

partial contents of recovered file fragment

farther into the file

4. Press **q** to exit the MORE command and return to the command prompt.

Isabel points out that you can use this technique to determine whether you want to keep the contents of a file like this. In cases where disk errors cause you to lose a valuable file, recovered file fragments may save you some time and effort in restoring your data.

Sorting ASCII Text Files

As Isabel and you talk further about redirection and filters, you learn that there are three other commands that are filters: one for sorting the contents of ASCII text files, and two others for locating information in ASCII text files.

The SORT filter can take input from a command or a file, sort the input, and then display the results. If you want to use an ASCII text file as the source for input, and then sort that input, use the following approach:

> **SORT** < *filename*

The SORT filter sorts the contents of the file starting with the first character on each line, comparing that character with the first character on the next line. If the first character on each line is identical, then it compares the second characters, sorting each line with respect to all other lines in a file from left to right. By default, the input is sorted in ascending order (from 0 to 9, and then from A to Z) using the ASCII code of the characters (although it ignores uppercase or lowercase). If you want to sort in descending order (in reverse order), you would use the **Reverse switch** (**/R**), as follows:

> **SORT /R** < *filename*

When you produced the Templates.txt file, you used the Order switch to arrange the directory listing in order by filename. You now want to display that same file information in reverse order by date (from the most recent file to the oldest file). Because the date is the first column in this ASCII text file, you can sort the contents of the file by date. If the date is the same for more than one file, then each line is sorted by the time. If the date and time are the same, then each line is next sorted by the file size. If the date, time, and file size are the same, then each line is sorted by the filename. Again, the sort is from left to right.

To redirect input from a file on disk to the SORT filter:

1. Type **sort /r < templates.txt** and then press **Enter**. The operating system redirects input from the Templates.txt file on disk to the SORT filter, and the SORT filter sorts the contents of the file so that file dates are listed in reverse order. See Figure 3-12. However, the output scrolled so fast within the window that you were probably unable to see the first part of the output.

| Figure 3-12 | SORTING REDIRECTED INPUT |

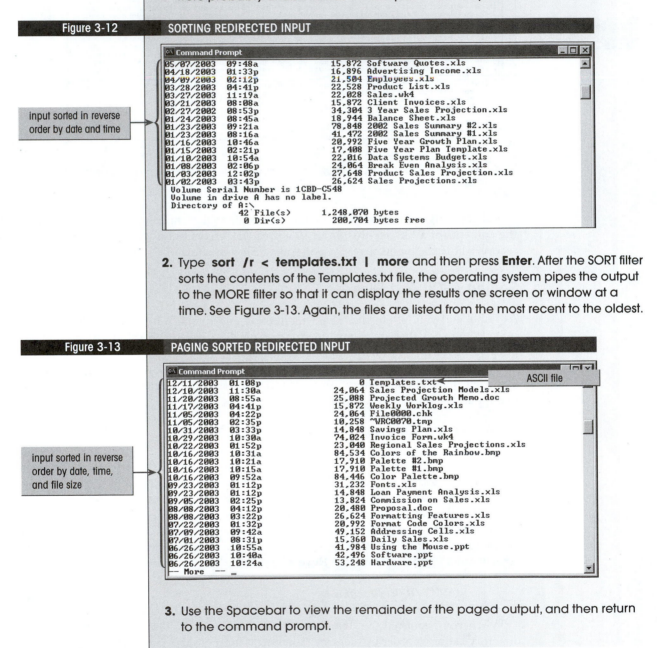

2. Type **sort /r < templates.txt | more** and then press **Enter**. After the SORT filter sorts the contents of the Templates.txt file, the operating system pipes the output to the MORE filter so that it can display the results one screen or window at a time. See Figure 3-13. Again, the files are listed from the most recent to the oldest.

| Figure 3-13 | PAGING SORTED REDIRECTED INPUT |

3. Use the Spacebar to view the remainder of the paged output, and then return to the command prompt.

The SORT filter provides a simple and easy mechanism for quickly sorting the contents of an ASCII text file from left to right.

REFERENCE WINDOW   **RW**

Sorting the Contents of ASCII Text Files with the SORT Filter
- Open a Command Prompt window.
- Change the default drive to the drive that contains the files you want to examine.
- Type SORT, press the Spacebar, type the name of the ASCII text file, press the Spacebar, type | (the pipe operator), press the Spacebar, type MORE, and then press Enter.
- Press the Spacebar to view each of the next screens or windows of sorted output and return to the command prompt.

The SORT filter works in the same basic way in other versions of Windows and different versions of MS-DOS and UNIX. In all these operating systems, you can also use SORT without redirecting input. For example, you could type sort /r templates.txt in the example above, without the "<" input redirection symbol. Again, enclose filenames containing spaces in quotation marks.

You can also use the pipe operator to send the output of another command to the SORT filter as input, as you did previously with the MORE command.

Searching the Contents of an ASCII Text File

After demonstrating the use of the SORT filter, Isabel shows you how to find information in an ASCII text file with the use of the FIND filter. She points out that you can use this filter to quickly search files that contain information about the company's collection of template files. For practice, Isabel suggests you list all the files that contain "Sales" in the filename and store the list of filenames in a new text file called "Sales Templates.txt".

The FIND filter searches one or more ASCII text files for a specific string of text (a set of characters, such as a filename or a setting), and then displays the results by file. The general syntax for this command is as follows:

FIND *"string" filename*

You must enclose the text that you specify as the string within quotation marks. Also, unless you specify otherwise, FIND is case sensitive, and therefore the string must be in the same case as that found in the file (or files).

To search for a text string in an ASCII text file:

1. Clear the window.

2. Type **find "Sales" Templates.txt** and then press **Enter**. The FIND filter searches the contents of the Templates.txt file (an ASCII text file), and lists the lines that contain the word "Sales." See Figure 3-14. The FIND filter has extracted a subset of the information contained in the file.

   TROUBLE? If the FIND filter reports that the parameter format is not correct, then you did not include the string within quotation marks. Repeat the command, and use the exact syntax shown.

   TROUBLE? If the FIND filter does not list any lines within the Templates.txt file, then you typed "Sales" in all uppercase, all lowercase or you did not capitalize the beginning "S" in "Sales." The FIND filter is case-sensitive. Repeat this step again, but use the exact case shown for the string, or recall the same command and add the Ignore switch (/I) so that the FIND filter ignores the case.

Figure 3-14   USING THE FIND FILTER TO LOCATE TEXT IN AN ASCII FILE

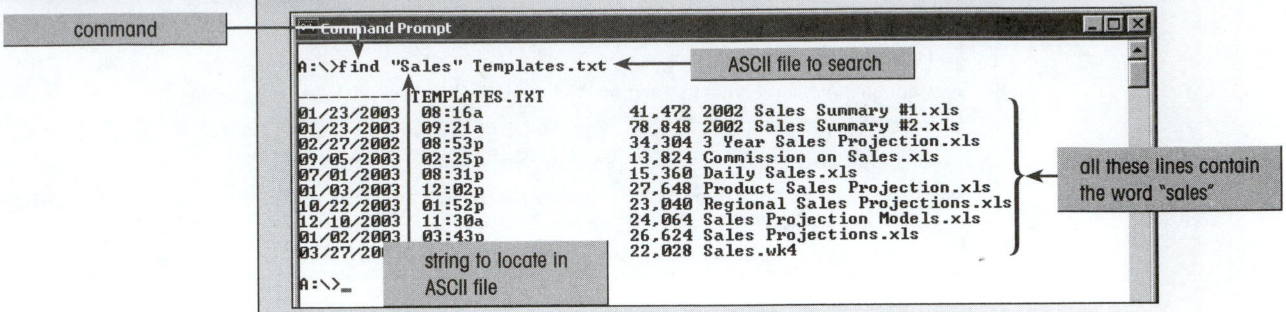

command

A:\>find "Sales" Templates.txt ← ASCII file to search

```
-------- TEMPLATES.TXT
01/23/2003   08:16a            41,472 2002 Sales Summary #1.xls
01/23/2003   09:21a            78,848 2002 Sales Summary #2.xls
02/27/2002   08:53p            34,304 3 Year Sales Projection.xls
09/05/2003   02:25p            13,824 Commission on Sales.xls
07/01/2003   08:31p            15,360 Daily Sales.xls
01/03/2003   12:02p            27,648 Product Sales Projection.xls
10/22/2003   01:52p            23,040 Regional Sales Projections.xls
12/10/2003   11:30a            24,064 Sales Projection Models.xls
01/02/2003   03:43p            26,624 Sales Projections.xls
03/27/200                      22,028 Sales.wk4

A:\>_
```

all these lines contain the word "sales"

string to locate in ASCII file

3. Clear the window, type **find "Sales" Templates.txt > "Sales Templates.txt"**, and then press **Enter**. You must use quotation marks around the string "Sales" and the filename "Sales Templates.txt" (because the latter contains a space). The operating system records the output of the FIND filter in an ASCII text file on disk.

   TROUBLE? If the FIND filter reports that the parameter format is not correct, then you did not include the string within quotation marks. Repeat the command, and use the exact syntax shown.

4. Type **type "Sales Templates.txt"** and then press **Enter**. TYPE displays the contents of the Sales Templates.txt file. See Figure 3-15. Notice that each of the lines in "Sales Templates.txt" contains the word "Sales."

   TROUBLE? If the command interpreter displays a message indicating that the system cannot find the file you specified, then you did not include quotation marks around the filename. Repeat the step using the exact syntax shown.

Figure 3-15   REDIRECTING OUTPUT OF THE FIND FILTER TO A FILE

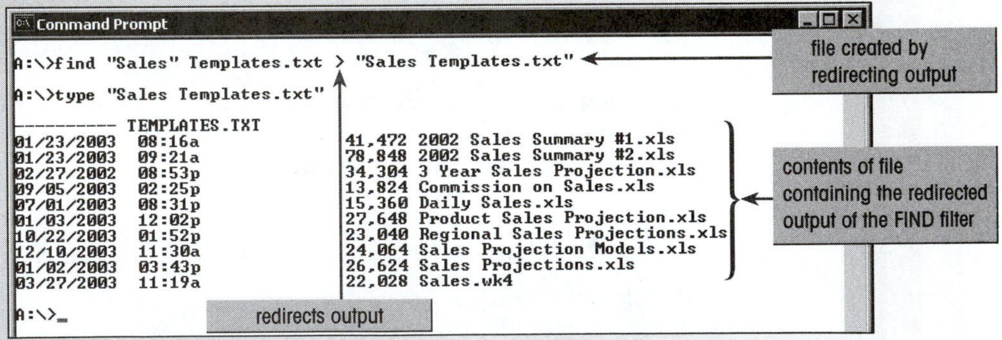

A:\>find "Sales" Templates.txt > "Sales Templates.txt" ←

A:\>type "Sales Templates.txt"

```
-------- TEMPLATES.TXT
01/23/2003   08:16a            41,472 2002 Sales Summary #1.xls
01/23/2003   09:21a            78,848 2002 Sales Summary #2.xls
02/27/2002   08:53p            34,304 3 Year Sales Projection.xls
09/05/2003   02:25p            13,824 Commission on Sales.xls
07/01/2003   08:31p            15,360 Daily Sales.xls
01/03/2003   12:02p            27,648 Product Sales Projection.xls
10/22/2003   01:52p            23,040 Regional Sales Projections.xls
12/10/2003   11:30a            24,064 Sales Projection Models.xls
01/02/2003   03:43p            26,624 Sales Projections.xls
03/27/2003   11:19a            22,028 Sales.wk4

A:\>_
```

file created by redirecting output

contents of file containing the redirected output of the FIND filter

redirects output

You can use the FIND filter in the same way in other versions of Windows and MS-DOS. For those operating systems that support long filenames, you will need to place quotation marks around filenames with spaces.

Windows 2000 and versions of Windows NT 4.0 also offer the FINDSTR command, a more powerful utility that can locate text strings using a set of specialized wildcards to match patterns, and which also has the ability to examine multiple files in the same pass.

REFERENCE **WINDOW** `RW`

Searching ASCII Text Files with the FIND Filter
- Open a Command Prompt window.
- Change the default drive to the drive that contains the files you want to examine.
- Type FIND, press the Spacebar, type the string (or text) you want to locate within quotation marks (required), press the Spacebar, type the name of the ASCII text file, and then press Enter.
- If you want to redirect output of the FIND filter to a file on disk, type FIND, press the Spacebar, type the string (or text) you want to locate within quotation marks (required), press the Spacebar, type the name of the ASCII text file, type > (the output redirection operator), press the Spacebar, type the name of the file that will store the output, and then press Enter.

Although you will find that you depend on the MORE filter when working in a command line environment, the SORT and FIND filters are also useful tools that you can call on when the need arises.

Appending Output to an ASCII Text File

Now that you are familiar with the use of the output and input redirection operators, Isabel shows you how to append, or add, the output of a command to an existing file by adding a list of all files with "Projection" in the filename to the file you made previously.

If you create an ASCII text file, and then find that you need to append output to the end of that same file, you can use the append redirection operator (>>), as follows:

[*command*] >> *filename*

You need to be careful when you use this redirection operator. If you accidentally type only one greater-than symbol rather than two, the operating system will overwrite the existing file.

If you need to append output to another file, you will probably also want to insert some blank lines between the output that already exists in the file, and the next output you append to that file. You can use the following command to add a blank line to the end of the file:

ECHO. >> *filename*

You can use the ECHO command to display messages or blank lines in a window or on the screen. If you follow the ECHO command with a period (or dot) without any space between ECHO and the period, then the operating system will display a blank line in the window or on the screen. Then, if you use the append redirection operator with this command and specify a filename, the operating system will add a blank line to the bottom of the file, because you are redirecting output from the display device.

To append output in a file on diskette:

1. Clear the window, type **echo. >> "Sales Templates.txt"** and check what you've typed. You must type the period (or dot) right after you type ECHO (no space is allowed). You also have to enclose the long filename within quotation marks because it contains a space. Press **Enter**. The operating system writes a blank line to the bottom of the file "Sales Templates.txt" and then displays the command prompt.

2. Press **F3** to recall the previous command and then press **Enter**. The operating system writes another blank line to the bottom of the same file.

3. Type **find "Projection" Templates.txt** and then press **Enter**. The FIND filter finds five lines in the Templates.txt file that contain the word "Projection". See Figure 3-16. Now that you've tested the command to make sure it works, you can recall the same command and append the output to the Sales Templates.txt file.

   TROUBLE? If the FIND filter reports that the parameter format is not correct, then you did not include the string within quotation marks. Repeat the command, and use the exact syntax shown.

   TROUBLE? If the FIND filter does not list any files, then you might have typed Projection in all uppercase or all lowercase (check the spelling as well). The FIND filter is case-sensitive. Repeat this step, but use the exact case shown for the string, or recall the same command and add the Ignore switch (/I) so the FIND filter ignores the case.

| Figure 3-16 | USING THE FIND FILTER TO SEARCH FOR TEXT IN AN ASCII FILE |

command

append output
redirection operator

appending a blank line
to the bottom of an
ASCII file

```
Command Prompt                                                    _ □ ×

A:\>echo. >> "Sales Templates.txt"

A:\>echo. >> "Sales Templates.txt"

A:\>find "Projection" Templates.txt

---------- TEMPLATES.TXT
02/27/2002   08:53p              34,304 3 Year Sales Projection.xls
01/03/2003   12:02p              27,648 Product Sales Projection.xls
10/22/2003   01:52p              23,040 Regional Sales Projections.xls
12/10/2003   11:30a              24,064 Sales Projection Models.xls
01/02/2003   03:43p              26,624 Sales Projections.xls

A:\>_
```

lines that contain the
word "Projection"

filename

4. Clear the window, type **find "Projection" Templates.txt >> "Sales Templates.txt"**, and then press **Enter**. The operating system appends the output of the FIND filter to the end of the "Sales Templates.txt" file.

   TROUBLE? If the FIND filter reports that the parameter format is not correct, then you did not include the string within quotation marks. Repeat the command, and use the exact syntax shown.

5. Type **more < "Sales Templates.txt"** and then press **Enter**. See Figure 3-17. Notice the two blank lines that you appended to this file before using the FIND filter to locate all lines with the word "Projection" and append the results to this file.

   TROUBLE? If the operating system displays a message indicating that the system cannot find the file you specified, then you did not include quotation marks around the long filename. Repeat the step using the exact syntax shown.

   TROUBLE? If you see lines that begin with a period (or dot), then you typed a space between ECHO and the period when you originally entered the command, rather than typing ECHO. with the period right after the command.

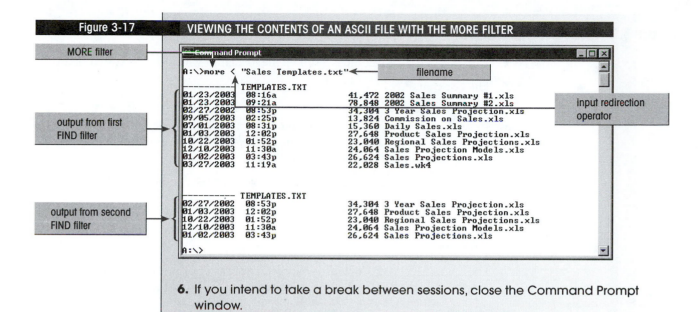

Figure 3-17 **VIEWING THE CONTENTS OF AN ASCII FILE WITH THE MORE FILTER**

6. If you intend to take a break between sessions, close the Command Prompt window.

If you use the append output redirection operator and specify a filename that does not already exist, Windows 2000 creates the file first, and then appends the output to the new file.

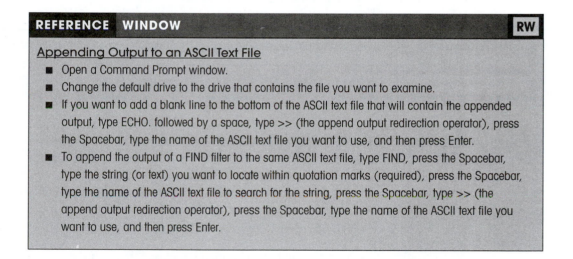

REFERENCE WINDOW **RW**

Appending Output to an ASCII Text File

- Open a Command Prompt window.
- Change the default drive to the drive that contains the file you want to examine.
- If you want to add a blank line to the bottom of the ASCII text file that will contain the appended output, type ECHO. followed by a space, type >> (the append output redirection operator), press the Spacebar, type the name of the ASCII text file you want to use, and then press Enter.
- To append the output of a FIND filter to the same ASCII text file, type FIND, press the Spacebar, type the string (or text) you want to locate within quotation marks (required), press the Spacebar, type the name of the ASCII text file to search for the string, press the Spacebar, type >> (the append output redirection operator), press the Spacebar, type the name of the ASCII text file you want to use, and then press Enter.

You can append output to a file on disk using the output redirection operator the same way in other versions of Windows, MS-DOS, and UNIX. For those operating systems that support long filenames, make sure you place quotation marks around filenames with spaces.

Piping, redirection, and filtering are three powerful tools that are often used in combination with each other to manage input and output in a command line environment.

Session 3.1 QUICK CHECK

1. A(n) _____ file is a simple file format in which data is stored as text.

2. The last character in an ASCII text file is a special type of code—a(n) _____ code.

3. To send output to another device other than the standard output device (the display device), you can _____, or change the destination of, that output and, for example, send the output to a file on disk.

4. You can use the _____ operator to redirect output to a file.

5. To view the contents of an ASCII text file, you use the _____ command.

6. A(n) _____ is a command that can modify the output of another command.

7. The _____ operator redirects the output produced by a command operation so that the output then becomes the input for another command.

8. You can use the _____ operator to redirect input from a file on disk.

9. You can use the _____ operator to redirect output and add it to the end of an existing file.

10. The standard input device is the _____, and the standard output device is the _____.

SESSION 3.2

In this session you will redirect the output of a command to a printer. You will also copy, rename, and delete individual files and groups of files on disk.

Redirecting Output to the Printer

Isabel asks you to print a list of the files on your diskette.

She tells you that besides redirecting the output of a command to a file, you can also send the output directly to the printer. Using this capability with the DIR command allows you to do something that Windows Explorer and My Computer cannot do—print a list of files in a directory.

To send the output of a command, such as DIR, to the printer, redirect the output as you have previously, but instead of typing a filename, specify the device name of your printer port. IBM designated LPT1 (Line Printer #1) as the default printer port on its original PCs. Today, most people still connect their printer to LPT1. If you work on a network, output to LPT1—you can also use the name PRN (for printer)—is more than likely captured and redirected to a network printer. LPT1 and PRN are reserved device names, which you cannot use as folder names or filenames. A **device name** is a name Windows 2000 assigns to one of the devices, or hardware components, in a computer system. Figure 3-18 lists device names used by Windows 2000. The NUL device, sometimes called the "Bit Bucket," is a special device that behaves like a perpetually empty file and discards any data you copy or redirect into it. All versions of Windows and MS-DOS use these device names.

Figure 3-18 **RESERVED DEVICE NAMES**

DEVICE NAME	MEANING	ASSIGNED TO
LPT1	Line Printer 1	First parallel port
LPT2	Line Printer 2	Second parallel port
LPT3	Line Printer 3	Third parallel port
PRN	Printer	First parallel port
COM1	Communications port 1	First serial port
COM2	Communications port 2	Second serial port
COM3	Communications port 3	Third serial port
COM4	Communications port 4	Fourth serial port
CON	Console unit	Monitor and keyboard
A:	Drive A	First floppy drive
C:	Drive C	First hard disk drive
NUL	NUL device	"Bit Bucket"

To send the current directory listing to the printer:

1. If necessary, open a Command Prompt window, and then change the foreground and background colors.

2. Make sure your Data Disk is in drive A, change the default drive to drive A, and then clear the window.

3. Make sure your printer is on.

4. Type **dir > prn** and then press **Enter**. The DIR command does not display output in the window, but rather redirects it to your printer port. See Figure 3-19. The print-out contains the directory listing for your Data Disk.

   TROUBLE? If Windows 2000 displays an error message and informs you that the system cannot write to the specified device, enter the command DIR > "Directory Listing.txt" to redirect the output to a file, and then use notepad to print a copy of "Directory Listing.txt".

   TROUBLE? If your printer does not print, check to see if your printer's indicators show that it has received data. You may need to eject the page manually, because the above command does not send a form-feed signal to the printer to eject the page automatically, as a word processor would.

Figure 3-19 **REDIRECTING OUTPUT OF A DIRECTORY LISTING TO A PRINTER**

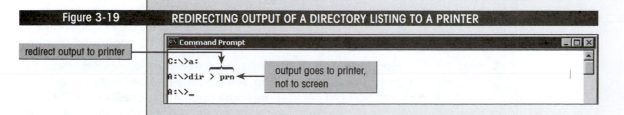

redirect output to printer

output goes to printer, not to screen

Knowing how to redirect output to your printer port is important if you need to troubleshoot a printer problem. In fact, if you are using the Print Troubleshooter in Windows Help, it will recommend that you use this technique as a starting point for troubleshooting the problem and testing the printer connection.

REFERENCE WINDOW   `RW`

Redirecting Output to a Printer
- Open a Command Prompt window.
- Change the default drive to the drive that contains the files with which you want to work.
- Type DIR, followed by a space, type **>** PRN, and then press Enter key.
- If necessary, eject the page from your printer manually.

As noted earlier, using redirection to send the output of a command line to the printer allows you to quickly print lists and reports not otherwise available in Windows, such as a list of filenames in a directory.

Other versions of Windows and MS-DOS redirect output to a printer in the same way. If a filename contains one or more spaces, you'll need to enclose it in quotation marks.

Copying Files

Isabel asks you to make a copy of the "Five Year Plan Template.xls" file and to revise it so that you have a new version. She asks you to name the new version "Five Year Plan Draft.xls."

You can use the COPY command to quickly copy the contents of an existing file into a new file on the same disk, and at the same time give the copy a new name. COPY is a versatile, internal command that you can use in a variety of ways. If you want to create a copy of a file from an existing file, the syntax is as follows:

COPY *source* [*destination*]

The original file that you copy is the **source file**—in this case, "Five Year Plan Template.xls." The new file that you produce from the copy operation is the **destination file**, or **target file**—in this case, "Five Year Plan Draft.xls."

If you copy a file and specify a filename that already exists, COPY automatically asks for verification before it overwrites the file. After you make a copy of a file, you should verify that the copy operation produced the file you wanted.

To copy the template file:

1. Type **set dircmd=/p /o** and then press **Enter** to specify default switches for the Directory command.

2. Type **copy "Five Year Plan Template.xls" "Five Year Plan Draft.xls"** and then press **Enter**. Because these filenames each contain spaces, you must place each filename within quotation marks. If the copy is successful, the COPY command displays the message "1 file(s) copied." and then you see the command prompt.

3. Type the command **dir Five*** and then press **Enter**. The file "Five Year Plan Draft.xls" is shown in the directory listing. See Figure 3-20. Note that the new file contains the same number of bytes and date and time of creation as "Five Year Plan Template.xls." Because you have not yet made any changes to "Five Year Plan Draft.xls," it is identical to "Five Year Plan Template.xls."

Figure 3-20	CREATING A COPY OF A FILE

set default DIR switches

```
Command Prompt                                                    _ □ ×

A:\>set dircmd=/p /o

A:\>copy "Five Year Plan Template.xls" "Five Year Plan Draft.xls"
        1 file(s) copied.

A:\>dir Five*
 Volume in drive A has no label.
 Volume Serial Number is F065-B557

 Directory of A:\

01/16/2003  10:46a            20,992 Five Year Growth Plan.xls
01/15/2003  02:21p            17,408 Five Year Plan Draft.xls
01/15/2003  02:21p            17,408 Five Year Plan Template.xls
        3 File(s)             55,808 bytes
        0 Dir(s)             185,856 bytes free

A:\>_
```

name of file to copy

check for new file

name of new file

files with the word "Five" at the beginning of the filename

You can also copy files from one drive to another, as well as from one directory to another directory. In Tutorial 4, you will examine some of these techniques for copying files.

REFERENCE   WINDOW   **RW**

Creating a Copy of a File

- Open a Command Prompt window.
- Change the default drive to the drive that contains the file you want to copy.
- Type COPY, followed by a space, type the name of the source file, press the Spacebar, and type the name of the destination or target file. If one or both of the filenames contain spaces, you must enclose them within quotation marks.

In other versions of Windows and MS-DOS, you would create a copy of a file in the same way, enclosing filenames in quotation marks when they include spaces.

Renaming Files

Isabel asks you to rename some of the files on your diskette so the filenames more clearly identify the contents of the files. Later, when you are facing deadlines, you will not need to spend valuable time figuring out which file to use.

You can use the RENAME command, or its abbreviated version, REN, to change the name of a file. If you use wildcards with this command, you can change the names of files in a group. By contrast, Windows Explorer and My Computer provide no way to rename a group of files in one step.

The general syntax for these internal commands is as follows:

RENAME [*drive:*][*path*]*filename1 filename2*

REN [*drive:*][*path*]*filename1 filename2*

When you specify *filename1* (the source filename), you must include the drive and path if the file is on another drive or in another directory. The **path** specifies the name of the directory, or sequence of directories that point to where the file is stored. You *never* specify a drive or path for *filename2* (the destination filename). If you do, the RENAME command displays an error message because it thinks you are attempting to move the file, and this command does not move files. If you use wildcards in *filename2*, the characters represented by the wildcards will be identical to the corresponding characters in *filename1*.

Renaming a Single File

You'd like to make the filename Proposal.doc more descriptive, and because this particular Microsoft Word file is a proposal for computer training, you'd like to rename it to "Computer Training Proposal.doc". You can enter the RENAME command using either of the following approaches:

REN Proposal.doc "Computer Training Proposal.doc"

REN Proposal.doc "Computer Training Proposal.*"
Or, because the disk has no other files named "Proposal," you could also use:

REN Proposal.* "Computer Training Proposal.*"

Again, note that you must use quotation marks when a filename contains spaces. If you substitute an asterisk wildcard for the extension in the destination file, REN assumes you want to use the same extension as the source file. In this case, the asterisk in the source filename substitutes for whatever file extension the first file contains, and the REN command keeps the same extension for the new filename. These features save keystrokes, but more importantly, they preserve the extension, which almost all Windows applications require for their data files.

To rename the Proposal.doc file from the command prompt:

1. Clear the window, type **dir *pro***, and then press **Enter** to verify the file exists. DIR lists all filenames containing the characters "pro," regardless of case. See Figure 3-21.

| Figure 3-21 | LOCATING THE FILE TO RENAME |

2. Type **ren Proposal.doc "Computer Training Proposal.*"** and then press **Enter**. REN assumes that you want to rename the file on the current drive and that the extension of the new filename is the same. REN will not let you rename a file if there is already a file by the new name that you want to use. You can also use RENAME instead of REN.

3. Type (or recall) **dir *pro*** and then press **Enter** to verify the change. When it renamed the file, REN changed the name, but kept the extension. See Figure 3-22.

Figure 3-22 | RENAMING A FILE

Figure 3-22 RENAMING A FILE

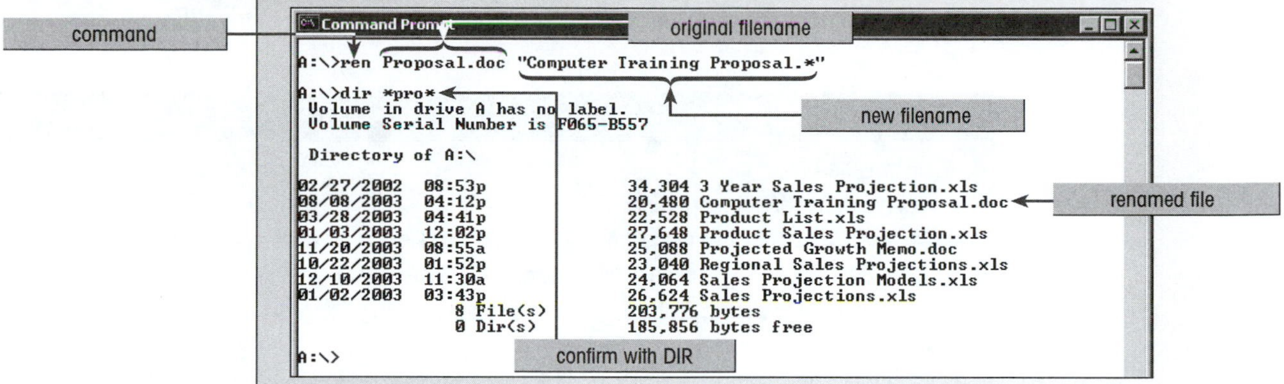

You can also rename a file using the MOVE command, which has a similar syntax to REN, except you can specify a different drive or path in addition to (or instead of) a new name, thus moving the file to a new location. You will learn more about the MOVE command in the next tutorial. Only the REN command, however, allows you to rename multiple files in one command line.

Renaming Multiple Files

Isabel asks you to use the "2002 Sales Summary" files as templates for the upcoming "2003 Sales Summary" files. She notes that you can rename both files in one step.

To rename both "2002 Sales Summary" files:

1. Clear the window, type **dir 2*** and then press **Enter** to verify that the files exist. DIR lists all filenames starting with the numeral "2"—"2002 Sales Summary #1.xls" and "2002 Sales Summary #2.xls."

2. Type **ren 2002* 2003*** and then press **Enter**. REN assumes you want to change only the first four characters of each filename, and preserves the rest of the filename, including the extensions.

3. Type (or recall) **dir 2*** and then press **Enter**. Figure 3-23 shows the change in filenames.

Figure 3-23 RENAMING MULTIPLE FILES

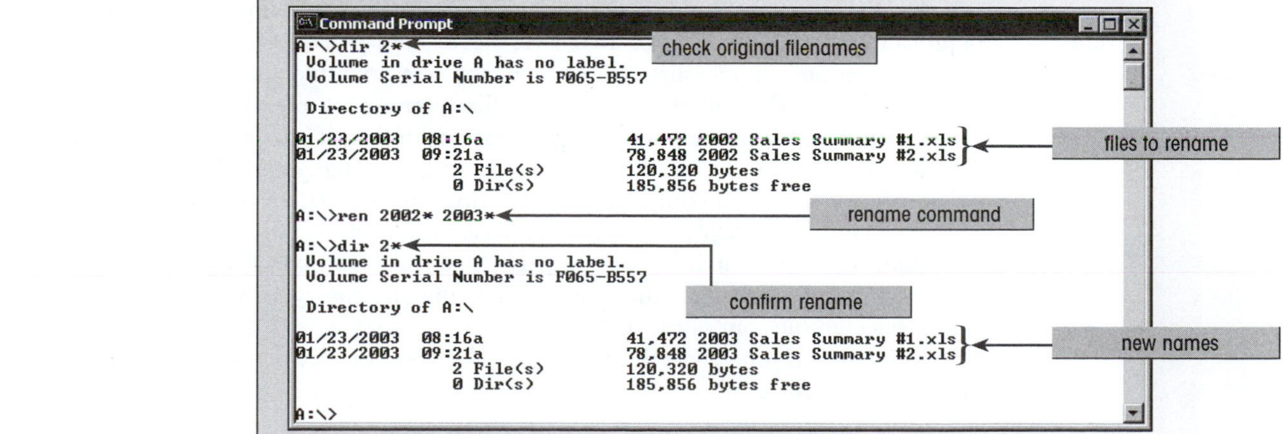

As noted earlier, if you are working in the graphical user interface, you can change the name of only one file at a time. By using REN in a Command Prompt window, you can save yourself a great deal of time and effort when you need to rename many different files.

REFERENCE WINDOW   **RW**

Renaming Files
- Open a Command Prompt window.
- Change the default drive to the drive that contains the file(s) you want to rename.
- Type REN, a space, the name of the original file, another space, and then the new name for the file. If you use wildcards in the new name, REN will keep the characters represented by the wildcards from the original name in the new name.
- To change the names of multiple files at once, type REN, a space, a matching pattern with wildcards to match the existing names, another space, and then a wildcard matching pattern to define which parts of the names you wish to change and which parts you wish to keep.

Other versions of Windows and MS-DOS contain a REN command that works the same way with single or multiple files, requiring quotation marks around filenames with spaces.

Deleting Files

You realize that there are a couple of files you do not need and you want to remove them from your diskette so they do not take up space. You can delete files from the command prompt with the DEL or ERASE commands. The general syntax is as follows:

DEL *filename*

ERASE *filename*

DEL and ERASE are simply two names for the same internal command, so use of either command name will produce the same result.

Deleting files from the command prompt is risky. If you use wildcards, you might inadvertently delete more files than you expect, including important document files you need. The Delete command does not ask if you are sure you want to delete a file or a group of files, except in one case. The only exception is when you enter DEL *.* at the command prompt. Then DEL will automatically ask you if you want to delete all the files in the directory.

Note: DEL and ERASE do *not* store deleted files in the Recycle Bin, and Windows 2000 does not provide any easy or reliable way to recover files deleted with the DEL or ERASE commands.

As a precautionary measure, you should first test your file specification with the DIR command. If the DIR command selects the files you expect, then you can use the DEL or ERASE command with the same file specification. In fact, if you use DEL (the more common choice), you can just recall the DIR command, and change "DIR" to "DEL".

You can also use the **Prompt for Verification switch**, (**/P**). When you use this switch, the Delete command displays a prompt and asks you to verify whether or not you want to delete the file. This switch becomes especially useful when you delete multiple files with wildcard patterns. It verifies that you are deleting the files you want, and allows you to remove selected files out of the matching group.

Because you no longer need the File0000.chk file, you decide to delete it, using the /P switch as a precaution.

To delete the file named File0000.chk:

1. Clear the window, type **dir file*** and then press **Enter** to verify that the file exists. There is only one file (the one you want to delete) that contains the characters "file" at the beginning of the filename. See Figure 3-24.

Figure 3-24	LOCATING THE FILE TO DELETE

```
Command Prompt                                                    _ □ X

A:\>dir file*                          check for file to delete
 Volume in drive A has no label.
 Volume Serial Number is F065-B557

 Directory of A:\

11/05/2003  04:22p                24,064 File0000.chk         file to delete
               1 File(s)          24,064 bytes
               0 Dir(s)          185,856 bytes free

A:\>_
```

2. Type **del file*** **/p** and then press **Enter**. DEL prompts for verification, displaying the filename and then the message "Delete (Y/N)?". See Figure 3-25.

Figure 3-25	DELETING A FILE

```
Command Prompt - del file* /p                                    _ □ X

A:\>dir file*
 Volume in drive A has no label.
 Volume Serial Number is F065-B557           command for
                                             deleting a file
 Directory of A:\

11/05/2003  04:22p                24,064 File0000.chk
               1 File(s)          24,064 bytes
               0 Dir(s)          185,856 bytes free

A:\>del file* /p
A:\File0000.chk, Delete (Y/N)?            Prompt for Verification
```

file to delete

3. Type **y** and then press **Enter**. DEL does not display any further messages.

4. To verify the deletion, type (or recall) **dir file*** and then press **Enter**. The DIR command verifies that the file File0000.chk no longer exists in the directory. See Figure 3-26.

Figure 3-26	VERIFYING A DELETED FILE

```
Command Prompt                                                    _ □ X

A:\>dir file*
 Volume in drive A has no label.
 Volume Serial Number is F065-B557

 Directory of A:\

11/05/2003  04:22p                24,064 File0000.chk
               1 File(s)          24,064 bytes
               0 Dir(s)          185,856 bytes free

A:\>del file* /p
A:\File0000.chk, Delete (Y/N)? y

A:\>dir file*                                  check for file again
 Volume in drive A has no label.
 Volume Serial Number is F065-B557

 Directory of A:\

File Not Found

A:\>_
```

delete confirmed

file no longer present

5. Close the Command Prompt window.

You could have also used ERASE to delete the file. Because ERASE is another name for DEL, it uses the same switches, including the Prompt for Verification switch.

REFERENCE WINDOW `RW`

Deleting Files

- Open a Command Prompt window.
- Change the default drive to the drive that contains the files you want to delete.
- Type DEL, press the Spacebar, type the name of the file to delete, press the Spacebar, type /P (the Prompt for Verification switch), and then press Enter. If you use wildcards and do not use the Prompt for Verification switch, DEL will remove all files that match the pattern you give.

If you delete a file from the command prompt and then check the disk that originally contained the file, the directory listing will no longer display the filename. Although you have deleted the file, the file actually still exists on the disk. When the Delete command deletes a file, it does not actually physically remove the file from the disk. Instead, it marks the file as deleted, which prevents the filename entry from appearing in the directory listing. The operating system then knows that it can use the space occupied by this deleted file if it needs that storage space for another file. The deleted file remains on disk until the operating system records the contents of a new file over all or part of that storage space. That means that if you find it necessary, you can acquire a third-party "undelete" utility to restore a file you have deleted. Although Windows 2000 does not include an "undelete" utility, other software products, such as Norton Utilities, include this utility as well as many other disk and file utilities.

Other versions of Windows and MS-DOS have the same Delete command, with the same quotation mark requirements as with other commands.

When combined with the DIR command, the TYPE, COPY, RENAME, and DEL commands assist you in one of the most important tasks you face when using a computer system—managing your files. Furthermore, some of these commands support features that are not available in the Windows 2000 graphical user interface, such as renaming multiple files.

Session 3.2 QUICK CHECK

1. A(n) _____ is a name Windows 2000 assigns to each of the devices, or hardware components, in a computer system.

2. If you want to redirect output to a printer, specify the name of your _____ as the output device.

3. _____ is the device name of the first parallel printer port (also called Line Printer #1).

4. When making a copy of a file, the file you copy is called the _____ file.

5. When making a copy of a file, the file that contains the new copy is called the _____ file.

6. One advantage of the REN command is that you can use wildcards to change the filename of _____ files.

7. When deleting a file, you should use the _____ switch.

8. When redirecting output to a parallel port, you can use _____ instead of LPT1 as the device name.

9. TYPE, COPY, RENAME, REN, DEL, and ERASE all have one feature in common—they are _____ commands.

10. You have to be careful when using _____ with the Delete or Erase commands.

OPERATOR AND COMMAND REFERENCE

OPERATOR	USE	BASIC SYNTAX	EXAMPLE
>	Redirects output to a file on disk, or to a printer	command > filename command > printer port	dir /o > templates.txt dir /o > prn
<	Redirects input from a file on disk	command < filename	more < templates.txt
|	Uses output of one command as the input for another command	command1 | command2	type templates.txt i more
>>	Appends output to the end of an existing file	command >> filename	find "Projection" Templates.txt >> "Sales Templates.txt"

COMMAND	USE	BASIC SYNTAX	EXAMPLE
TYPE	Displays the contents of a text file (or files)	TYPE filename	type config.nt
MORE	Displays output one screen at a time	command | MORE MORE < filename MORE filename	type templates.txt i more more < templates.txt more templates.txt
SORT	Sorts the contents of an ASCII text file	command | SORT SORT < filename SORT filename	type templates.txt i sort sort < templates.txt sort templates.txt
FIND	Displays or changes the system date	FIND "string" filename	find "Sales" Templates.txt
COPY	Creates new copies of one or more files	COPY source [destination]	copy "Five Year Plan Template.xls" "Five Year Plan Draft.xls"

OPERATOR	USE	BASIC SYNTAX	EXAMPLE
RENAME	Changes the name of one or more files	RENAME [drive:][path] filename1 filename2	rename Proposal.doc "Computer Training Proposal.doc"
REN		REN [drive:][path]filename1 filename2	ren Proposal.doc "Computer Training Proposal.doc"
DEL ERASE	Deletes one or more files	DEL filename ERASE filename	del *.chk erase *.chk

Items shown in italics and not enclosed within square brackets are required parameters. (See TYPE command.)
Items shown in italics and enclosed within square brackets are optional parameters. (See REN command.)

REVIEW ASSIGNMENTS

Another staff member requests a report that lists the files with templates for spreadsheet solutions. Isabel asks you to create an ASCII text file that contains a list of Excel spreadsheets on the templates disk, verify the contents of the file using the TYPE command as well as the MORE, SORT, and FIND filters, and then append a list of Lotus 1-2-3 spreadsheets on the templates disk. She also asks you to provide the file on a separate disk, and keep a copy of the file for later use.

As you complete each step, write down the commands you use, as well as the answer to each question, so that you can submit them to your instructor.

1. Insert the Data Disk that you used in the tutorial into drive A.

2. Open a Command Prompt window and change the default drive to drive A.

3. Display a directory listing of all the files on your Data Disk that contain the "xls" file extension. What command did you enter to perform this operation?

4. After you have verified that this command selects just files with the "xls" file extension, recall the previous command and redirect the output to a file on disk called "Spreadsheet Solutions.txt." What command did you enter to perform this operation?

5. Use the TYPE command to view the contents of this file, and page the output one screen or window at a time with the MORE filter. What command did you enter to perform this operation? What is the name of the first file listed? View the remainder of the output and return to the command prompt.

6. Redirect input from the "Spreadsheet Solutions.txt" file on disk to the MORE filter. What command did you enter to perform this operation? View the remainder of the output and return to the command prompt.

7. Redirect input from the "Spreadsheet Solutions.txt" file on disk to the SORT filter, and page the output one screen or window at a time with the MORE filter. What command did you enter to perform this operation? What is the name of the first file in the sorted list? How is the information sorted? View the remainder of the output and return to the command prompt.

8. Use the FIND filter to search the "Spreadsheet Solutions.txt" file for files that include the word "Summary" in the filename. What command did you enter to perform this operation? What are the names of the files located by the FIND filter?

9. Use the ECHO command and the append output redirection operator to add two blank lines to the bottom of the "Spreadsheet Solutions.txt" file. What command did you enter to perform this operation?

10. Display a directory listing of all files with the "wk4" file extension in alphabetical order by filename. What command did you enter to perform this operation?

11. Recall the previous command, and append the output to the bottom of the "Spreadsheet Solutions.txt" file. What command did you enter to perform this operation?

12. You decide to give your file a more specific name, so you rename it to "Spreadsheet Solution Files.txt." What command did you enter to perform this operation?

13. Create a copy of the "Spreadsheet Solution Files.txt" file, and name it "Backup of Spreadsheet Solution Files.txt." What command did you enter to perform this operation?

14. Delete the Templates.txt and "Sales Templates.txt" files from your Data Disk, using the Prompt for Verification switch to confirm that you are deleting the right file. What command(s) did you enter to perform this operation?

15. Close the Command Prompt window, and remove the diskette from the drive.

16. Submit a copy of the "Spreadsheet Solutions File.txt" file and your answers to the above questions, either as a printout, on diskette, or by e-mail, as your instructor requests, along with any other requested documentation.

CASE PROBLEMS

Case 1. Preparing a Report Using Redirection at Stratton Graphics Eve Stratton, owner of Stratton Graphics, and her staff specialize in the design of 3-D images and company presentations for the Web sites of her business clients. So she can develop new proposals, presentations, and graphics for projects with short turnaround times, she relies on an important set of files. She asks you to prepare and print a report that summarizes the types of files on the disk by file type and file size.

As you complete each step, write down the commands you use, as well as the answer to each question so that you can submit them to your instructor.

1. Open a Command Prompt window.

2. Insert your Data Disk into drive A, and then make that drive the default drive.

3. Display a directory listing of your Data Disk *in alphabetical order by file extension*, and redirect the output to a file on your Data Disk with the name "Stratton Graphics.txt." What command did you enter for this operation?

4. Verify that the operating system created the "Stratton Graphics.txt" file on diskette by redirecting input from the file and displaying one screen or window at a time. What command did you enter for this operation? What is the name of the first file listed in this file? View the remainder of the input, and return to the command prompt.

5. Append two blank lines to the bottom of the "Stratton Graphics.txt" file. What two commands did you enter for these operations?

6. Display another directory listing of your Data Disk *in order by file size*, from the largest to the smallest file, and append the output to the "Stratton Graphics.txt" file. What command did you enter for this operation?

7. Verify that the operating system appended the output to the "Stratton Graphics.txt" file by redirecting input from this file on disk and displaying the input one screen or window at a time. What command did you enter for this operation? View the remainder of the input, and return to the command prompt.

8. Display a directory listing of all files with the "xls" file extension in alphabetical order, and redirect the output to your printer port. What command did you use to perform this operation?

9. Submit a copy of the "Stratton Graphics.txt" file, your printed output of all files with the "xls" file extension, and your answers to the above questions, either as printout, on diskette, or by e-mail, as your instructor requests, along with any other requested documentation.

Case 2. Using Filters at Bayview Travel Service Bayview Travel Service is a small travel agency that arranges personal, group, and escorted tours for its customers, as well as handling worldwide reservations and tickets. Toby Landucci, the financial analyst at Bayview Travel Service, has developed a set of computer files for use in his job over the last fiscal year. For the upcoming year's budget projection, he wants to first make a copy of the diskette containing his budget files and then to prepare and print a list of files he plans to adapt for the new year. He asks you to document the list of files that he currently uses and then prepare and print a report that lists the files he will use for next year's budget analysis.

As you complete each step, write down the commands you use, as well as the answer to each question, so that you can submit them to your instructor.

1. Insert your Data Disk into drive A.

2. Open a Command Prompt window.

3. Change the default drive to the drive containing your Data Disk.

4. Display a directory listing of your Data Disk in alphabetical order by filename, and redirect the output to a file on your Data Disk with the name "Bayview Travel.txt." What command did you enter for this operation?

5. Verify that the operating system created the "Bayview Travel.txt" file on disk by redirecting input from the file and displaying it one screen or window at a time. What command did you enter for this operation? What is the name of the second file listed? View the remainder of the input, and return to the command prompt.

6. Use the FIND filter to search "Bayview Travel.txt" for "xls" in the filename, and page the output one screen by a time. What command did you enter for this operation? What is the first file in this selection?

7. After you test the FIND filter and verify that it is selecting the files you need, use the FIND filter to select the same listings, but this time redirect the output to a file on disk with the name, "Financial Analyses.txt." What command did you enter for this operation?

8. Redirect input using the "Financial Analyses.txt" file on disk to the SORT filter, and display the output one full window at a time. What command did you enter for this operation? What is the name of the first file displayed in the sorted listing? View the remainder of the input, and return to the command prompt.

9. Display a directory listing of all files with the "xls" file extension in alphabetical order, and redirect the output to your printer port.

10. Submit a copy of the "Bayview Travel.txt" and "Financial Analyses.txt" files, your printed output of all files with the "xls" file extension, and your answers to the above questions, either as printout, on diskette, or by e-mail, as your instructor requests, along with any other requested documentation.

Case 3. Copying Presentations at HiPerform Enterprises After experiencing an unprecedented increase in customers over the last year, James Everett, the owner and manager of HiPerform Enterprises, decides to apply for a business loan to expand his business. He asks you to make a copy of his templates disk, and then assemble copies of the documents that he will need to develop a business plan, which he then can include with his application for a business loan.

As you complete each step, write down the commands you use, as well as the answer to each question, so that you can submit them to your instructor.

1. Insert your Data Disk into drive A.

2. Open a Command Prompt window.

3. Make a copy of your Data Disk. What command did you enter to perform this operation?

4. Change the default drive to the drive containing your Data Disk.

5. On the duplicate of your Data Disk that you just made, free up storage space on your diskette for the new files, by deleting all the files with the file extension "txt," "bmp," "chk," and "tmp." What commands did you enter for these operations?

6. Produce a directory listing of the current drive that displays alphabetically all files whose filenames start with the words "Five Year" and which contain the "xls" file extension. What command did you enter for this operation? What are the names of the files that meet these criteria?

7. Copy the "Five Year Growth Plan.xls" file, and create a new file with the name "Five Year Sales Projection.xls." What command did you enter for this operation?

8. Recall the previous Directory command, and verify that Windows 2000 created a new file by making a copy of an existing file.

9. Using a similar approach, make a new copy of the file "Balance Sheet.xls" with the name "Company Balance Sheet.xls," and a new copy of the file "Loan Payment Analysis.xls" with the name "Loan Analysis.xls". What commands did you enter for these operations?

10. Change the name of the "Loan Analysis.xls" file to "Bank Loan Analysis.xls." What command did you enter for this operation?

11. Display a directory listing of all files on this diskette with the "xls" file extension in alphabetical order by filename, and redirect the output to your printer port. What command did you enter for this operation?

12. Submit your printed output of all files with the "xls" file extension, and your answers to the above questions, either as printout, on diskette, or by e-mail, as your instructor requests, along with any other requested documentation.

Case 4. Managing Files at Turing Enterprises Each year Melissa Turing, owner of Turing Enterprises, creates a copy of the diskette that contains her business files and then updates the files for the upcoming year. She asks you to make a copy of her diskette, remove files she no longer needs, rename files to reflect the current year, and then make copies of files that she can adapt for new ventures this next year.

As you complete each step, write down the commands you use, as well as the answer to each question, so that you can submit them to your instructor.

1. Insert your Data Disk into drive A.

2. Open a Command Prompt window.

3. Make a duplicate copy of your Data Disk.

4. Change the default drive to the drive containing your Data Disk.

5. On the duplicate copy, delete all the files with the "bmp" "chk" "doc" "tmp" "txt" and "wk4" file extensions. What commands did you enter to perform these operations?

6. Change the name of "Balance Sheet.xls" to "Turing Balance Sheet.xls," "Client Invoices.xls" to "Turing Client Invoices.xls," and "Weekly Worklog.xls" to "Turing Weekly Worklog.xls". What commands did you enter for these operations?

7. Change the names of the files "2003 Sales Summary #1.xls" and "2003 Sales Summary #2.xls" to "2003 Trips Summary #1.xls" and "2003 Trips Summary #2.xls" using one command in one step. What command did you enter to perform this operation?

8. Copy "Data Systems Budget.xls" to "Turing Budget Projection.xls," and copy "Software.ppt" to "Mediterranean Excursions.ppt." What commands did you enter for these operations?

9. Display a directory listing of all files on this diskette with the "xls" file extension in alphabetical order by filename, and redirect the output to your printer port. What command did you enter for this operation?

10. Submit your printed output of all files with the "xls" file extension, and your answers to the above questions, either as printout, on diskette, or by e-mail, as your instructor requests, along with any other requested documentation.

QUICK | CHECK ANSWERS

Session 3.1

1. ASCII
2. end-of-file (EOF)
3. redirect
4. output redirection
5. TYPE
6. filter
7. pipe
8. input redirection
9. append output redirection
10. keyboard, screen (or monitor or video display device)

Session 3.2

1. device name
2. printer port
3. LPT1
4. source
5. destination (or target)
6. multiple (or more than one)
7. Prompt for Verification (or/P)
8. PRN
9. internal
10. wildcards

OBJECTIVES

In this tutorial you will learn to:

- Examine the concept and use of the full path

- Create and change directories

- Move files to directories

- List and copy files in directories

- Delete files in directories

- Navigate a directory structure

- View, print, and save a directory tree

USING DIRECTORIES AND SUBDIRECTORIES

Organizing Company Files at SolarWinds

CASE

SolarWinds Unlimited

The staff members at SolarWinds depend on the availability of templates for a wide variety of uses—spreadsheet projections, sales summaries, budget analyses, workflow analyses, employee payroll, graphics, presentations, and training. Many different staff members have worked with Isabel to develop the templates that they need and to develop an approach that enables her staff to organize, track, and locate those templates quickly.

In the event you need to navigate, reorganize, and manage the directory structure of a disk in a command-line environment, Isabel wants you to organize the SolarWinds template files using basic directory management commands of the Windows 2000 command line.

SESSION 4.1

In this session, you will examine the importance of using directories to manage files on a hard disk, learn the concept, importance, and use of the full path. You will create and open directories, as well as move and copy files to directories.

Managing Files

Isabel asks you to assist her with the important task of developing a system for organizing and tracking template files needed by her staff. Over the years, the number and types of templates have increased significantly, and managers are increasingly emphasizing the importance of using templates wherever possible to develop complex documents, meet tight deadlines, and provide consistency in the appearance of all company documents. In order to develop your command-line file management skills, Isabel gives you a diskette containing template files used by the SolarWinds staff so that you can practice organizing files as you would on the hard drive.

File management is one of the major tasks faced by any user of a computer system. This task is more complicated on a hard disk because of the enormous storage capacity of the disk and the number of files stored on it. To assist you in this task, Windows 2000 and other operating systems allow you to group related files together in a directory on a disk. You can then work with each group of files as a separate unit, independent of all other files.

A **directory**, also known as a **folder,** acts as a container for files and other directories. Physically, it is actually a special type of file that contains information about the files and other directories it tracks. The term **directory** actually has two meanings. First, it refers to any directory on a disk drive: the root directory or any of its subdirectories. The **root directory** is the first directory created on a disk by an operating system or formatting utility. The operating system refers to it with a backslash (\ ) symbol. Second, as you have already seen in Tutorial 2, the term "directory" also refers to the output of the Directory (DIR) command. In the first three tutorials, you worked in the root directory of either drive C or drive A. When you used the Directory command, you viewed the contents of each of those directories.

The use of directories on a hard disk allows the operating system, software applications, and you to use that storage space effectively. Figure 4-1 shows an example of part of the directory structure of a drive on a hard disk. At the top of a directory structure is the root directory for drive C. Below the root directory, there are directories for installed software as well as directories for documents. A directory contained within, or "below," another directory is called a **subdirectory** of the other directory. (A subdirectory, or subfolder, is subordinate to another directory, or folder.) Conversely, a directory containing, or "above," another directory is called the **parent directory** of the other directory. A parent directory can have many subdirectories, but a subdirectory can have only one parent directory. Just as you can call a person a parent or a child, you can also call a directory a parent directory or a subdirectory, depending on the context.

The Windows 2000 installation program creates directories, such as "Documents and Settings," "Program Files," "Recycled," and "WINNT," for use by the operating system and software applications. The "Documents and Settings" directory contains data files and settings for each user of the computer. The "Program Files" directory contains subdirectories such as "Accessories," "Internet Explorer," "Outlook Express," and "Microsoft Office," for various types of software. The WINNT directory (which stands for "Windows NT," the original name for Windows 2000) contains most of the important Windows 2000 operating system files.

Each of these directories in turn may contain subdirectories. For example, the Microsoft Office directory shown in Figure 4-1 might contain Office and Templates subdirectories. The Recycled directory is a hidden system directory for storing files deleted from the hard disk. The WINNT directory folder contains the Windows 2000 operating system, organized into a myriad of subdirectories, for example, "Fonts," "Help," "History," "System32," "Temporary Internet Files," and "Web" directories, to name a few.

Figure 4-1	PARTIAL DIRECTORY STRUCTURE OF A DISK

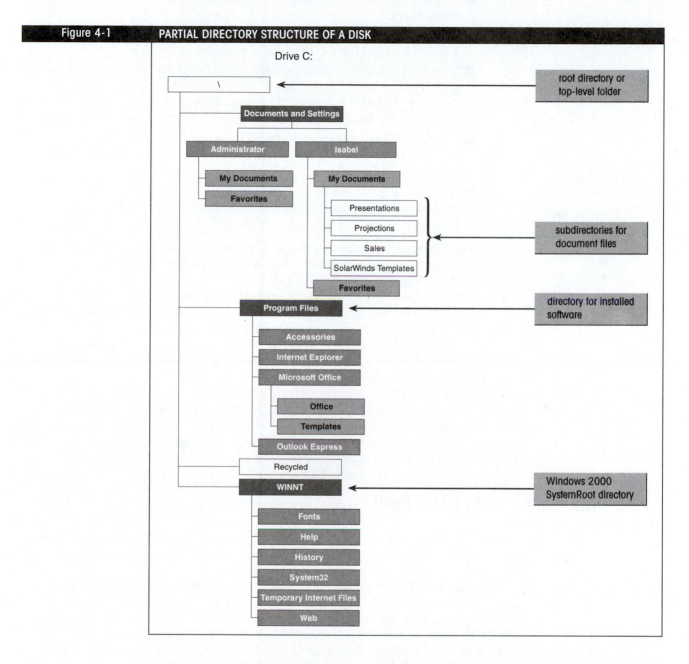

If you store document files on your hard disk drive, as most people do, then you can organize those documents into directories. As shown in Figure 4-1, the "Documents and Settings" directory folder contains a subdirectory for each defined local user of the computer (for example, "Isabel"), which in turn contains subdirectories including "My Documents" and "Favorites." You would store your files in your own "My Documents" directory, and you might create subdirectories such as those named "Presentations," "Projections," and "Sales," where you would store other documents that you create and use in your job.

As you can also tell from this figure, a typical hard disk drive has directories at different levels within the overall directory structure of the disk:

■ The first level is the root directory, represented in the figure by a backslash symbol (\ ).

■ The second level consists of the "Documents and Settings," "Program Files," "Recycled," and "WINNT" directories.

■ The third level consists of the directory folders for the local users of the computer ("Administrator" and "Isabel" in this case), "Accessories," "Internet Explorer," "Microsoft Office," "Outlook Express," "Fonts," "Help," "History," "System32," "Temporary Internet Files," and "Web" directories.

■ The fourth level consists of the "My Documents" and "Favorites" directories for each of the computer's users, and the "Office" and "Templates" subdirectories under "Microsoft Office."

■ The fifth level consists of the "Presentations," "Projections," "Sales," and "SolarWinds Templates" subdirectories under Isabel's "My Documents" directory.

The actual directory structure of a disk is far more complicated than can be illustrated in a figure; however, the important point is that files are organized into directories at different levels within the directory structure of a disk.

If you organize your hard disk into directories, store files in the appropriate directory, and maintain the directories, you can locate files easily and quickly. By approaching file management in an organized way, you can work more productively.

Before you tackle the larger task of organizing the files on a hard disk, Isabel has asked you to start with the files on your templates diskette. She points out that the diskette would correspond to your "My Documents" directory folder on the hard drive. Although you use directories on hard disks, you can also create directories on a diskette and on other types of disks, such as Zip disks and recordable CDs. Once you are familiar with the process of creating directories and moving or copying files to directories, then you are in a better position to evaluate and reorganize how you store document files on a hard disk. Before you can work with directories, you must understand the concept and use of the full path.

The Importance of the Full Path

As you start the process of organizing the template files into directories, Isabel emphasizes the importance of understanding the concept and use of the full path so that you can work effectively and efficiently with directories on a disk.

Whether you work from the desktop in the graphical user interface or from the Command Prompt window, Windows 2000 uses the full path to locate and load programs, as well as to locate and open directories and files. The **full path**, originally called the **MS-DOS path**, is a notation that identifies the exact location of a directory or file on a disk. The full path includes the name of the drive that contains the directory or file, the sequence of directory name(s) that identifies the location of a directory or file, and the name of the directory or file. For example, when you open a Command Prompt window, Windows 2000 displays the full path of the current drive and directory in the command prompt itself (C:\>). The current drive and directory is the root directory (or top-level folder) of drive C. If you change the default drive from drive C to drive A, then the full path of the current drive and directory is the root directory of drive A (A:\>). As shown in Figure 4-2, the first backslash symbol identifies the root directory of the drive in each case.

Figure 4-2	ABSOLUTE AND RELATIVE PATHS

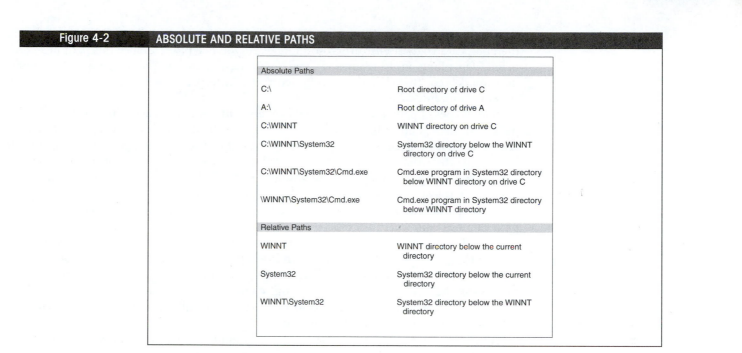

Absolute Paths	
C:\	Root directory of drive C
A:\	Root directory of drive A
C:\WINNT	WINNT directory on drive C
C:\WINNT\System32	System32 directory below the WINNT directory on drive C
C:\WINNT\System32\Cmd.exe	Cmd.exe program in System32 directory below WINNT directory on drive C
\WINNT\System32\Cmd.exe	Cmd.exe program in System32 directory below WINNT directory
Relative Paths	
WINNT	WINNT directory below the current directory
System32	System32 directory below the current directory
WINNT\System32	System32 directory below the WINNT directory

Windows 2000 is installed in a directory called the **SystemRoot** folder. In most installations, the *SystemRoot* folder is named WINNT on drive C. In that case, the full path to the WINNT directory is: C:\WINNT. This path identifies the drive name first (C:—drive names always consist of a letter followed by a colon), then a backslash (\ ) identifying the root directory containing the WINNT directory, and finally the actual name of the WINNT directory. If Windows 2000 was installed as an upgrade from a previous version of Windows, it may be installed in the Windows directory on drive C of your computer instead of in WINNT. Then, the full path for the Windows directory would be: C:\Windows.

Within the WINNT (or Windows) directory, program and supporting files are organized into different subdirectories. One of those subdirectories is the System32 directory, which contains important system files and programs. If your Windows SystemRoot directory is named WINNT, then the full path to the System32 directory is: C:\WINNT\System32.

This path indicates that the System32 directory is below the WINNT directory, which is in turn below the root directory of drive C. In a path that specifies a set of connected subdirectories, the subdirectory names are separated from each other by a backslash (\ ). All of the backslashes—other than the one that follows the drive name—are separators between two connected subdirectories. Only the backslash after the drive name refers to the root directory.

As you learned in Tutorial 1, the name of the program that Windows 2000 opens when you choose Command Prompt on the Accessories menu is Cmd.exe. If your Windows SystemRoot directory is named WINNT, then the full path for that program file is: C:\WINNT\System32\Cmd.exe.

This path indicates that the Cmd.exe program file is stored in the System32 directory, which is below the WINNT directory, which is in turn below the root directory of drive C. In this path, all of the backslash symbols except for the first one, are separators. The second backslash separates two subdirectory names, and the third backslash separates a directory name from a filename. As mentioned in Tutorial 1, files like Cmd.exe with the file extension "exe" are **executable** files, or files that contain program code that Windows 2000 can load (or copy) into memory (or RAM) and run.

If a path contains a long filename with spaces for a directory or a file, then you might need to enclose the entire path in quotation marks so Windows 2000 knows it is one specification; otherwise, it might interpret the spaces as separating different parts of a command line. For example, if you have Office 2000 installed on your computer, it is more than likely installed in the Program Files folder. The path to the folder containing Office 2000 would then be: C:\Program Files\Microsoft Office. If you need to reference this path in a command (depending on the command), you might need to enclose the full path within quotation marks so that Windows 2000 correctly interprets the command, as follows: "C:\Program Files\Microsoft Office"

These types of paths are also referred to as **absolute paths**, because they spell out the full path, and there is no ambiguity as to the location of the directory or file. An absolute path always includes a backslash (\ ) before the name of the first directory, meaning that it begins at the root directory. For example, C:\Documents and Settings\Isabel\My Documents\Projections specifies an absolute path. When you work in a command-line environment, you can also use a relative path. A **relative path** makes assumptions about the location of a directory or file, always starting from the current drive and directory. A relative path cannot begin with a backslash. For example, if you use just the path Projections in a command, then the command will assume that the Projections directory is below the current working directory of the current drive (whatever drive that might be). If your current working directory is Isabel's "My Documents" directory on drive C (C:\Documents and Settings\Isabel\My Documents), then the command will assume that the **Projections** directory is located below that directory, and that the full path is: "C:\Documents and Settings\Isabel\My Documents\Projections".

When you enter commands at the command prompt that operate on directories or files (or both), you can use either an absolute or a relative path to specify the directories and files. The advantage of the relative path is that it saves time and keystrokes. As you work with directories in this tutorial, you will try different methods for using absolute and relative paths.

Except where noted, all of the commands you will use in this tutorial are available in all versions of Windows and MS-DOS.

Getting Started

You will need to make a new copy of Data Disk #1 so that you can organize the files into directories. You cannot use the same diskette that you used in the last tutorial, because you deleted files on that disk. Also, you renamed files and created new files using the COPY command. So you can perform all the operations in this tutorial, and so your screen views match those shown in the figures, you will make a new copy of Data Disk #1 in the following steps. When you create your new copy of Data Disk #1, you can reuse your last duplicate of the diskette. (Remember to keep your original version of the Data Disk #1 intact so you can make a copy whenever necessary.)

To make the task of reorganizing the files into directories easier, Isabel recommends that you also print a directory listing in alphabetical order by filename.

To prepare your diskette:

1. Open a Command Prompt window, set colors if necessary, and clear the window.

2. Follow the instructions provided by your instructor for making a copy of Data Disk #1.

3. Change the default drive to A.

4. Print an alphabetical directory listing of drive A using the DIR command with the Order switch and redirecting its output to the printer. If necessary, eject the page manually.

5. Remove your hard copy from the printer.

By using an alphabetical listing of filenames, you can more easily spot similarities in file-names so that you can use wildcards in your file specification and move groups of files at once, rather than having to move them one at a time.

Deleting Files from a Diskette

Before you reorganize the template files, you decide to delete files that you no longer need. Deleting extraneous files will also ensure that you have enough storage space on the diskette for the operations you need to perform.

To delete files you no longer need:

1. Clear the window, type **del *.tmp /p** and then press **Enter**. The Delete command asks you to verify that you want to delete ~WRC0070.tmp. See Figure 4-3.

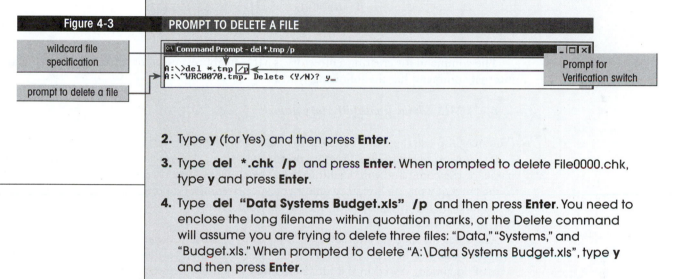

Figure 4-3	PROMPT TO DELETE A FILE

wildcard file specification

prompt to delete a file

Prompt for Verification switch

```
A:\>del *.tmp /p
A:\~WRC0070.tmp, Delete (Y/N)? y_
```

2. Type **y** (for Yes) and then press **Enter**.

3. Type **del *.chk /p** and press **Enter**. When prompted to delete File0000.chk, type **y** and press **Enter**.

4. Type **del "Data Systems Budget.xls" /p** and then press **Enter**. You need to enclose the long filename within quotation marks, or the Delete command will assume you are trying to delete three files: "Data," "Systems," and "Budget.xls." When prompted to delete "A:\Data Systems Budget.xls", type **y** and then press **Enter**.

As step 4 above points out, the DEL command can delete multiple files whose names are separated by spaces in the command line. Therefore, make sure you place quotation marks around filenames containing spaces. You should develop the habit of using the **Prompt for Verification switch (/P)** whenever you delete files. This switch provides a margin of safety and safeguards against accidentally deleting the wrong file or files.

Creating **Directories**

After discussing with Isabel how best to organize files on your templates disk, you decide to organize your files in groups based on their type of use. For example, you want to store all PowerPoint presentations in a directory called "Presentations". Next, using your printed copy of the directory listing, you prepare a sketch of the directory structure for the types of files contained on the templates diskette, as shown in Figure 4-4. After you reorganize this disk, all the files will be located in five different directories so that you can easily find a file when you need it.

Figure 4-4   **SKETCH OF PROPOSED DIRECTORY STRUCTURE**

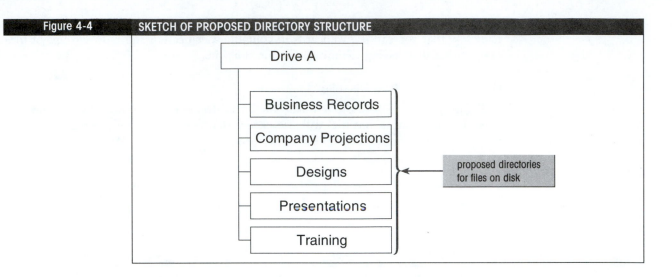

The command for creating a directory is MD (an abbreviation for Make Directory). This internal command has the following syntax:

MD [*drive*:][*path*]*directory name*

(You may also use the name MKDIR for this command, as in UNIX.)

If you want to create the directory on another drive, you must specify the alternate drive name, or the command will default to the current drive. The directory will likewise default to the current working directory unless you specify another directory path. To change locations, identify the directory path, such as the root directory, where you want the new directory to be located.

The rules for naming a directory are the same as those for naming a file, although most directories do not have an extension as part of their name. Just as a filename identifies the type of document stored in the file, a directory's name describes the types of files that you will store in the directory.

Before you create a subdirectory, you should check the current directory shown in the command prompt so that you create a new directory in the right place.

You decide to start by creating the Presentations directory first.

To create a directory:

1. Clear the window, type **md Presentations** and then press **Enter**. The Make Directory command creates a directory below the root directory of the disk drive containing your diskette and displays the command prompt. If you perform this operation from another drive, such as drive C, you would include the drive name and path before the directory name (for example, md A:\ Presentations). Also, if the disk contains a file with the same name as the one you want to use as the directory name, the Make Directory command will display a message and note that a directory or file by that name already exists.

2. Type **dir /ad** and then press **Enter**. The Directory command displays information about the new directory but does not list any files on the disk, because you used the Attribute switch with the parameter for displaying only directories. See Figure 4-5. The <DIR> marker verifies that Presentations is a directory.

| Figure 4-5 | MAKING A DIRECTORY |

Make Directory command
name of directory
switch for displaying only directories
directory marker
new directory

```
Command Prompt                                                  _ □ ×

A:\>md Presentations

A:\>dir /ad
 Volume in drive A has no label.
 Volume Serial Number is F065-B557

 Directory of A:\

12/18/2003  07:02p    <DIR>          Presentations
              0 File(s)              0 bytes
              1 Dir(s)      264,192 bytes free

A:\>
```

The Directory command's Attribute switch with the directory parameter (/AD) is useful when you need to screen out all the files in a directory and focus on the subdirectories.

REFERENCE WINDOW   RW

Creating a Directory:

■ Open a Command Prompt window, and then change to the drive where you want to create the directory.

■ If you want to create a subdirectory below the root directory of the drive, type MD, press the Spacebar, type the name of the new directory, and then press Enter.

■ Type DIR /AD and then press Enter to view a list of directories on the disk so you can verify that you created the directory.

Although the MKDIR name for this command works exactly like MD, most people use MD because it saves keystrokes. Because UNIX uses "mkdir," but not "md," those familiar with that operating system might be more comfortable with the longer name.

Changing the Current Working Directory

Isabel notes that another advantage of working within a directory is that you can work with files in that directory without having to type the directory name with each command. That simplifies many types of file operations.

Once you create a directory, you can use the CD (Change Directory) command to switch to that directory, and make it the new current working directory (also known as the current directory). This internal command has the following syntax:

CD [*drive:*][*path*]directory name

(You may also use the name CHDIR for this command. UNIX uses "cd".)

As long as a Command Prompt window remains open, the command interpreter maintains a current working directory for each drive. When you switch drives, you go to whatever directory you most recently set on that drive. If you do not specify a drive name, you remain on the same drive, but you change the current working directory to the one you specify in the Change Directory command. If you haven't used the CD command to change the current directory of a particular drive, you'll switch to the drive's root directory. When you close the Command Prompt window, you lose all the current directory settings.

When you specify the path, you are telling the Directory command the name of the directory to which you want to change, and its location relative to a higher directory, such as the root directory.

After you change to a new directory, you can work more easily with the files stored in it. You will now change to the Presentations directory that you just created and examine its contents.

To change to the Presentations directory:

1. Clear the window, type **cd Presentations** and then press **Enter**. After the Change Directory command changes to the Presentations directory, the command interpreter (Cmd.exe) updates the command prompt to show the full path of what is now the current directory, A:\Presentations. See Figure 4-6. A:\Presentations indicates that Presentations is a subdirectory below the root directory of the diskette in drive A. That subdirectory is now the current directory.

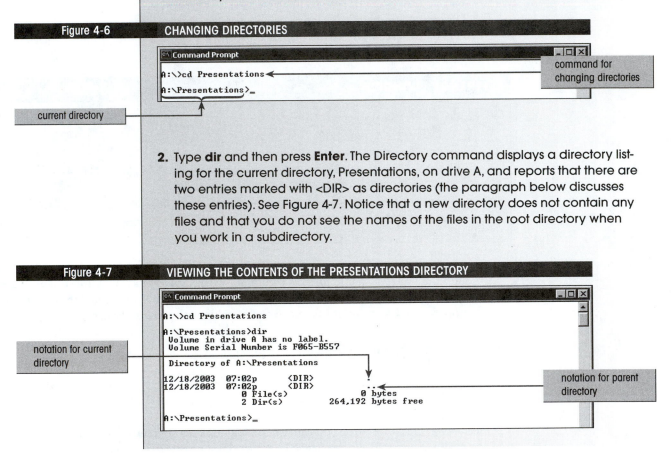

| Figure 4-6 | CHANGING DIRECTORIES |

Command Prompt

A:\>cd Presentations ◄──────────── command for changing directories

A:\Presentations>_

current directory

2. Type **dir** and then press **Enter**. The Directory command displays a directory listing for the current directory, Presentations, on drive A, and reports that there are two entries marked with <DIR> as directories (the paragraph below discusses these entries). See Figure 4-7. Notice that a new directory does not contain any files and that you do not see the names of the files in the root directory when you work in a subdirectory.

| Figure 4-7 | VIEWING THE CONTENTS OF THE PRESENTATIONS DIRECTORY |

Command Prompt

A:\>cd Presentations

A:\Presentations>dir
 Volume in drive A has no label.
 Volume Serial Number is F065-B557

 Directory of A:\Presentations

12/18/2003 07:02p   <DIR>   .
12/18/2003 07:02p   <DIR>   ..
              0 File(s)   0 bytes
              2 Dir(s)   264,192 bytes free

A:\Presentations>_

notation for current directory

notation for parent directory

Whenever the operating system creates a directory, it always creates two entries within the directory. The first entry, named "." (pronounced "dot"), acts as a kind of alias (or alternate name) for the current directory. The second entry, named ". ." (pronounced "dot dot"), refers to the parent directory, which contains the current directory and is located one level higher. On your diskette, for example, the parent directory of Presentations is the root directory. With the exception of the root directory of a drive, every directory has a parent directory. Windows 2000 uses the "." and ". ." entries to keep track of the current directory and the parent directory as you move or navigate from one directory to another. When entering commands at the command prompt, you may use these aliases anywhere in place of the name of the current directory or the parent of the current directory. For example, if you were in "C:\Documents and Settings\Isabel\My Documents\Presentations," and you wanted to switch to the parent directory (My Documents), you could just type cd . . instead of cd \Documents and Settings\Isabel\My Documents.

Now that you have created one of the directories planned for this diskette, you want to move the appropriate files to this directory. To simplify this operation, you decide to return to the root directory where these files are currently stored. Again, you use the CD or CHDIR commands. For the root directory's name, you use the notation that identifies the root directory—the backslash (\ ).

To return to the root directory:

1. Clear the screen, type **cd ** and then press **Enter**. The Directory command updates the command prompt and shows the root directory of drive A as the current directory. See Figure 4-8. If you prefer to reduce keystrokes, you do not have to leave a space between "cd" and the backslash.

   TROUBLE? If the Directory command informs you that the syntax of your command is incorrect, then you may have typed a slash (/) instead of a backslash (\ ). Enter the command again.

Figure 4-8	CHANGING TO THE ROOT DIRECTORY

Change Directory command switches to root directory →

```
Command Prompt                                    _ □ ×

A:\Presentations>cd \  ←──────────────────────────────────    symbol for root directory
A:\>_
```

2. Type **dir /o /p** and then press **Enter**. The Directory command lists directories (in this case, there is only one) in alphabetical order, then lists files in alphabetical order. See Figure 4-9.

Figure 4-9	DISPLAYING THE CURRENT DIRECTORY

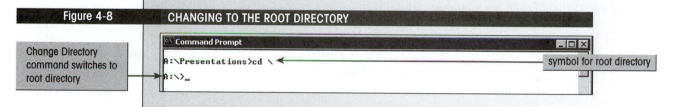

command →

```
Command Prompt - dir /o /p                        _ □ ×
Volume in drive A has no label.
Volume Serial Number is F065-B557

Directory of A:\

12/18/2003  07:02p    <DIR>         Presentations
01/23/2003  08:16a          41,472 2002 Sales Summary #1.xls
01/23/2003  09:21a          78,848 2002 Sales Summary #2.xls
02/27/2002  08:53p          34,304 3 Year Sales Projection.xls
07/09/2003  09:42a          49,152 Addressing Cells.xls
04/18/2003  01:33p          16,896 Advertising Income.xls
05/30/2003  11:22a          22,016 Andre's Employee Payroll.xls
06/26/2003  09:30a          52,736 Application Software.ppt
01/24/2003  08:45a          18,944 Balance Sheet.xls
01/08/2003  02:06p          24,064 Break Even Analysis.xls
03/21/2003  08:08a          15,872 Client Invoices.xls
10/16/2003  09:52a          84,446 Color Palette.bmp
10/16/2003  10:31a          84,534 Colors of the Rainbow.bmp
09/05/2003  02:25p          13,824 Commission on Sales.xls
07/01/2003  08:31p          15,360 Daily Sales.xls
04/09/2003  02:12p          21,504 Employees.xls
01/16/2003  10:46a          20,992 Five Year Growth Plan.xls
01/15/2003  02:21p          17,408 Five Year Plan Template.xls
09/23/2003  01:12p          31,232 Fonts.xls
Press any key to continue . . . _
```

directory listed before files

files listed in alphabetical order by filename

3. Press the **Spacebar** to view each of the next screens and to return to the command prompt. Recall that these files were not displayed when you viewed a directory listing of the Presentations directory. Now the Directory command does not display the contents of the Presentations directory, only the contents of the root directory.

REFERENCE WINDOW   **RW**

<u>Changing the Current Working Directory</u>

■ At the command prompt, type CD, press the Spacebar, type the path and name of the directory, and then press Enter.

■ To return to the root directory, type CD, press the Spacebar, type \ (a backslash), and then press Enter.

This command, CD \, is one of the most useful commands in a command-line environment, because it will switch you to the root directory of the current drive—no matter which directory you start from.

Moving Files to Another Directory

After examining the directory, you realize that all the files that you want to move to the Presentations directory have one feature in common, the same file extension, "ppt" (an abbreviation for PowerPoint Presentation).

You can use the MOVE command (an external command) to move these files in one step. If you want to move one or more files from one directory to another, you use the following syntax:

**MOVE [*drive:*][*path*]*filespec destination*

The drive name, path, and filespec (short for file specification) identify the source file or files you want to move to another location. You must specify the drive name for the source file or files if they are located on another drive. You must also specify the path if it is different from that of the current directory. The filespec might be a specific filename or a wildcard pattern. The destination includes the name of the directory where you want to move the files. The destination might also include a drive name and path. If you are moving only one file, you can also specify a new filename for that file. If you are moving a group of files, the destination must be the directory name that will contain the group; you cannot specify new filenames.

For example, to move a file by the name of Cashflow.xls from the root directory of drive A to the Business directory on drive A, you would enter this command:

MOVE Cashflow.xls Business

To move all the files with the "xls" file extension from the root directory of drive A to the Business directory on drive A, you would enter this command:

MOVE *.xls Business

To move a file named Cashflow.xls from the current directory on drive C to the current directory on drive A (that is, whatever directory you most recently made current on drive A with the CD command), you would enter this command:

MOVE Cashflow.xls A:

As you will discover, the MOVE command is quite versatile.

To move all the files with the "ppt" extension to the Presentations directory:

1. Clear the window.

2. Type **move *.ppt Presentations** and then press **Enter**. The MOVE command displays the names of the files that it moves when you use a wildcard in the file specification for the source files. See Figure 4-10. Notice also that all of the files have the same file extension.

Figure 4-10	MOVING FILES TO A DIRECTORY

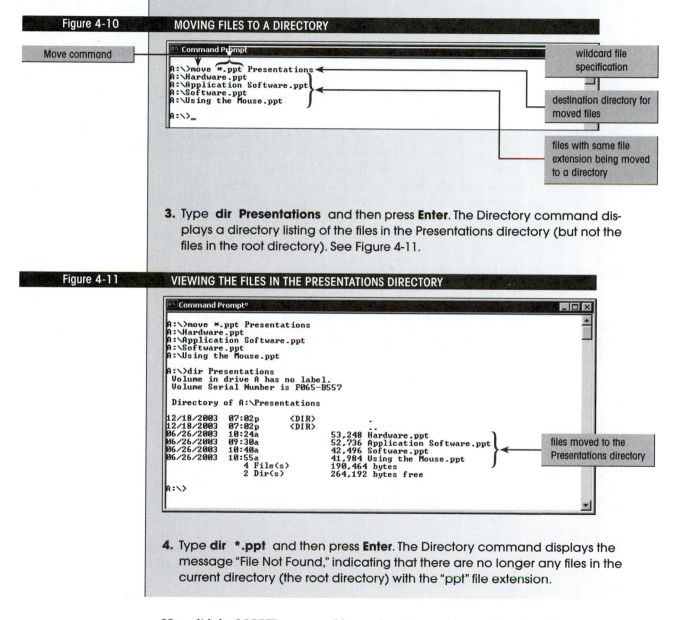

Move command

wildcard file specification

destination directory for moved files

files with same file extension being moved to a directory

3. Type **dir Presentations** and then press **Enter**. The Directory command displays a directory listing of the files in the Presentations directory (but not the files in the root directory). See Figure 4-11.

Figure 4-11	VIEWING THE FILES IN THE PRESENTATIONS DIRECTORY

files moved to the Presentations directory

4. Type **dir *.ppt** and then press **Enter**. The Directory command displays the message "File Not Found," indicating that there are no longer any files in the current directory (the root directory) with the "ppt" file extension.

How did the MOVE command know that Presentations referred to the name of a directory? The MOVE command examines the contents of the root directory and locates the directory named Presentations. It then moves the files you specified to that directory.

REFERENCE WINDOW   **RW**

Moving a Group of Files to Another Directory

- Open a Command Prompt window.
- Change the default drive to the drive that contains the file or files you want to move.
- If necessary, use the Make Directory (MD) command to create a new directory for the files you want to move.
- Type MOVE, press the Spacebar, type a file specification that uses wildcards to select a group of files (such as all files with the same file extension), press the Spacebar, type the name of the directory where you want to move the files, and then press Enter. You might need to specify the drive name and path for the source or destination.
- To verify the move, type DIR, press the Spacebar, type the name of the directory where you moved the files, and then press Enter.

In this instance, you could have also used \Presentations for the destination, to indicate that it is a subdirectory of the root directory. If you do not specify the backslash (\ ) for the root directory and if the current directory is the root directory (as is the case here), the MOVE command (like other commands) assumes the Presentations subdirectory is located in the current directory (which is the root directory). Likewise, you could have also specified the destination as A:\Presentations. By using a relative path ("Presentations"), the MOVE command assumed that the Presentations subdirectory is located in the current directory on the current drive.

Copying Files to Another Directory

Isabel asks you to use the command line to create a Designs directory folder and place the bitmap graphics files (containing "bmp" file extensions) in it. She informs you that staff members also need one of the files, "Colors of the Rainbow.bmp", in the Presentations directory. She recommends you use the COPY command to put a duplicate of this file into the Presentations directory, and then move the original file, along with the rest of the bitmap files, into the new Designs directory.

To copy a file into one directory, and then move it to another directory as part of a group:

1. Check the command prompt to make sure you are at the root directory of drive A; if not, change the default drive and, if necessary, type **cd ** and then press **Enter** to change to the root directory.

2. Clear the window.

3. Type **dir *.bmp** and then press **Enter** to list the bitmap files. Notice that you can uniquely specify "Colors of the Rainbow.bmp" with just the first six characters, "Colors." See Figure 4-12.

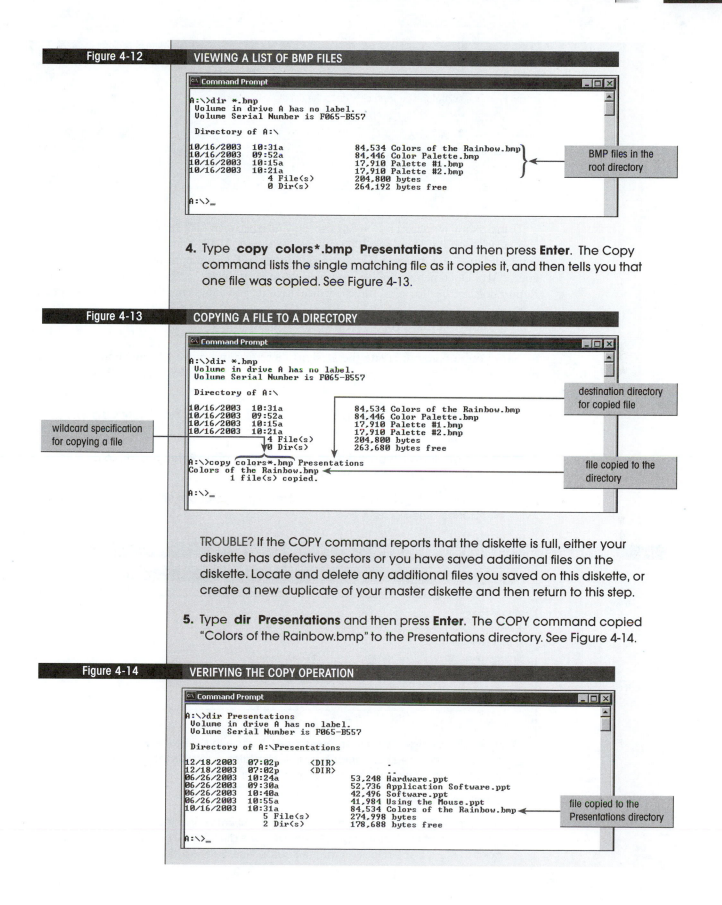

| Figure 4-12 | VIEWING A LIST OF BMP FILES |

```
A:\>dir *.bmp
 Volume in drive A has no label.
 Volume Serial Number is F065-B557

 Directory of A:\

10/16/2003  10:31a            84,534 Colors of the Rainbow.bmp
10/16/2003  09:52a            84,446 Color Palette.bmp
10/16/2003  10:15a            17,910 Palette #1.bmp
10/16/2003  10:21a            17,910 Palette #2.bmp
               4 File(s)         204,800 bytes
               0 Dir(s)          264,192 bytes free

A:\>_
```

BMP files in the root directory

4. Type **copy colors*.bmp Presentations** and then press **Enter**. The Copy command lists the single matching file as it copies it, and then tells you that one file was copied. See Figure 4-13.

| Figure 4-13 | COPYING A FILE TO A DIRECTORY |

```
A:\>dir *.bmp
 Volume in drive A has no label.
 Volume Serial Number is F065-B557

 Directory of A:\

10/16/2003  10:31a            84,534 Colors of the Rainbow.bmp
10/16/2003  09:52a            84,446 Color Palette.bmp
10/16/2003  10:15a            17,910 Palette #1.bmp
10/16/2003  10:21a            17,910 Palette #2.bmp
               4 File(s)         204,800 bytes
               0 Dir(s)          263,680 bytes free

A:\>copy colors*.bmp Presentations
Colors of the Rainbow.bmp
        1 file(s) copied.

A:\>_
```

destination directory for copied file

wildcard specification for copying a file

file copied to the directory

TROUBLE? If the COPY command reports that the diskette is full, either your diskette has defective sectors or you have saved additional files on the diskette. Locate and delete any additional files you saved on this diskette, or create a new duplicate of your master diskette and then return to this step.

5. Type **dir Presentations** and then press **Enter**. The COPY command copied "Colors of the Rainbow.bmp" to the Presentations directory. See Figure 4-14.

| Figure 4-14 | VERIFYING THE COPY OPERATION |

```
A:\>dir Presentations
 Volume in drive A has no label.
 Volume Serial Number is F065-B557

 Directory of A:\Presentations

12/18/2003  07:02p    <DIR>          .
12/18/2003  07:02p    <DIR>          ..
06/26/2003  10:24a            53,248 Hardware.ppt
06/26/2003  09:30a            52,736 Application Software.ppt
06/26/2003  10:40a            42,496 Software.ppt
06/26/2003  10:55a            41,984 Using the Mouse.ppt
10/16/2003  10:31a            84,534 Colors of the Rainbow.bmp
               5 File(s)         274,998 bytes
               2 Dir(s)          178,688 bytes free

A:\>_
```

file copied to the Presentations directory

REFERENCE WINDOW   **RW**

Copying Files to Another Directory

■ From the command prompt, change to the directory that contains the file or files you want
  to copy.
■ Type COPY, press the Spacebar, type the name of the file you want to copy or enter a file specification with wildcards to copy a group of files, press the Spacebar, type the path and name of the
  directory to which you want to copy the file(s), and then press Enter.

Using a similar approach, you can also copy files between disk drives. This option becomes particularly useful if Windows 2000 will not start up normally and you can only work from a command line. For example, if your current drive was C:, your current working directory was your "My Documents" folder, and you wanted to copy a file named "Final Project Report.doc" to the "Reports" directory on a diskette, you could enter the following command:

copy "Final Project Report.doc" a:\Reports

Now you're ready to create the Designs directory and move all the "bmp" files to this directory.

To create the Designs directory and move "bmp" files to this directory:

1. Clear the window, type **md Designs**, and then press **Enter**. The Make Directory
   command creates this directory.

2. Type (or recall) **dir /ad** and then press **Enter**. Your diskette now contains two
   directories. See Figure 4-15.

Figure 4-15	ADDING A NEW DIRECTORY

```
A:\>md Designs ◄─────────────────────────────                   creates a new directory
                                                                 named Designs
A:\>dir /ad
 Volume in drive A has no label.
 Volume Serial Number is F065-B557

 Directory of A:\

12/18/2003  07:02p    <DIR>          Presentations
12/18/2003  07:19p    <DIR>          Designs ◄──────            new directory
               0 File(s)             0 bytes
               2 Dir(s)        178,688 bytes free

A:\>_
```

3. Type **dir Designs** and then press **Enter**. Notice that, like the Presentations
   directory you created earlier, this directory also contains the two standard
   entries marked as directories ("." and ".."), but no files.

4. Clear the window.

5. Type **move *.bmp Designs** and then press **Enter**. The MOVE command lists
   the names of the files it copies to the Designs directory when you use a wildcard in the file specification for the source files. See Figure 4-16.

Figure 4-16 | **MOVING FILES TO A DIRECTORY**

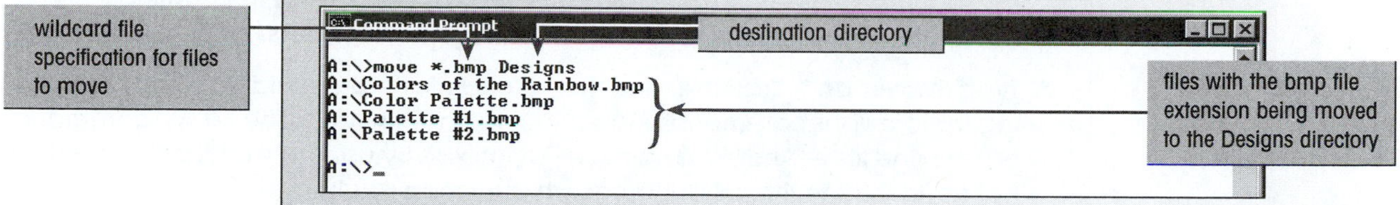

wildcard file specification for files to move

destination directory

```
Command Prompt
A:\>move *.bmp Designs
A:\Colors of the Rainbow.bmp
A:\Color Palette.bmp
A:\Palette #1.bmp
A:\Palette #2.bmp

A:\>_
```

files with the bmp file extension being moved to the Designs directory

6. Type (or recall) **dir Designs** and then press **Enter**. The Designs directory contains the four files that the MOVE command moved to this directory. See Figure 4-17.

Figure 4-17 | **VIEWING THE FILES IN THE DESIGNS DIRECTORY**

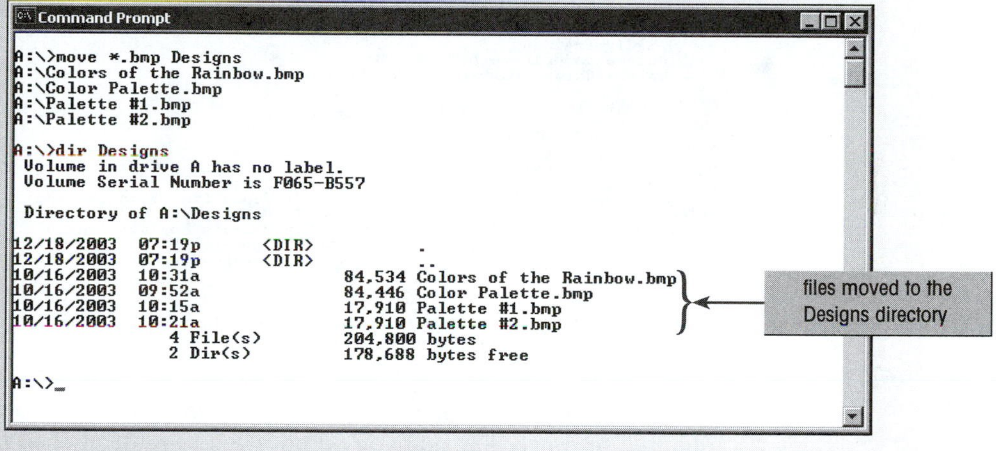

```
Command Prompt
A:\>move *.bmp Designs
A:\Colors of the Rainbow.bmp
A:\Color Palette.bmp
A:\Palette #1.bmp
A:\Palette #2.bmp

A:\>dir Designs
 Volume in drive A has no label.
 Volume Serial Number is F065-B557

 Directory of A:\Designs

12/18/2003  07:19p    <DIR>          .
12/18/2003  07:19p    <DIR>          ..
10/16/2003  10:31a            84,534 Colors of the Rainbow.bmp
10/16/2003  09:52a            84,446 Color Palette.bmp
10/16/2003  10:15a            17,910 Palette #1.bmp
10/16/2003  10:21a            17,910 Palette #2.bmp
               4 File(s)        204,800 bytes
               2 Dir(s)         178,688 bytes free

A:\>_
```

files moved to the Designs directory

You can use the COPY and MOVE commands to make sure that you have copies of the files you need in the correct directories.

Organizing Training Templates

On your templates disk, you have a set of templates that are used for employee training sessions on the use of Microsoft Excel. You decide to place those files in a Training directory.

To organize templates used for training:

1. Check the command prompt to make sure you are at the root directory of drive A; if not, change the default drive to drive A and, if necessary, type **cd ** and then press **Enter** to change to the root directory.

2. Clear the window, type **md Training** and then press **Enter** to create a Training directory.

3. Type **move "Addressing Cells.xls" Training** and then press **Enter**. (Make sure you place the long filename of the file you are copying within quotation marks; otherwise, the MOVE command will report that you used the incorrect syntax.) The MOVE command moves the file, but unlike moving a group of files, it does not display the name of the file. Also, you could have performed the copy more easily by using the asterisk wildcard. If you had examined your hardcopy of the files on this disk, you would have discovered that there is only one file that starts with the characters "Add"—so you could have used Add* instead of "Addressing Cells.xls" for the file specification of the source file.

4. Type **move fo* Training** and then press **Enter**. This time, the MOVE command moved three files—Fonts.xls, "Format Code Colors.xls", and "Formatting Features.xls". All of these filenames start with the characters "fo".

5. Type **move an* Training** and then press **Enter** (you could do this by recalling the previous command and replacing "fo" with "an"). The MOVE command moves one file—"Andre's Employee Payroll.xls". By using a wildcard, you did not need to type the full filename with quotation marks.

6. Clear the window, type **dir Training** and then press **Enter**. The Directory command lists the five files you moved to this directory. See Figure 4-18.

Figure 4-18   VIEWING THE FILES IN THE TRAINING DIRECTORY

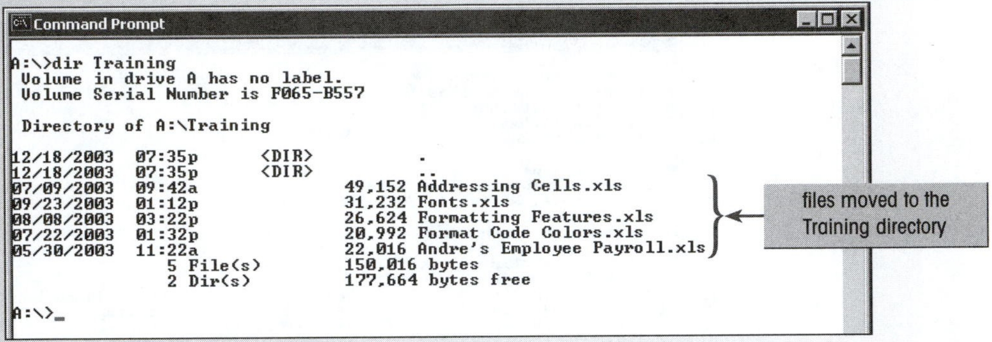

By using wildcards to take advantage of similarities in filenames, you can reduce the time required to move files, and you do not need to remember to put quotation marks around long filenames.

Moving Files from the Parent Directory

Next, you decide to create a Business Records directory and then move templates used for creating files that track business transactions into this directory.

To organize templates into the Business Records directory:

1. Check the command prompt to make sure you are at the root directory of drive A; if not, change the default drive to drive A and, if necessary, type **cd ** and then press **Enter** to change to the root directory.

2. Clear the window, type **md "Business Records"** and then press **Enter**. The Make Directory command creates this directory. You need to enclose the long directory name within quotation marks; otherwise, the Make Directory command will create two directories—one called Business, and the other called Records.

3. Use the DIR command to display a directory listing of your diskette. Your diskette now includes a directory named "Business Records."

   TROUBLE? If your directory listing shows two directories, one named Business and the other named Records, and if you do not have a directory named "Business Records," then you did not enclose "Business Records" within quotation marks when you entered the MD command in the previous step. Repeat the previous step, place quotation marks around the directory name, and then display a directory listing to verify that you completed it correctly.

TROUBLE? If you want to remove the directories named Business and Records, type RD Business, then press Enter, and then type RD Records and then press Enter. This use of the Remove Directory (RD) command removes empty directories.

4. Type **move L*** **"Business Records"** and then press **Enter**. The MOVE command moves "Loan Payment Analysis.xls" to the Business Records directory. Because this file is the only one whose filename starts with the letter "L," you can use a wildcard to move the file with a minimal amount of effort.

TROUBLE? If the MOVE command informs you that the syntax of your command is incorrect, repeat this step, and make sure you enclose the directory name within quotation marks.

5. Type **move i*** **"Business Records"** and then press **Enter** (you may accomplish this by recalling the previous command and changing the "L" to an "i"). The MOVE command moves "Invoice Form.wk4"—the only file that starts with an "i"—to the Business Records folder. Editing the previous command saves time and effort, and results in fewer errors, especially when entering and working with long filenames with spaces.

6. Type **move w*** **"Business Records"** and then press **Enter** (again, you can recall and edit the previous command). The MOVE command moves "Weekly Worklog.xls," the only file that starts with a "w," to the Business Records folder.

7. Type **move d*** **"Business Records"** and then press **Enter**. The MOVE command moves "Daily Sales.xls," the only file that starts with a "d," to the Business Records folder.

8. Type **cd Business Records** and then press **Enter**. The Change Directory command changes to the Business Records directory. See Figure 4-19. Note that you did not need to type the quotation marks around "Business Records" for this command. The CD command doesn't require quotation marks, because it expects just a single target directory name. It therefore assumes that multiple words separated by spaces are all part of the target name.

Figure 4-19	MOVING FILES TO THE BUSINESS RECORDS DIRECTORY

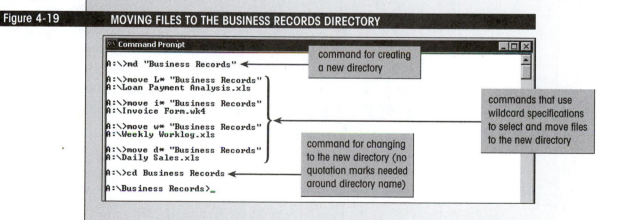

9. Clear the window, type **dir** and then press **Enter**. The Directory command shows the four files that you moved to this folder. See Figure 4-20.

Figure 4-20   VIEWING THE FILES IN THE BUSINESS RECORDS DIRECTORY

```
Command Prompt                                                    _ □ ×

A:\Business Records>dir
 Volume in drive A has no label.
 Volume Serial Number is F065-B557

 Directory of A:\Business Records

12/18/2003  07:37p    <DIR>          .
12/18/2003  07:37p    <DIR>          ..
09/23/2003  01:12p            14,848 Loan Payment Analysis.xls
10/29/2003  10:30a            74,024 Invoice Form.wk4
11/17/2003  04:41p            15,872 Weekly Worklog.xls
07/01/2003  08:31p            15,360 Daily Sales.xls
               4 File(s)        120,104 bytes
               2 Dir(s)         177,152 bytes free

A:\Business Records>_
```

files moved to the "Business Records" directory

After checking the contents of this directory, you realize that you need to include three other files in it. Since you are already in the directory, you decide to work from there instead of returning to the root directory.

To copy files from the parent directory:

1. Clear the screen, type **move "Savings Plan.xls"** and then press **Enter**. The MOVE command informs you that it cannot find the file you specified. See Figure 4-21. Like other commands, the MOVE command assumes that "Savings Plan.xls" is stored in the current directory (which is now the Business Records directory) because you did not specify the path where the file is stored.

Figure 4-21   THE IMPORTANCE OF SPECIFYING THE PATH

current directory

```
Command Prompt                                                    _ □ ×

A:\Business Records>move "Savings Plan.xls"
The system cannot find the file specified.

A:\Business Records>
```

MOVE command cannot find the file because it assumes the file is in the current directory

2. Type **move "\Savings Plan.xls"** and then press **Enter**, making sure you include the backslash (\ )—the name of the root directory—before the "S" in Savings this time. (You can recall and edit the previous command to do this.)

3. Type (or recall) **dir** and then press **Enter**. The MOVE command moved "Savings Plan.xls" from the root directory to the current directory. See Figure 4-22.

Figure 4-22	SPECIFYING THE PATH FOR A FILE

revised MOVE command now includes the path of the file

MOVE command moved the file using the path

4. Type **move \"Product List.xls"** and then press **Enter**. The MOVE command moves Product List.xls to this directory. Note that you can place the quotation marks around either the entire file specification, or around just the long filename.

5. Type **move *.wk4** and then press **Enter**. The MOVE command moves Sales.wk4, the only file with the "wk4" file extension, to this directory.

6. Type **move *t.xls** and then press **Enter**. The MOVE command moves Balance Sheet.xls, the only file with a "t" before an "xls" file extension, to this directory.

7. Type **move \c*** and then press **Enter**. The MOVE command copies two files from the root directory to the current directory. Again, for the file specification, all you need to type is the minimum amount of information needed to locate the files with the asterisk wildcard, plus the path that indicates where the files are stored. See Figure 4-23 for a summary of these operations.

Figure 4-23	MOVING FILES TO THE CURRENT DIRECTORY

quotation marks placed only around the filename rather than the full path

because you did not specify a destination, the MOVE command moves the file to the current directory

file specification for the source files includes the path

8. Type **dir** and then press **Enter**. You have now moved the five additional files you want to store in this directory.

Instead of working from a printed copy of a directory listing, you can use the Directory command to remind you of the names of the files in the current directory so you can use the right wildcard specification to move or copy a specific file or group of files.

If you want to copy a file from the parent directory to the current subdirectory, but leave the original file in the parent directory, you can use the same techniques with the COPY command that you used above with the MOVE command.

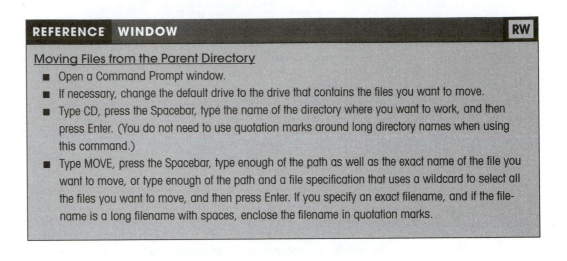

REFERENCE WINDOW   **RW**

Moving Files from the Parent Directory
- Open a Command Prompt window.
- If necessary, change the default drive to the drive that contains the files you want to move.
- Type CD, press the Spacebar, type the name of the directory where you want to work, and then press Enter. (You do not need to use quotation marks around long directory names when using this command.)
- Type MOVE, press the Spacebar, type enough of the path as well as the exact name of the file you want to move, or type enough of the path and a file specification that uses a wildcard to select all the files you want to move, and then press Enter. If you specify an exact filename, and if the filename is a long filename with spaces, enclose the filename in quotation marks.

By taking advantage of the fact that commands use the current drive if you do not specify otherwise, you can simplify and streamline file operations in a command-line environment. In contrast, by specifying enough of the path, you can guarantee that commands locate the file you need, without displaying an error and requiring more work on your part to correct the problem and complete the operation.

Completing the Directory Structure

You only have one more directory to create, and then you can move all the remaining files to that directory.

To complete the reorganization of your Data Disk:

1. Clear the window, type **cd ..** (two periods) and then press **Enter**. You return to the root directory. See Figure 4-24. Although you could have referred to the root directory by using the backslash (by entering the command CD \), this command also works. The "dot dot" instructs the Change Directory command to move to the parent directory of the current directory. In this case, the parent directory of the "Business Records" directory is the root directory. Unlike the backslash (\), which can bypass many different levels to get directly to the root directory, "dot dot" only moves up one level.

Figure 4-24	CHANGING TO THE PARENT DIRECTORY

notation for parent directory

```
Command Prompt
A:\Business Records>cd ..
A:\>_
```

Change Directory command changes to the root directory (the parent directory of Business Records)

2. Type **dir /o** and then press **Enter**. You now have four directories, and the remaining files (all ones with the "xls" file extension) are the ones you want to move to the last directory you will now create. See Figure 4-25.

Figure 4-25   VIEWING THE CONTENTS OF THE ROOT DIRECTORY

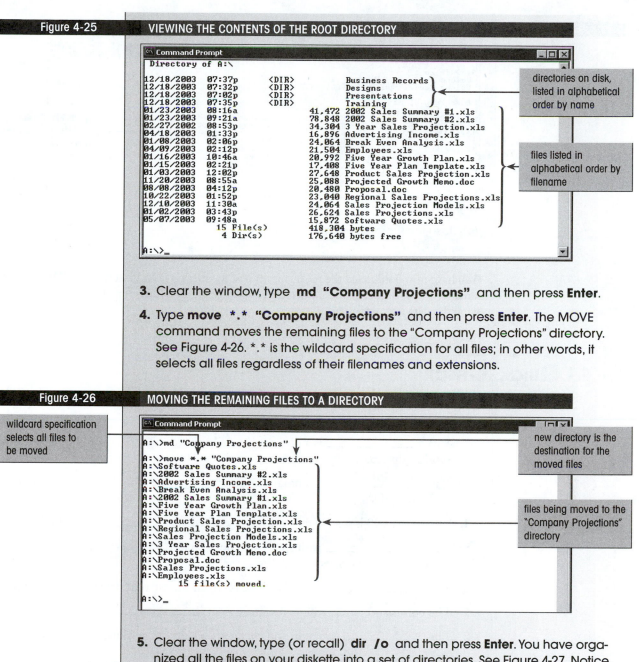

3. Clear the window, type **md "Company Projections"** and then press **Enter**.

4. Type **move *.* "Company Projections"** and then press **Enter**. The MOVE command moves the remaining files to the "Company Projections" directory. See Figure 4-26. *.* is the wildcard specification for all files; in other words, it selects all files regardless of their filenames and extensions.

Figure 4-26   MOVING THE REMAINING FILES TO A DIRECTORY

5. Clear the window, type (or recall) **dir /o** and then press **Enter**. You have organized all the files on your diskette into a set of directories. See Figure 4-27. Notice that the directory listing acts as a "table of contents" for the diskette. Also note that, even though you used *.* as the file specification for the source files in the previous step, the MOVE command did not move your directories, only your files.

Figure 4-27   VIEWING THE CONTENTS OF THE ROOT DIRECTORY

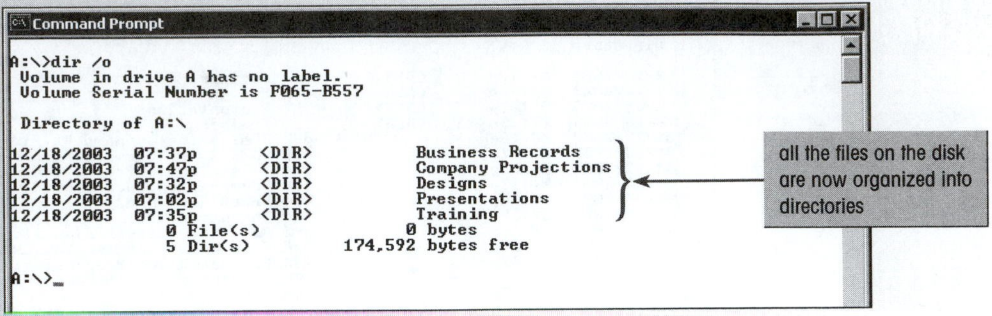

```
Command Prompt                                                    _ □ ✕

A:\>dir /o
 Volume in drive A has no label.
 Volume Serial Number is F065-B557

 Directory of A:\

12/18/2003  07:37p    <DIR>          Business Records
12/18/2003  07:47p    <DIR>          Company Projections
12/18/2003  07:32p    <DIR>          Designs
12/18/2003  07:02p    <DIR>          Presentations
12/18/2003  07:35p    <DIR>          Training
               0 File(s)              0 bytes
               5 Dir(s)         174,592 bytes free

A:\>_
```

all the files on the disk are now organized into directories

6. Close the Command Prompt window.

You have now completed the reorganization of the files on your diskette at the Windows 2000 command line as Isabel requested, creating appropriate new directory folders and copying or moving the data files into them.

Session 4.1 QUICK CHECK

1. The _____ is the first directory created on a disk by an operating system or formatting utility.

2. A(n) _____ is a directory that is subordinate to, and contained within, another directory.

3. The _____ is a notation that identifies the exact location of a directory or file on a disk.

4. Windows 2000 is installed in a directory called the _____ folder.

5. A(n) _____ path spells out the full path, and there is no ambiguity as to the location of the directory or file.

6. A(n) _____ path always starts from the current drive and directory.

7. The command for creating a directory is _____.

8. The _____ command changes the current working directory.

9. The ". ." entry in a directory listing refers to the _____.

10. You can use the _____ command to move files to another location.

SESSION 4.2

In this session, you will copy files within the same directory. You will display a graphical representation of the directory structure of your disk, explore additional techniques for navigating up and down the directory structure, and save a copy of the directory tree display.

Copying Files within a Directory

Isabel asks you to create sales summary template files for 2003, following the format of the same files for 2002. Your new "Company Projections" directory folder already contains 2002 sales summary files. To save time and effort, you decide to copy these files so you can modify them later. Because you will use these two groups of files in conjunction with each other, you want to keep them in the same directory. When you copy a file within the same directory, you must give it a new name, because a directory cannot contain two files or subdirectories with the same name.

To copy the sales summary files within the "Company Projections" directory:

1. Open a Command Prompt window, set colors if necessary, insert the copy of Data Disk #1 that you used in Session 4.1 in drive A, and make drive A the current drive.

2. Clear the screen, type **cd com*** and then press **Enter**. The Change Directory command changes to the "Company Projections" directory, because only "Company Projections" matched your wildcard specification "com*" (if there had been more than one matching directory, you would have switched to whichever directory came first in the directory listing's arbitrary disk order). The command prompt should now contain the name of the "Company Projections" directory folder.

3. Type **copy 2002* 2003*** and then press **Enter**. The COPY command copies two files and produces two new files with new filenames beginning with "2003".

4. Type **dir 200*** and then press **Enter** to view the new files. See Figure 4-28. Now there are four files that begin with "200" in the "Company Projections" directory folder.

Figure 4-28	COPYING FILES WITHIN A DIRECTORY

change directory with wildcard matches only "Company Projections"

```
A:\>cd com*

A:\Company Projections>copy 2002* 2003*
2002 Sales Summary #2.xls
2002 Sales Summary #1.xls
        2 file(s) copied.

A:\Company Projections>dir 200*
 Volume in drive A has no label.
 Volume Serial Number is F065-B557

 Directory of A:\Company Projections

01/23/2003  09:21a           78,848 2002 Sales Summary #2.xls
01/23/2003  08:16a           41,472 2002 Sales Summary #1.xls
01/23/2003  09:21a           78,848 2003 Sales Summary #2.xls
01/23/2003  08:16a           41,472 2003 Sales Summary #1.xls
               4 File(s)        240,640 bytes
               0 Dir(s)          54,272 bytes free

A:\Company Projections>
```

copy matching files, changing the first four characters

wildcard matches both sets of filenames

original files

new files

5. Type **cd ** and then press **Enter** to return to the root directory to review your work.

Note that copying files within one directory has no effect on files with similar names in any other directories.

REFERENCE WINDOW   **RW**

<u>Copying Files within a Directory</u>
- Open a Command Prompt window.
- If necessary, change the default drive to the drive that contains the files you want to copy.
- Type CD, press the Spacebar, type the name of the directory where you want to work, and then press Enter. (You do not need to use quotation marks around long directory names when using this command.)
- Type COPY, press the Spacebar, type the name of the file you want to copy, or type a file specification that uses a wildcard to select all the files you want to copy, type a name or filespec for the name(s) of the new files, and then press Enter. If you specify an exact filename, and if the filename is long, enclose the filename in quotation marks.
- Type DIR and then press Enter to verify that the copy operation worked.

You can perform file operations, such as COPY, within a directory without affecting files in any other directories.

Viewing a Directory Structure

You want to view a graphical representation of the partially completed directory structure of your diskette. You can use the TREE command to display a directory tree from the command prompt. A **directory tree** is a diagrammatic representation of the directory structure of a hard disk or diskette. It shows the current directory and all subdirectories below the current directory. The TREE command is an external command with the following syntax:

TREE [*drive:*][*path*]

If you do not specify a drive or path, the TREE command assumes you want to view the directory structure of the current drive, starting with the current directory. If you want the directory tree to include the root directory and all subdirectories, you must start from the root directory or specify the root directory as the path. If you want to view the directory tree of another drive, or that of a specific directory of a hard disk or diskette, you must specify the other drive name and/or directory path.

To view a directory tree of your Data Disk #1:

1. Check the command prompt to make sure you are at the root directory of drive A; if not, you can get to the root directory by typing **cd /d a:** and pressing **Enter**. The **Drive Switch (/d)** switch changes the current drive in addition to changing the designated current working directory for the drive.

2. Clear the window.

3. Type **tree** and then press **Enter**. TREE displays a diagrammatic representation of the directory structure of your diskette. See Figure 4-29. Next to the name of the drive, TREE displays a dot (.) to indicate that the directory tree starts at the current directory. The directory tree shows the five subdirectories under the root directory.

Figure 4-29   DISPLAYING A DIRECTORY TREE

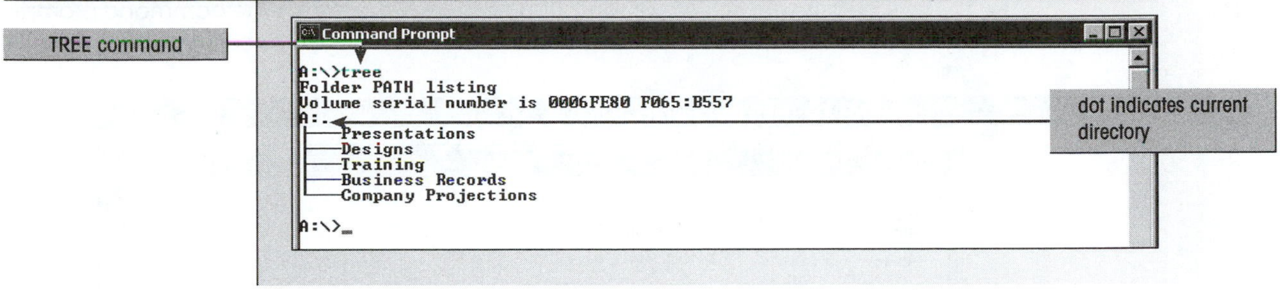

TREE command

```
Command Prompt

A:\>tree
Folder PATH listing
Volume serial number is 0006FE80 F065:B557
A:.
    ┌──Presentations
    ├──Designs
    ├──Training
    ├──Business Records
    └──Company Projections

A:\>_
```

dot indicates current directory

In this directory tree, you see the relationship of the subdirectories to the root directory. As you construct or revise the directory structure of your hard disk or diskettes from the command prompt to meet your changing needs, you can quickly view the directory structure to verify directory operations and to refresh your memory of the disk's directory structure.

REFERENCE   WINDOW   **RW**

Displaying the Directory Tree of a Disk or Directory

- Open a Command Prompt window.
- If necessary, change the default drive to the drive that contains the files you want to view.
- Type CD, press the Spacebar, type the name of the directory folder from which you want to start, and then press Enter. (You do not need to use quotation marks around long directory names with this command.)
- Type TREE and then press Enter.
- If necessary, you scan scroll your Command Prompt window back to see more of the TREE display.
- If you cannot scroll back to the start of the display, type TREE | MORE to pause the display after each page screen.

The TREE command gives you a quick overview of a directory folder structure. Later, you'll save a copy of a TREE display to a file, but first you'll practice moving between directories on your hard drive.

Navigating a Directory Tree

Now you want to learn how to navigate within a directory folder tree at the command prompt. There are two techniques you can use; you can change to a directory in one step by specifying its full path, or you can traverse the directory tree one subdirectory at a time by specifying the directory's name.

You want to examine directories of your hard drive. First, because you want to make sure that your computer contains some new fonts that you've installed on your hard disk, you are going to change to the Windows 2000 Fonts directory by specifying its full path and then check the contents of this directory.

To change to the Fonts directory in one step:

1. Type **cd /d c:\win*\fonts** and then press **Enter**. The "/d" changes your default drive to C as well as changing your current directory folder. See Figure 4-30. Again, each drive maintains its own current default directory in a Command Prompt

window. "Win*" will match your Windows 2000 SystemRoot directory name as long as it begins with the letters "win," such as Windows or WinNT. The command prompt shows that the current directory is the Windows 2000 Fonts directory.

Figure 4-30 | **CHANGING TO THE FONTS DIRECTORY**

```
Command Prompt                                              _ □ ×
A:\>tree
Folder PATH listing
Volume serial number is 0006FE80 F065:B557
A:.
├────Presentations
├────Designs
├────Training
├────Business Records
└────Company Projections

A:\>cd /d c:\win*\fonts

C:\WINNT\Fonts>
```

new current directory

CD command changes to the Fonts directory on drive C

TROUBLE? If you get an error message saying, "The filename, directory name, or volume label syntax is incorrect," your Windows 2000 SystemRoot directory name may not begin with the letters "win" (or it might be on another volume with a different drive letter). List your root directory's subdirectories by typing **dir c:\ /ad** and pressing **Enter**. Look for the name of your SystemRoot directory folder and substitute its name for "win*" in the step above. If you have trouble identifying your Windows 2000 SystemRoot folder name, ask a lab assistant or instructor.

2. Type **dir /o /p** and then press **Enter** to view the files in this directory. When prompted, use the Spacebar to view the remainder of the directory listing.

3. Type **cd ** and then press **Enter**. As you can tell from the command prompt, the CD command moved the current working directory up two directories to the root directory.

REFERENCE WINDOW | **RW**

Changing to Another Drive and Directory
- Open a Command Prompt window.
- If necessary, change the default drive to the drive that contains the files you want to copy.
- Type CD, press the Spacebar, type the /D switch, press the Spacebar, type the full path (with or without wildcards) of the drive and directory where you want to work, and then press Enter.

The enhanced features of the Change Directory command in Windows 2000 now allow you to not only change directories, but also change drives.

Stepping Down a Directory Tree

You next want to examine the Windows 2000 SystemRoot and the System32 directories. Again, the SystemRoot directory is typically C:\WINNT or, if you have an upgraded system, C:\Windows. The System32 directory folder contains most of the command prompt utility programs you use. You can step down the directory tree one directory at a time.

To change to the Windows 2000 SystemRoot directory and then to the System32 subdirectory:

1. Clear the window, type **cd win*** and then press **Enter** (substitute your Windows 2000 SystemRoot directory name for "win*" if necessary; if your SystemRoot is on another drive, add /d and the drive letter as well). The command prompt shows that the current directory is the Windows 2000 directory.

2. Recall (or type) **dir /o /p** and then press **Enter**. DIR displays a list of the subdirectories below your Windows 2000 SystemRoot directory folder. See Figure 4-31. As you can tell from this directory listing, the Windows SystemRoot directory contains many different subdirectories for the Windows 2000 program and supporting files.

| Figure 4-31 | DISPLAYING THE CONTENTS OF THE SYSTEMROOT DIRECTORY |

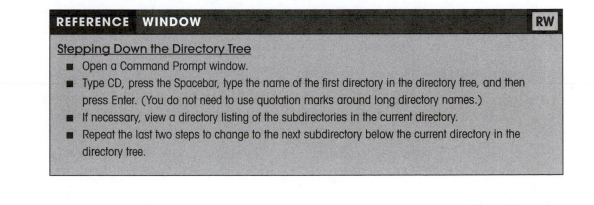

3. Use the Spacebar to view the remainder of the directory listing. The Windows directory also contains important operating system files as well as directories.

4. Type **cd system32** and then press **Enter**. The command prompt shows that the current directory is the System32 directory, which is positioned below the Windows 2000 directory.

5. Recall (or type) **dir /o /p** and then press **Enter** to view the files in this directory.

6. Use the Spacebar to view the next screen of the directory listing, and then use **Ctrl+C** to interrupt the Directory command and return to the command prompt. If you examined the entire directory listing for the directory used on the computer in Figure 4-31, you would find that it contains 26 directories and over 1,400 files. The number of directories and files on your computer system might differ.

REFERENCE WINDOW   **RW**

Stepping Down the Directory Tree
- Open a Command Prompt window.
- Type CD, press the Spacebar, type the name of the first directory in the directory tree, and then press Enter. (You do not need to use quotation marks around long directory names.)
- If necessary, view a directory listing of the subdirectories in the current directory.
- Repeat the last two steps to change to the next subdirectory below the current directory in the directory tree.

To change to a directory, you can step down the directory tree one directory at a time, or if you know the full path to a directory, you can switch to that directory in one step.

Stepping Up the Directory

You first want to return to the Windows 2000 SystemRoot folder and then to the root directory. If you change to a subdirectory and then want to move one level higher in the directory tree to its parent directory, you can use this variation of the Change Directory command:

CD ..

Because ". ." (dot dot) refers to the parent directory of the current directory, you can change to a parent directory without specifying its full path. In the following steps you will return to the root directory, one directory level at a time.

To change to the parent directory of System32:

1. Clear the screen, type **cd ..** and then press **Enter**. The command prompt shows that the current directory is the Windows 2000 SystemRoot directory (probably C:\WINNT). See Figure 4-32. You can now use this same command to move to the parent directory of the SystemRoot directory.

Figure 4-32	STEPPING UP THE DIRECTORY TREE

parent directory of system32

root is the parent of the WINNT directory

```
Command Prompt                                          _ □ ×
C:\WINNT\system32>cd ..
C:\WINNT>_
```

two dots indicate the parent directory

2. Type **cd ..** and then press **Enter**. The command prompt shows that you are at the root directory. See Figure 4-33.

Figure 4-33	CHANGING TO THE ROOT DIRECTORY

parent directory of the current directory

root directory

```
Command Prompt                                          _ □ ×
C:\WINNT\system32>cd ..
C:\WINNT>cd ..
C:\>
```

REFERENCE WINDOW   RW

Stepping Up a Directory Tree
- Open the Command Prompt window.
- Type CD, press the Spacebar, type .. and then press Enter.
- If necessary, view a directory listing of the subdirectories in the current directory.
- Repeat the last two steps to change to the next subdirectory in the directory tree above the current directory.

Next, you want to change to the Media subdirectory folder (containing sound files), examine the files included with Windows 2000 for use as sound events, and switch to the Fonts subdirectory to check for additional fonts before returning to the root directory. Later, you can install the additional sound files and fonts that you need on your computer for your next project.

To traverse the subdirectories of the Windows 2000 directory folder:

1. Type **cd c:\win*\media** and then press **Enter**. The command prompt shows that the current directory folder is Media.

2. Recall (or type) **dir   /o /p** and then press **Enter** to view the files in this directory. When prompted, press the Spacebar to view the remainder of the directory listing.

3. Clear the screen, type **cd ..\fonts** and then press **Enter**. This command changes to the Fonts directory, which is below the parent directory of your current working directory. See Figure 4-34. Because the Fonts directory is under the same parent directory, you can reference the parent directory by using "dot dot." Directories that are located in the same level of the directory tree are called **parallel directories**. You could also enter "cd \win*\fonts" to achieve the same result.

Figure 4-34	CHANGING TO A PARALLEL DIRECTORY

new directory on the same level as the previous directory

move up to the parent directory

move down to another subdirectory of the parent

4. Type **cd ** and then press **Enter** to return to the root directory.

You can use the same techniques to navigate a more complex directory structure elsewhere on your hard disk in order to locate client or business files.

Saving a Directory Tree Display

You want to save a copy of the directory tree that includes the files contained in each of the directories of your new templates diskette. If you reorganize your templates diskette later, you can use this documentation to help you in planning the changes you intend to make. Likewise, if you reorganize a disk and then change your mind later, you can quickly reconstruct the directory structure and restore your business files to the original directories.

Earlier, you used the TREE command to view a directory tree at the command prompt. You can use a variation of the same command to view filenames by directory. You can then save a copy of the directory tree display by redirecting that output to a file. The **Filename switch (/F)** displays the directory tree and lists the filenames in each directory. When you save this information, you can also include the **ASCII switch (/A)**, so that any program or printer can reproduce it, even if the program cannot display the graphics lines in TREE's regular directory display. If you use the ASCII switch, TREE substitutes other symbols for the graphics lines. Let's try it.

To display and save a directory tree of your Data Disk:

1. Be sure drive A contains your Data Disk. Check the command prompt to make sure you are at the root directory of drive A; if not, move there in one step by typing **cd /d a:** and pressing **Enter**.

2. Clear the window, type **tree /f | more** and then press **Enter**. The MORE filter displays the first page of output from the TREE command. See Figure 4-35. The directory tree displays and lists the filenames in each directory.

Figure 4-35	VIEWING A DIRECTORY TREE WITH FILENAMES

3. Use the Spacebar to view the remainder of the directory tree and return to the command prompt.

4. Type **tree /f /a > treefile.txt** and then press **Enter**. As you've seen earlier, you can redirect the output of any command to a file or device by using the output redirection operator (>) and the name of the file or device.

5. Type **treefile.txt** and then press **Enter**. If necessary, maximize the Notepad window. Because you typed the data file name (treefile.txt) without specifying a command, and because Windows 2000 associates the "txt" extension with the Notepad program, Windows opens Notepad and opens treefile.txt. See Figure 4-36. Notice that ASCII symbols are used instead of graphical lines to show the directory tree and the relationship of directories to each other.

Figure 4-36   **VIEWING A SAVED DIRECTORY TREE USING NOTEPAD**

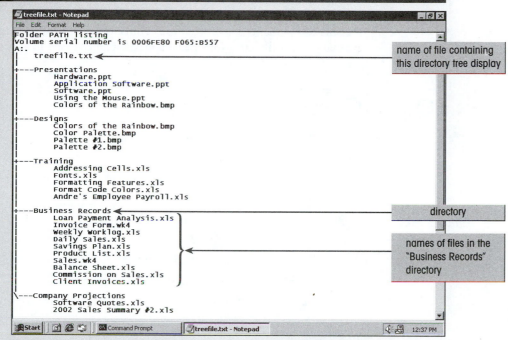

```
treefile.txt - Notepad
File  Edit  Format  Help
Folder PATH listing
Volume serial number is 0006FE80 F065:B557
A:.
|      treefile.txt
|
+---Presentations
|          Hardware.ppt
|          Application Software.ppt
|          Software.ppt
|          Using the Mouse.ppt
|          Colors of the Rainbow.bmp
|
+---Designs
|          Colors of the Rainbow.bmp
|          Color Palette.bmp
|          Palette #1.bmp
|          Palette #2.bmp
|
+---Training
|          Addressing Cells.xls
|          Fonts.xls
|          Formatting Features.xls
|          Format Code Colors.xls
|          Andre's Employee Payroll.xls
|
+---Business Records
|          Loan Payment Analysis.xls
|          Invoice Form.wk4
|          Weekly Worklog.xls
|          Daily Sales.xls
|          Savings Plan.xls
|          Product List.xls
|          Sales.wk4
|          Balance Sheet.xls
|          Commission on Sales.xls
|          Client Invoices.xls
|
\---Company Projections
           Software Quotes.xls
           2002 Sales Summary #2.xls
```

name of file containing this directory tree display

directory

names of files in the "Business Records" directory

Start   Command Prompt   treefile.txt - Notepad   12:37 PM

6. In Notepad, scroll up and down to view the tree display of your diskette.

7. If requested by your instructor, print this directory tree file from Notepad.

8. Exit Notepad after you examine the directory tree.

9. Note that you can also provide another person with treefile.txt by delivering the diskette, or by sending the file by e-mail.

For a quick overview of the directory structure of a hard disk or diskette, use the TREE command at the command prompt. You can then locate specific directories and periodically evaluate the organization of directories on diskettes or hard disks.

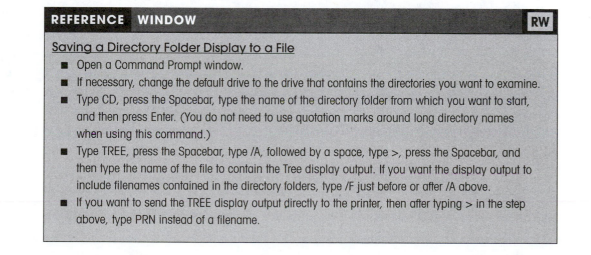

REFERENCE WINDOW   **RW**

Saving a Directory Folder Display to a File

- Open a Command Prompt window.
- If necessary, change the default drive to the drive that contains the directories you want to examine.
- Type CD, press the Spacebar, type the name of the directory folder from which you want to start, and then press Enter. (You do not need to use quotation marks around long directory names when using this command.)
- Type TREE, press the Spacebar, type /A, followed by a space, type >, press the Spacebar, and then type the name of the file to contain the Tree display output. If you want the display output to include filenames contained in the directory folders, type /F just before or after /A above.
- If you want to send the TREE display output directly to the printer, then after typing > in the step above, type PRN instead of a filename.

The TREE command is a useful tool for providing an overview of the directory structure of a disk and for use before, during, and after the process of reorganizing it. You also can rely on it as a navigational aide as you step up and down the directory tree.

Isabel compliments you on your use of directory commands to organize the template files and says that the new directory folder layout makes it much easier to locate and work with related files.

Session 4.2 QUICK | CHECK

1. When you copy a file within the same directory, you must give it a(n) _____.

2. A(n) _____ is a diagrammatic representation of the directory structure of a hard disk or diskette.

3. Next to the name of the drive, TREE may display a dot (.) to indicate that the directory tree starts at the _____ directory.

4. The _____ option of the CD command changes your current default drive as well as changing your current working directory folder.

5. If you change to a subdirectory and then want to move one level higher in the directory tree to its parent directory, you can use the command _____.

6. The _____ switch of the TREE command displays the directory tree and lists the filenames in each directory.

7. If you use the _____ switch, the TREE command substitutes other symbols for the graphics lines.

COMMAND REFERENCE

COMMAND	USE	BASIC SYNTAX	EXAMPLE
CD	Changes the current working directory	CD [drive:][path]directory name CHDIR [drive:][path]directory name	cd \Documents and Settings cd Projections cd \
CD . .	Changes to the parent directory above the current directory	CD . .	cd . .
MD	Creates (or makes) a new directory	MD [drive:][path]directory name MKDIR [drive:][path]directory name	md Presentations
MOVE	Moves one or more files to another drive and/or directory	MOVE [drive:][path]filespec destination	move *.bmp Designs
TREE	Displays a diagram of the directory tree; the /F switch adds filenames to the display; the /A switch displays with ASCII characters only	TREE [drive:][path] [/F] [/A]	tree a:\ /f /a

Items shown in italics and not enclosed within square brackets are required parameters
Items shown in italics and enclosed within square brackets are optional parameters

REVIEW ASSIGNMENTS

One of your co-workers at SolarWinds, Judith, wants to organize her document template files into directories by document type so she can quickly locate templates for a specific type of application. She asks you to help her create the directories and move the files to the directories on that disk.

As you perform the following steps, record your answers to any questions so you can submit them to your instructor.

1. Open a Command Prompt window.

2. Make a copy of the original Data Disk #1(do not use the Data Disk you used in the tutorial). You can use DISKCOPY to copy over the diskette that you used in the tutorial.

3. Change the default drive to drive A.

4. Specify default switches for the Directory command in the Windows environment so that this command displays filenames in alphabetical order first by file extension, then by the main part of the filename, one screen at a time. What command did you enter for this operation?

5. Display a directory listing of your new Data Disk, and verify that filenames are arranged alphabetically, first by file extension, then by the main part of the filename. If necessary, change the default switches for the Directory command in the Windows environment.

6. Delete the files named File0000.chk and ~WRC0070.tmp using the Prompt for Verification switch. What commands did you enter to perform these operations?

7. Create a directory named Images, and move bitmapped image files with the "bmp" file extension to this directory. What commands did you enter for these two operations? How did you verify this operation?

8. Create a directory named "Word Templates"; copy the files with the "doc" file extension to this directory; verify that the copy operation worked; and then delete the document files with the "doc" file extension from the root directory. What commands did you enter for these four operations?

9. Create a directory named Presentations; change to the Presentations directory; and then move files with the "ppt" file extension from the root directory to this directory. What commands did you enter for these three operations?

10. Change to the root directory; create a directory named "Lotus Templates"; and then move files with the "wk4" file extension to this directory. What commands did you enter for these three operations?

11. Create a directory named "Excel Templates"; change to the "Excel Templates" directory; and then move files with the "xls" file extension to this directory. What commands did you enter for these three operations?

12. Change to the root directory, and display the directory structure of your diskette on screen. What commands did you enter for these two operations?

13. Change to the "Excel Templates" directory, and display the directory contents. Now, using one command, change to the "Word Templates" directory. Display the "Word Templates" directory contents. What commands did you enter for these four operations?

14. Change to the root directory. Create a text file that contains the directory structure of the diskette, with no line-drawing characters, and includes all filenames in each directory. Display the resulting text file with Notepad. What commands did you enter for these three operations?

CASE PROBLEMS

Case 1. Organizing Client Files at The Perfect Match   The Perfect Match, an employment agency, hires temporary employees to assist their clients in the preparation of documents. Corey Tanner, the Office Manager, asks you to organize the spreadsheet documents on one of their clients' disks, and to prepare documentation for that client so her employees can easily find the files on the disk.

As you perform the following steps, record your answers to any questions so you can submit them to your instructor.

1. Open a Command Prompt window.

2. Make a copy of the original Data Disk #1 (do not use the Data Disk you used in the tutorial). You can use DISKCOPY to copy over the diskette that you used in the tutorial.

3. Change the default drive to drive A.

4. Specify default switches for the Directory command in the Windows environment so this command displays filenames in alphabetical order first by file extension, then by the main part of the filename, one screen at a time. What command did you enter for this operation?

5. Display a directory listing of your new Data Disk, and verify that filenames are arranged alphabetically first by file extension, then by the main part of the filename. If necessary, change the default switches for the Directory command in the Windows environment.

6. Delete the files named File0000.chk and ~WRC0070.tmp using the Prompt for Verification switch. What commands did you enter to perform these operations?

7. Display all the files with the file extension "bmp." What command did you enter for this operation? Recall that command, and change the DIR command to DEL, and then delete all these files.

8. Repeat this same process to view, then delete, all the files with the "doc," "ppt," and "wk4" file extensions. What commands did you use to view and then delete these three types of files?

9. Display a directory of your disk. The only files that remain are those with the "xls" file extension.

10. Using Figure 4-37 as a guideline, create a subdirectory named "Spreadsheet Templates" in the root directory of the disk. What command did you enter for this operation?

11. Move all the files with the "xls" file extension from the root directory to the "Spreadsheet Templates" subdirectory. What command did you enter for this operation?

12. Change to the "Spreadsheets Templates" subdirectory. What command did you enter for this operation?

13. Create a directory named "Business Records", and then move the files shown under it in Figure 4-37 to that directory. List the commands you used to move the files. *Note*: Use wildcards wherever possible to reduce the number of steps and commands that you need to enter.

14. Create the remaining directories shown in Figure 4-37, and move the remaining files to the directories shown in Figure 4-37.

15. Change to the "Sales Summaries" directory and then, using a wildcard, copy the two files that begin with "2002" to produce two new files that begin with "2003" in the filenames. Repeat the process to produce two other new files that begin with "2004" in the filenames. What command did you enter to change to this directory? What commands did you enter to create copies of the two files that begin with "2002?"

16. In the root directory of your diskette, create an ASCII file containing a directory tree, which shows the final directory structure of your Data Disk with a list of the files in each directory. What command did you enter for this operation? If your instructor requests a printed copy of this file, then open the file in Notepad and print it, or redirect the contents of this file to your printer port.

| Figure 4-37 | ORGANIZING CLIENT FILES AT THE PERFECT MATCH |

Spreadsheet Templates

Business Records

Balance Sheet.xls
Client Invoices.xls
Commissions on Sales.xls
Daily Sales.xls
Data Systems Budget.xls
Employees.xls
Loan Payment Analysis.xls
Product List.xls
Software Quotes.xls
Weekly Worklog.xls

Projections

3 Year Sales Projection.xls
Advertising Income.xls
Break Even Analysis.xls
Five Year Growth Plan.xls
Five Year Plan Template.xls
Product Sales Projection.xls
Regional Sales Projections.xls
Sales Projection Models.xls
Sales Projections.xls

Sales Summaries

2002 Sales Summary #1.xls
2002 Sales Summary #2.xls

Training

Addressing Cells.xls
Andre's Employee Payroll.xls
Fonts.xls
Format Code Colors.xls
Formatting Features.xls
Savings Plan.xls

Case 2. Preparing Projections at Fast Track Trainers   The end of Fast Track Trainers' fiscal year is quickly approaching, and Samantha Kuehl wants to create a diskette with sales projections and summaries for the next five years. She asks you to make a copy of her working disk and then create directories for FY 2002 and FY 2003 (FY stands for Fiscal Year). After copying the files with the current years' sales summaries and sales projections to the FY 2002 directory, she asks you to make duplicate copies of these same files and copy them to the FY 2003 directory. She also asks that you update the filenames so that the fiscal year is clear from the filename.

As you perform the following steps, record your answers to any questions so you can submit them to your instructor.

1. Open a Command Prompt window.

2. Make a copy of the original Data Disk #1 (do not use the Data Disk you used in the tutorial). You can use DISKCOPY to copy over the diskette that you used in the tutorial.

3. Change the default drive to drive A.

4. Specify default switches for the Directory command in the Windows environment so that this command displays filenames in alphabetical order first by file extension, then by the main part of the filename, one screen at a time. What command did you enter for this operation?

5. Display a directory listing of your new Data Disk, and verify that filenames are arranged alphabetically first by file extension, then by the main part of the filename. If necessary, change the default switches for the Directory command in the Windows environment.

6. Display all the files with the file extension "bmp." What command did you enter for this operation? Recall the command, change the DIR command to DEL, and then delete all these files. What is the final revised command that you used to delete these files?

7. Repeat this same process to view and then delete all the files with the "chk," "doc," "ppt," "tmp," and "wk4" file extensions.

8. Display a directory of your disk. The only files that remain are those with the "xls" file extension.

9. Create a subdirectory named "FY 2002" in the root directory of the disk. What command did you enter for this operation?

10. Copy "2002 Sales Summary #1.xls" and "2002 Sales Summary #2.xls" to the "FY 2002" directory. What command did you enter for this operation?

11. Copy "Sales Projections.xls" to the "FY 2002" directory and, in the process, change the filename to "2002 Sales Projections.xls". What command did you enter for this operation?

12. Create a subdirectory named "FY 2003" in the root directory of the disk.

13. From the root directory, copy the files in the "FY 2002" directory to the "FY 2003" directory, and during the copy operation, change the first part of the filename from "2002" to "2003". What command did you enter for this operation?

14. Delete the remaining files in the root directory of drive A. What command did you enter for this operation?

15. In the root directory of your diskette, create an ASCII file containing a directory tree that shows the final directory structure of your Data Disk with a list of the files in each directory. What command did you enter for this operation? If your instructor requests a printed copy of this file, then open the file in Notepad and print it, or redirect the contents of this file to your printer port.

Case 3. Preparing for Computer Training Workshops at HiPerform Systems   HiPerform Systems is a small business in Ipswich, Massachusetts, that sells and services computer systems and hard disk drives. James Everett, owner of HiPerform Systems, would like to offer introductory computer courses to customers who buy HiPerform computers. James gives you a copy of a work diskette and asks you to reorganize it, creating and using different folders for the PowerPoint presentation files, bitmap images, and selected spreadsheets he plans to use in his courses.

As you perform the following steps, record your answers to any questions so that you can submit them to your instructor.

1. Open a Command Prompt window.

2. Make a copy of the original Data Disk #1 (do not use the Data Disk you used in the tutorial). You can use DISKCOPY to copy over the diskette that you used in the tutorial.

3. Change the default drive to drive A.

4. Specify default switches for the Directory command in the Windows environment so that this command displays filenames in alphabetical order first by file extension, then by the main part of the filename, one screen at a time. What command did you enter for this operation?

5. Display a directory listing of your new Data Disk, and verify that filenames are arranged alphabetically first by file extension, then by the main part of the filename. If necessary, change the default switches for the Directory command in the Windows environment.

6. Display all the files with the file extension "doc." What command did you enter for this operation? Recall the command, change the DIR command to DEL, and then delete these files. What is the final revised command that you used to delete these files?

7. Repeat this same process to view, then delete, all the files with the "chk," "tmp," and "wk4" file extensions.

8. Display a directory of your disk. The only files that should remain are those with the "xls," "bmp," and "ppt" file extensions.

9. Create a directory named "Computer Courses" in the root directory of the disk. What command did you enter for this operation?

10. Move all the files with the "ppt" file extension from the root directory to the "Computer Courses" directory. What command did you enter for this operation?

11. Move "Fonts.xls" and "Software Quotes.xls" from the root directory to the "Computer Courses" directory. What command did you enter for this operation?

12. Create a subdirectory named Images in the root directory of the disk. What command did you enter for this operation?

13. Move all the files with the "bmp" file extension from the root directory to the Images directory. What command did you enter for this operation?

14. Delete the remaining files in the root directory of drive A. What command did you enter for this operation?

15. In the root directory of your diskette, create an ASCII file containing a directory tree that shows the final directory structure of your Data Disk with a list of the files in each directory. What command did you enter for this operation? If your instructor requests a printed copy of this file, then open the file in Notepad and print it, or redirect the contents of this file to your printer port.

Case 4. *Investigating Advertising Images at Turing Enterprises*   Melissa Turing, owner of Turing Enterprises, plans to prepare a Web site advertising the company's tour packages for women, and she wants to use and enhance the outdoor images in the Windows 2000 Wallpaper directory folder in her advertising. But before she uses these images, she wants to get permission from Microsoft so that she can avoid copyright infringement. Melissa asks you to copy the image files to a folder on a diskette and prepare a file listing the file-names so she can refer to them when she contacts Microsoft.

As you perform the following steps, record your answers to any questions so that you can submit them to your instructor.

1. Open a Command Prompt window.

2. Place a blank diskette in drive A. If you have completed the tutorial thus far, you can reformat your duplicate of Data Disk #1.

3. Change the default drive to drive A.

4. Display a directory listing of your Data Disk, and verify that your diskette is blank.

5. Create a subdirectory named "Windows Images" in the root directory of the disk. What command did you enter for this operation?

6. Change to your new "Windows Images" directory folder. What command did you enter for this operation?

7. Change to the root directory of drive C in one step. What command did you enter for this operation?

8. Change to your Windows directory folder. What command did you enter for this operation?

9. From your Windows directory, change to the Wallpaper subdirectory under the Web directory using one command. What command did you enter for this operation?

10. Copy all the files in the Wallpaper directory to the "Windows Images" directory on drive A. What command did you enter for this operation?

11. Change the default drive to drive A.

12. In the root directory of your diskette, create an ASCII file containing a directory tree, which shows the final directory structure of your Data Disk with a list of the files in each directory. What command did you enter for this operation? If your instructor requests a printed copy of this file, then open the file in Notepad and print it, or redirect the contents of this file to your printer port.

13. Display a directory of the Web Wallpaper folder on drive C, and verify that you have all of the images that you copied to your diskette. What command did you enter for this operation?

14. Delete all the files in the "Windows Images" folder. What command did you enter for this operation?

QUICK | CHECK ANSWERS

Session 4.1

1. root directory
2. subdirectory
3. full path
4. SystemRoot
5. absolute
6. relative
7. MD
8. CD
9. parent directory
10. MOVE

Session 4.2

1. new name
2. directory tree
3. current
4. /D
5. CD . .
6. /F or the Filename switch
7. /A or the ASCII switch

WINDOWS XP COMMAND-LINE UPDATE

Overview

The Windows XP Appendix provides you with the information you need to complete the tutorials in the Microsoft Windows 2000 MS-DOS Command Line book using Windows XP Professional or Windows XP Home Edition. This appendix covers new features, describes differences between Windows 2000 and Windows XP, and provides additional help for you to complete the tutorial steps. Each tutorial in this appendix uses the following icons to help you quickly orient yourself and find the information you need.

NEW A new topic that expands on the coverage in a tutorial and focuses on new features of Windows XP and operating system software, or that replaces the comparable section for completing a set of steps, such as Starting Windows XP.

UPDATE An update to tutorial steps that describes differences between Windows 2000 and Windows XP.

HELP Additional information to help you complete a step or resolve a problem you might encounter.

New Topics

Working in the Windows XP command-line environment is remarkably similar to that for Windows 2000 Professional. Because Windows XP is an upgrade to Windows 2000, improvements have been made to the GUI (graphical user interface), some features have been replaced, and features have been added. This appendix includes the following additional topics on new features of Windows XP Professional and Windows XP Home Edition that extend the coverage provided in the first tutorial:

TUTORIAL	NEW TOPICS
Tutorial 1: Opening Command Line Sessions	PC Operating Systems:
	The Windows ME Operating System
	The Windows XP Operating System
	The Convergence of the Windows 9x and Windows NT Product Lines
	Starting Windows XP
	The Windows XP Desktop
	Changing to Windows Classic Style
	Changing to Web Style
	Logging Off, or Turning Off, Your Computer

OPENING COMMAND LINE SESSIONS

Session 1.1

This session provides an overview of the role of operating system software, the types of operating systems used on PCs, and the importance of developing a skill set that enables you to work with different operating systems in today's dynamic business environments. This additional section expands on Tutorial 1 and provides information about the Windows ME and Windows XP operating systems, as well as the convergence of Microsoft's two product lines for desktop operating systems.

Because individuals who use this updated book may be new to Windows XP or may not have taken a comprehensive course that covers features of Windows XP, this tutorial provides an overview of the new Windows XP GUI, describes how to perform basic operations that are different than previous versions of Windows (such as logging onto your computer, switching between Web style and Windows Classic view, and shutting down your computer), and describes how to work with basic Windows tools, such as the Start menu, taskbar, folder windows, and task-oriented dynamic menus. In addition, although most of your work will be in a Command Prompt window, some tutorials cover related features of the GUI for comparison.

PC Operating Systems

After the introduction of Windows 2000 Professional, Microsoft developed and released the Windows ME and Windows XP operating systems, which built on the successes of previous versions of Windows and also introduced many new and important features. Like other operating systems, Windows XP Professional and Windows XP Home Edition complete the startup process, configure and customize your computer, display a user interface, provide support services to programs, handle input and output, manage the file system and system resources (such as memory), resolve system errors and problems (if possible), provide Help, and include utilities for optimizing and troubleshooting your computer.

The Windows ME Operating System

The Windows ME operating system, or Millennium Edition (Windows Version 4.900.3000), was designed as an upgrade for Windows 98 users and incorporated features of Windows 2000 Professional, and marked the next step in the development of the Windows 9x product line. Windows ME was also intended to be a bridge for upgrading to the Windows NT product line from Windows 95 and Windows 98. **Windows 9x** refers to the operating system product line that includes Windows 95, Windows 98, and Windows ME. See *Figure A1-1*. This product line was designed primarily for the home user. In contrast, the Windows NT product line includes Windows NT Workstation 4.0 and Windows 2000 network operating systems that are more commonly used in business environments. Over the years, Microsoft has indicated it would eventually combine the two different product lines into a single product line. If you start with Windows 95 in *Figure A1-1* and go from right to left down the table, you are looking at the order in which the products in the two different lines were released. Also, there were prior versions of the Windows NT product line before Windows NT Workstation 4.0.

Figure A1-1	WINDOWS DESKTOP OPERATING SYSTEM PRODUCT LINES
WINDOWS 9X PRODUCT LINE	**WINDOWS NT PRODUCT LINE**
Windows 95	Windows NT Workstation 4.0
Windows 98	Windows 2000
Windows ME	Windows XP

One of the important features introduced in Windows ME is the System Restore feature. This feature creates **system checkpoints** which saves changes to system files, device drivers, and system settings on your computer system. If you run into a problem, you can "roll back" your computer system and restore it to an earlier working, or trouble free, state. For example, if you encounter problems when installing a new application or modifying a hardware configuration, you can roll back your computer to the point just before you installed the software or modified the hardware configuration, and restore a previous configuration that worked without any problems.

Another new component in Windows ME is the **Home Networking Wizard** which is designed to step a user through the process of setting up a home network, enabling Internet Connection Sharing so that networked computers connect to the Internet via one computer, and choosing which files and printers to share on a network.

Windows ME includes **Windows Movie Maker** for editing and enhancing video and home movies; an enhanced **Windows Media Player** for listening to music CDs with on-screen visualizations of sounds, creating music libraries, playing movies, listening to Internet radio stations, and customizing the appearance of Windows Media Player with the use of **skins** (a design scheme for changing the look of Windows Media Player); **WebTV** for viewing television programs broadcast over the Internet with a TV tuner card (a feature originally introduced in Windows 98); and the **Windows Image Acquisition** technology for obtaining images from a scanner or digital camera. Not surprisingly, these technologies are also incorporated into the Windows XP operating system.

The Windows XP Operating System

The Windows XP (for "Experience") operating system marks another important and major change in the development of the Windows operating system. Windows XP supports and enhances many of the features included in previous versions of Windows, includes major changes to the graphical user interface, and introduces many new features.

In October 2001, Microsoft released the following three versions of Windows XP:

- **Windows XP Professional Edition** (Windows Version 2002, or Windows Version 5.1.2600) for business users and for advanced users who prefer to use it on their home computer system,

- **Windows XP Home Edition** (Windows Version 2002, or Windows Version 5.1.2600) for home users and users of entertainment-based computer systems, and

- **Windows XP 64-Bit Edition** for scientific, engineering, business, and other types of resource-intensive applications, such as those required for handling special effects in movies and 3D animation.

Windows XP 64-Bit Edition is designed for use with Intel's new Itanium processor that supports up to 16 GB (gigabytes) of RAM, and up to 16 TB (terabytes) of virtual memory. The **Itanium** processor is capable of performing up to 20 operations simultaneously, and can preload data into virtual memory for faster access and processing.

For users of prior Windows versions, the most obvious change in Windows XP Professional and Windows XP Home Editions is the redesign of the GUI. For new installations of Windows XP, Microsoft has simplified the desktop by removing all icons except the Recycle Bin. The Start menu is now the primary way by which you access resources on your computer system. In addition to e-mail and Internet access links, the Start menu lists the five most recently used programs. You still access installed software through the All Programs menu on the Start menu. In addition, you can open the My Documents, My Computer, My Pictures, My Music, and Control Panel folders as well as the enhanced Help and Support Center from the Start menu. You will also see My Network Places and Printers and Faxes on the Start menu in Windows XP Professional, but not Windows XP Home Edition. However, you can modify the Start Menu to display these two options, and you can add Favorites to the Start menu in both versions of Windows XP.

The Control Panel is organized into a new view called **Category view** that provides links to common tasks for customizing and configuring your computer. When you are working in a folder window, Windows XP uses **dynamic menus** to display menu options related to your current task, and links to other places on your computer where you might want to work. For example, if you are working in a folder that contains document files, the dynamic menus list options for working with files, such as copying, moving, renaming, and deleting files. Also, **Tiles view** (Large Icons view in previous versions of Windows), which combined with the **Show in Groups** option, organizes the contents of a folder window by file type. If a folder contains Microsoft Word and Microsoft Excel files, Windows XP can group all the Word document files together and all the Microsoft Excel files together so that you can easily locate what you need to use. Within the My Pictures folder and other folders designated for images, **Filmstrip view** displays thumbnail views of images contained within the files in the folder as well as a full-screen view of whichever thumbnail you select.

Rather than setting aside a taskbar button for each document you open in each application, Windows XP uses **taskbar grouping** to provide access to all open documents of a certain type (such as Word documents) under one taskbar button. For example, if you open different documents with the same application, Windows XP combines all the documents' taskbar buttons into one taskbar button labeled with the name of the application. When you click this taskbar button, Windows XP displays a pop-up list of the document names so you can select the document you want to use. Another advantage of taskbar grouping is that you can perform the same operation on all documents that you open with the same application. For example, you can right-click a taskbar button, and then close all documents opened in the same application.

Here are some of the other new features available in both the Windows XP Professional and Home Editions:

- **Dynamic Update**—The Setup program used to install Windows XP can now check Microsoft's Windows Update Web site for important system updates and download them before it installs Windows XP. This guarantees that the operating system files on your computer are current.

■ **Performance enhancements**—Windows XP starts up more quickly, performs better, uses system resources and memory more efficiently, and shuts down faster than other versions of Windows.

■ **Fast User Switching**—You do not need to log off if someone else needs to use the computer. Instead, another user can log onto their user account while you remain logged onto your account. After the other user logs off, you can switch back to your user account and continue working with any open applications and documents.

■ **Enhanced multimedia features and capabilities with Windows Movie Maker**—You can capture, edit, and organize video clips from a digital video camera or an analog camera so you can create and share home movies on your computer. You can use the **Scanner and Camera Wizard** to scan images or download them from a camera and automatically store those images in your My Pictures folder. Within the enhanced **My Pictures** folder, you can organize and preview digital photos as well as order prints using a Web service. You can use the enhanced **Windows Media Player** to play CDs and DVDs, burn CDs, and organize music files in the **My Music** folder.

■ **Internet Explorer 6**, an enhanced and improved version of Microsoft's Web browser, and **Windows Messenger,** an instant messaging application that allows you to find out who is online, send an instant message, engage a group of friends in an online conversation, invite someone who is online to play a game, dial a contact's computer, send one or more files to someone else, and, if you have a HotMail account, receive a notification when new e-mail arrives.

■ **Credential Manager**—This tool secures and automatically provides your user name and password to applications (such as e-mail software), services (such as your ISP), and Web sites that request that information so that you do not have to repeatedly specify the same information.

■ **System Restore**—As noted earlier, Windows XP periodically saves information regarding changes to the configuration of your computer system, operating system files, and device drivers, so that if you make a change to your computer and then encounter a problem, you can "roll back" your computer system to an earlier functioning state.

■ **Device Driver Rollback**—This tool replaces a newly installed device driver that does not work properly with a previously working version of that same device driver.

■ **Side-by-side DLLs**—Windows XP maintains different versions of the same DLL (Dynamic Link Library) program files used by different applications. This feature prevents problems caused by replacing a DLL file used by several different applications when installing a new application.

■ **Internet Connection Firewall**—This feature protects your computer from intruders and hackers while you are connected to the Internet.

■ **Remote Assistance**—A technical support person, colleague, or friend can remotely connect to your computer to assist you with a project or to troubleshoot a problem. Note that both systems must be using Windows XP.

■ **Network Setup Wizard**—This feature steps you through the process of creating a home network so your computers can share peripherals (such as a printer), software, files, and use Internet Connection Sharing to share a single Internet connection.

- **Help and Support Center**—Microsoft has expanded and enhanced the Help system in Windows XP so that you can find information on your local computer or on the Web.

Here are some additional features and capabilities of Windows XP Professional:

- **Remote Desktop**—This tool allows you to access and use another computer from a computer running Windows 95 or later. For example, you can use Remote Desktop to access your office computer from your home computer, or vice versa.

- **Encrypting File System**—This feature, introduced in Windows 2000 Professional, augments the NTFS file system and enables you to encrypt files with a randomly generated key. This feature provides a high level of security.

- **Network Location Awareness**—This new Windows XP service allows the operating system and applications to determine when a computer has changed its network location.

- **User State Migration Tool**—Administrators can use this tool to migrate a user's data, operating system settings, and application settings from one computer to another computer with Windows XP Professional.

- **Wireless 802.1x networking support**—This feature improves performance for wireless networks.

- **Enhanced processor and memory support**—Window XP Professional now supports two symmetric processors and up to 4 GB of RAM. In a computer that uses **symmetric multiprocessing**, programs or tasks can be processed simultaneously by multiple microprocessors.

Not surprisingly, Windows XP Professional and Windows XP Home Edition provide increased performance and support for setting up, configuring, securing, administering, and troubleshooting networks. In addition, Windows XP Professional and Windows XP Home Edition offer enhanced Internet and Web technologies, and protection for the Windows XP operating system and operating environment, which are important factors in providing the best possible support in a business environment.

The Convergence of the Windows 9x and Windows NT Product Lines

As noted earlier, the different versions of the Windows operating systems fall into two major product lines: Windows 9x and Windows NT product lines (see *Figure A1-1*). Each of these product lines reflects the differences in the needs of Microsoft's home user base and its business user base. Over the years, Microsoft has worked to merge the two product lines into a single Windows operating system. This transition not only requires successfully merging technologies in the different product lines, but also meeting the more complex networking and security needs of businesses, while appealing to home users who want simplicity and access to entertainment-oriented multimedia technologies. With the development of Windows XP, Microsoft is moving much closer to that goal.

The rapid changes in hardware technologies and in the Internet and World Wide Web are reflected in changing operating system technologies. *Figure A1-2* illustrates the introduction of operating systems and operating environments over a 20-year period from 1981-2001. As *Figure A1-2* shows, the primary operating system used by PCs over this time period was DOS, having been used for more than twice as long as the different versions of the Windows operating systems. In contrast, there were six major upgrades of the DOS operating system over a 14-year period, and Microsoft has upgraded the Windows operating system six times in a six-year period. The pace of development and change in operating system technology in the future will be as rapid as it was in the past, and coincide with rapid changes in the Internet, World Wide Web, and hardware technologies.

Figure A1-2 PC OPERATING SYSTEMS & OPERATING ENVIRONMENTS

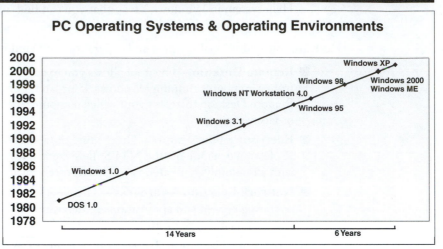

Session 1.2

The second session leads you through the process of opening a command-line session and using basic commands. Although Windows XP Professional and Windows XP Home Edition provide new features and no longer include certain features found in Windows 2000 Professional, the command-line environment in both versions is almost identical to that of Windows 2000. However, because the process for logging on your computer, working with the Windows XP desktop and Start menu, using Web style, opening a command-line session, and logging off your computer can differ from that for Windows 2000, the following material describes how to complete these operations using Windows XP. This section also explains differences that you can encounter when working within the Windows XP command-line environment.

Starting Windows XP

If you are using Windows XP Professional or Windows XP Home Edition, complete the following steps to log onto your computer, and then read the subsequent sections that describe the Windows XP desktop and how to switch between Web style and Windows Classic style.

> ### To log on to your computer:
>
> **1.** Power on your computer, and if you have a dual-boot or multiple-boot system, select Windows XP Professional or Windows XP Home Edition from the OS Choices startup menu. While starting up, your computer might briefly display information about startup operations and technical specifications for your computer, or you might see a splash logo for your computer's manufacturer. Eventually, Windows XP displays a Welcome screen and prompts you to select your user name, as shown in *Figure A1-3*, or it might display a Log On to Windows dialog box instead.
>
> TROUBLE? If you are working in a computer lab, your instructor and lab support staff will supply you with a user name and password.

TROUBLE? If you do not see a Welcome screen or a Log On to Windows dialog box, then Windows XP has automatically logged you onto your computer.

TROUBLE? If you do not see the Welcome screen, this feature is turned off, and you log onto your computer using the standard Log On to Windows dialog box.

TROUBLE? If you are working on a network domain, you might need to press Ctrl+Alt+Del before you can log onto your computer.

Figure A1-3	WINDOWS XP WELCOME SCREEN

2. If Windows XP displays a Welcome screen, click your **user account** icon, and if Windows XP prompts you for your password, type your **password**, and then press the **Enter** key or click the **Next** ➜ button. If Windows XP displays a Log On to Windows dialog box, enter your **user name** (if necessary), type your **password** (if you use a password), and then press the **Enter** key, or click the **OK** button. Windows XP loads your personal settings and then displays the desktop. See *Figure A1-4*. If you purchased a computer that was customized by the manufacturer, or if you or someone else has already customized your computer, your desktop will differ from the one shown in this figure.

TROUBLE? If you do not remember your password, and if you are logging onto your computer from the Welcome screen, you can click the Password Hint ? button, and Windows XP will display a hint to remind you of your password if you specified a hint or provided one to your network administrator.

TROUBLE? If Windows XP displays an MSN Explorer dialog box informing you that no one is set up to use MSN Explorer on your computer and prompting you to click "Add New User" to create a user account, click the Close ⊗ button in the MSN Explorer dialog box, and then click the Close ⊠ button in the MSN dialog box. Unfortunately, Windows XP might continue to redisplay these dialog boxes periodically, and you might need to close them to continue working with your computer. If Windows XP displays a "Take a tour of Windows XP" informational Help balloon, click its Close button ⊠.

| Figure A1-4 | WINDOWS XP DESKTOP |

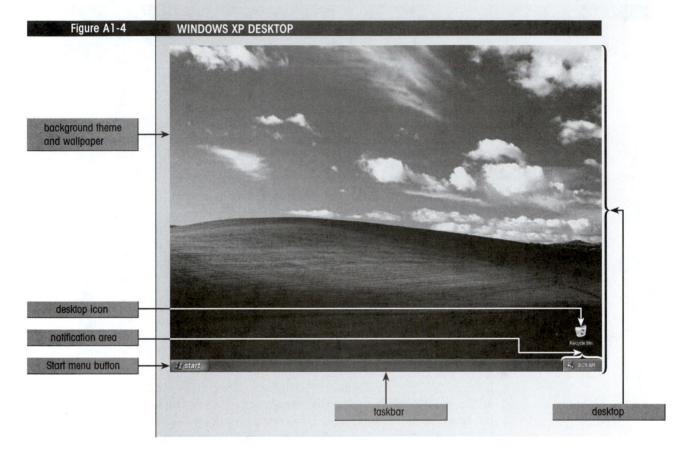

If your computer is a member of a network **domain**, a group of computers on a network that share a common directory database, each user is assigned to a group, which in turn provides each user with rights and permissions granted to the group by the network administrator. Each domain has a unique name and is administered as a unit with common rules and procedures. A **group** can consist of a set of users, computers, contacts, and even other groups. A **right** is a task that a user can perform on a computer or within a domain. For example, the administrator might grant a user the right to log onto a computer locally. A **permission** is a rule that determines which users can access an object and how they can access that object. For example, a network administrator might grant some users the permission to use a printer and others the permission to use and manage the printer.

In a domain, a user can belong to any of the following groups: Administrators, Power Users, Users, Backup Operators, Guests, or Replicator.

■ **Administrators Group**—Users have full access to the computer and can install an operating system, update or upgrade the operating system, configure and troubleshoot the operating system, manage the security of the computer system, and back up and restore the computer system.

- **Power Users Group**—Users can install software that does not modify the operating system, customize or make changes to some system settings and system resources (such as power options), and create and manage local user accounts and groups.

- **Users Group**—Users cannot modify the operating system, its settings, or data belonging to other users, and therefore this account is considered the most secure.

- **Backup Operators Group**—Users can back up and restore files on a computer, but cannot change security settings.

- **Guests Group**—Users can log onto a computer and use the computer, but with limits.

- **Replicator Group**—Users can replicate files across a domain.

The same types of user groups are also found in Windows 2000 Professional.

Instead of belonging to a domain, users might belong to a **workgroup**, which consists of a group of computers that provide users with access to printers and other shared resources, such as shared folders, on the network. Or a user might have a user account on a standalone computer that is not connected to other computers within a network. On a workgroup or standalone computer, there are three types of user accounts: Computer Administrator, Limited, and Guest.

- **Computer Administrator**—Users can make changes to the computer system, including creating and removing other user accounts, install software, and access all files on a computer. Windows XP creates a Computer Administrator account for you during installation, and uses the Administrator password you provide during setup.

- **Limited**—Users cannot install hardware or software, or change the account name or account type. A member with this type of account can use software already installed on the computer, and can make some changes to their account, such as changing their password or picture.

- **Guest**—An account that allows users who do not already have a user account to log onto and use the computer. There is no password for a Guest account.

If you are the only user for a computer, your user account is a Computer Administrator account that gives you full access to the computer. If you create multiple accounts when you install Windows XP, each account is a Computer Administrator account. However, it is a good idea to create another account with limited access, and to use that account, especially when you connect to the Internet, in order to prevent unauthorized access and changes to your system. If you log onto your computer as an Administrator and then connect to the Internet, a hacker who gains access to your computer has full access to your computer system. You are also vulnerable to **Trojan horses**, programs that appear to be *bona fide* programs, but which are designed to retrieve information from your computer, such as user names and passwords, and then transmit that information to others who then can subsequently access your computer via an Internet connection.

To further protect your computer, use a password that contains at least 7 to 14 characters, and that contains letters of the alphabet (both uppercase and lowercase), numerals, and symbols. Use at least one symbol as the second through sixth character. Your password should not be a common name or word, and you should not repeat previously used passwords. Although Windows XP supports passwords that are up to 127 characters long, use passwords that are 7 to 14 characters long if you have other computers in your network that are running either Windows 95 or Windows 98, because they do not support longer passwords.

The Windows XP Desktop

Windows XP uses the desktop as the starting point for accessing and using the resources and tools on your computer. With previous versions of Windows, the desktop contained icons for My Computer, My Documents, My Network Places (called Network Neighborhood in Windows 95, and Network in Windows 98), Internet Explorer, Microsoft Outlook, and the Recycle Bin. If you upgrade from a previous version of Windows, your Windows XP desktop contains the same icons as before. If you purchase a new computer with Windows XP Professional or Home Edition, the Recycle Bin is the only icon on the desktop, unless the manufacturer customized the desktop. However, you can still place the standard desktop icons found in previous versions of Windows on the desktop, and you can add shortcuts to the desktop. As you install software and hardware, icons for those products might also be placed on the desktop.

Microsoft has reorganized the Start menu in Windows XP so that the Start menu consists of two panels, each separated into groups. See *Figure A1-5*. On the left panel of the Start menu shown in *Figure A1-5*, Internet MSN Explorer and E-mail with Microsoft Outlook are listed above the separator line in an area called the **pinned items list**. Items in this area always remain on the Start menu. Your e-mail option might indicate that you use MSN Explorer instead of Microsoft Outlook.

Under the separator line, Windows XP lists the most frequently used programs in an area called the **most frequently used programs list**. Located at the bottom of the left panel, you can display the All Programs menu from which you can choose a system tool, such as Windows Update, or open an application.

From the right panel, you can open the My Documents, My Pictures, My Music, My Computer, or My Network Places folders, or use My Recent Documents, if displayed, to open a recently used document. You can also open the Control Panel or Printers and Faxes folders, connect to MSN Explorer, or display all connections. With Windows XP Home Edition, you might not have a Connect To option (though it can be added to the Start menu). You can open the Help and Support Center, which has been expanded to provide you with access to not only Help but also system settings. Search has been expanded so that you can search for pictures, music, video, documents, files, folders, computers, people, or even information in the Help and Support Center. As with previous versions of Windows, you can use Run to open a program, folder, document, or Web site.

You can also log off and turn off your computer from the Start menu. As you can see with this new release, the focal point has shifted from the desktop to the Start menu.

Figure A1-5   WINDOWS XP START MENU

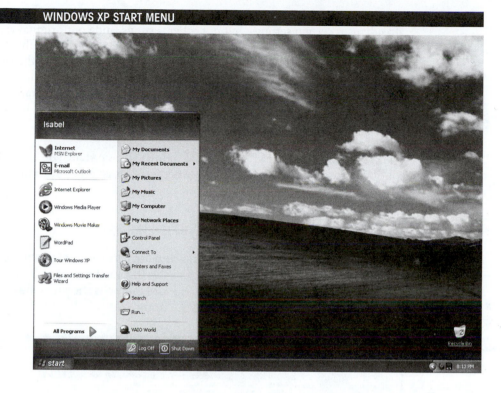

In addition to displaying the Start button and **notification area** (formerly called the system tray), the taskbar retains the same features and functions found in earlier versions of Windows. The notification area contains not only the current time, but also icons for programs loaded in the background. If you have not used an icon in the notification area for a while, Windows XP hides the icon. You can click the Show Hidden Icons ⓒ button to display icons that are hidden from view.

Although Microsoft has redesigned the desktop, Start menu, and taskbar, you should feel at home with Windows XP, because you still have access to the same basic Windows user interface and the same basic features found in previous versions of Windows.

Changing to Windows Classic Style

Windows XP provides you with a new way of interacting with your computer called **Web style**. With Web style, you can navigate your computer as you would navigate the World Wide Web using hypertext links. You select an object by pointing to the object (you do not need to click the object to select it) and you open an object with a single click as you would with a hypertext link.

In contrast, earlier versions of Windows defaulted to the Windows Classic view or style originally found in Windows 95. That meant you clicked an object to select it, and you double-clicked an object to open it.

Although these two different styles do not affect the way in which you work within a command-line environment, you should be familiar with these styles so that you can choose the style that best suits your needs.

If you or the organization for which you work prefer that you use the Windows Classic style, you can switch to that style by making four changes to the user interface:

■ Apply the Windows Classic theme

■ Change the Start menu style to the Windows Classic Start menu

■ Apply the Windows Classic folders option

■ Select the option for double-clicking icons to open objects

As you perform the following tutorial steps, you might discover that your computer already uses certain settings, but not other settings, and your original view of the user interface was a mix of Web style and Windows Classic style. Remember which settings your computer uses so that you can restore those settings at the end of the tutorial.

If you are working in a computer lab, make sure you have permission to change desktop settings. If necessary, ask your instructor or technical support staff before you complete these steps. If you are not allowed to change desktop settings, read, but do not complete, the steps in this section. However, review the figures so that you are familiar with the features described in these steps.

If your computer already uses the Windows Classic style, you can still work through the following tutorial steps to determine whether all four types of changes have been made to the user interface.

To apply the Windows Classic theme:

1. Right-click an empty area of the desktop, and then click **Properties** from the shortcut menu. Windows XP opens the Display Properties dialog box as shown in *Figure A1-6*. The name of the current theme is shown in the Theme list box. Note which theme is used on your computer.

Figure A1-6	CHOOSING A DESKTOP THEME

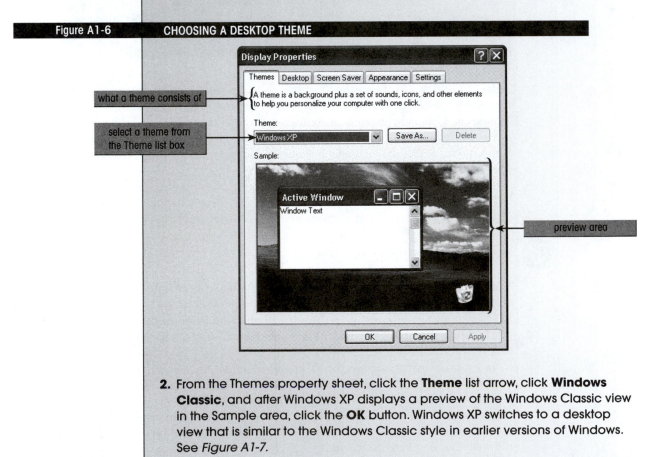

what a theme consists of

select a theme from the Theme list box

preview area

2. From the Themes property sheet, click the **Theme** list arrow, click **Windows Classic**, and after Windows XP displays a preview of the Windows Classic view in the Sample area, click the **OK** button. Windows XP switches to a desktop view that is similar to the Windows Classic style in earlier versions of Windows. See *Figure A1-7*.

Figure A1-7	WINDOWS CLASSIC DESKTOP THEME

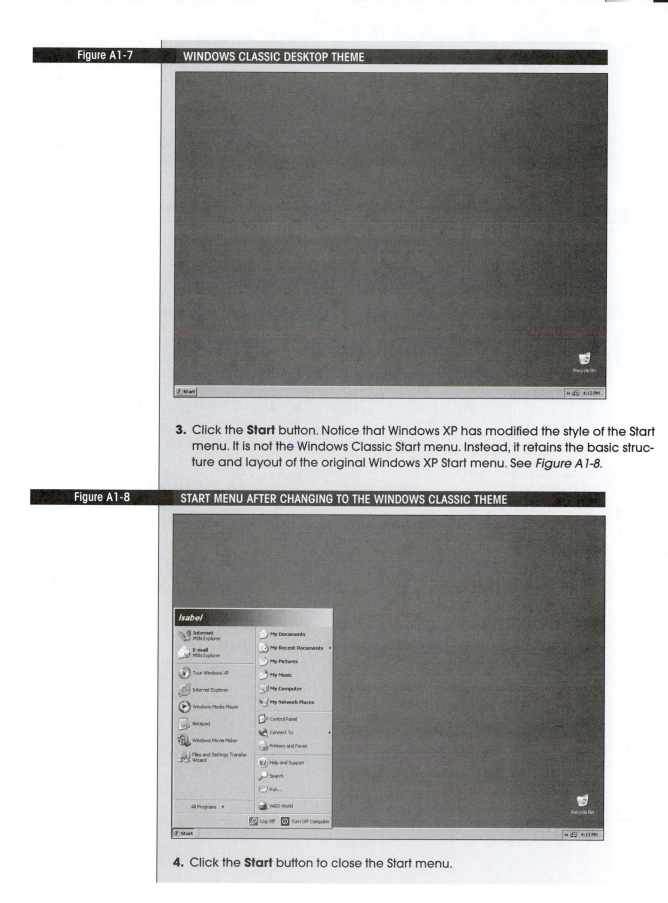

3. Click the **Start** button. Notice that Windows XP has modified the style of the Start menu. It is not the Windows Classic Start menu. Instead, it retains the basic structure and layout of the original Windows XP Start menu. See *Figure A1-8*.

Figure A1-8	START MENU AFTER CHANGING TO THE WINDOWS CLASSIC THEME

4. Click the **Start** button to close the Start menu.

The next step is to change the Start menu style to the Windows Classic Start menu. You can use the Start Menu property sheet to switch between the Windows XP Start menu style and the Windows Classic Start menu, and to customize the appearance of the Start menu.

To change the Start menu style:

1. Right-click the **Start** button, click **Properties**, and after Windows XP opens the Taskbar and Start Menu Properties dialog box, click the **Start Menu** tab if it is not already selected. See *Figure A1-9.*

Figure A1-9	START MENU PROPERTY SHEET

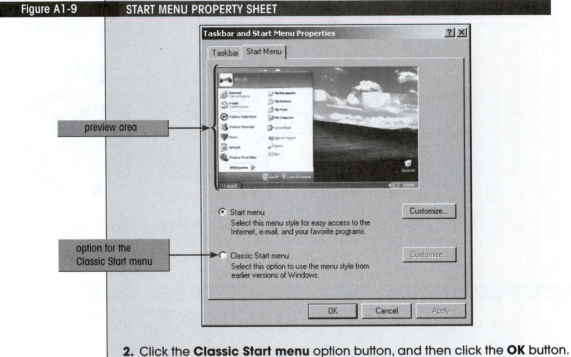

preview area

option for the Classic Start menu

2. Click the **Classic Start menu** option button, and then click the **OK** button. Windows XP adds icons for My Documents, My Computer, and My Network Places on the desktop. In the Windows XP Home Edition, you will also see an icon for Internet Explorer added to the desktop.

3. Click the **Start** button. Notice that the Start menu's appearance, structure, lay-out, and options appear more like the Start menu found in earlier versions of Windows. Windows XP, however, still retains the new Windows XP icons. See *Figure A1-10.*

Figure A1-10	VIEWING THE WINDOWS CLASSIC START MENU

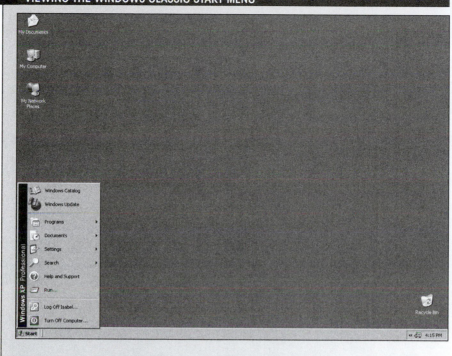

4. Click the **Start** button to close the Start menu.

Before you change to the Windows Classic folders view, examine the My Documents folder so that you can compare the task-oriented view found in Web style with the Windows Classic folders view. In the **task-oriented view**, Windows XP uses dynamic menus to display links to common folder tasks and other locations on your computer.

To change to Windows Classic folders and enable double-clicking:

1. Double-click the **My Documents** icon on the desktop. Windows XP displays the contents of the folder in task-oriented view. For this folder, Windows XP provides links to common File and Folder Tasks, as well as links to Other Places on your computer. See *Figure A1-11*.

Figure A1-11	TASK-ORIENTED VIEW WITH DYNAMIC MENUS

dynamic menu with task-oriented list

dynamic menu with links to other locations

2. Close the My Documents window.

3. Click the **Start** button, point to **Settings**, click **Control Panel**, and after Windows XP opens the Control Panel window, click **Switch to Classic View** in the Control Panel dynamic menu. Windows XP retains the dynamic menus so that you can switch back to Category View.

4. Double-click the **Folder Options** icon. Windows XP opens the Folder Options dialog box. See *Figure A1-12.*

Figure A1-12   FOLDER OPTIONS DIALOG BOX

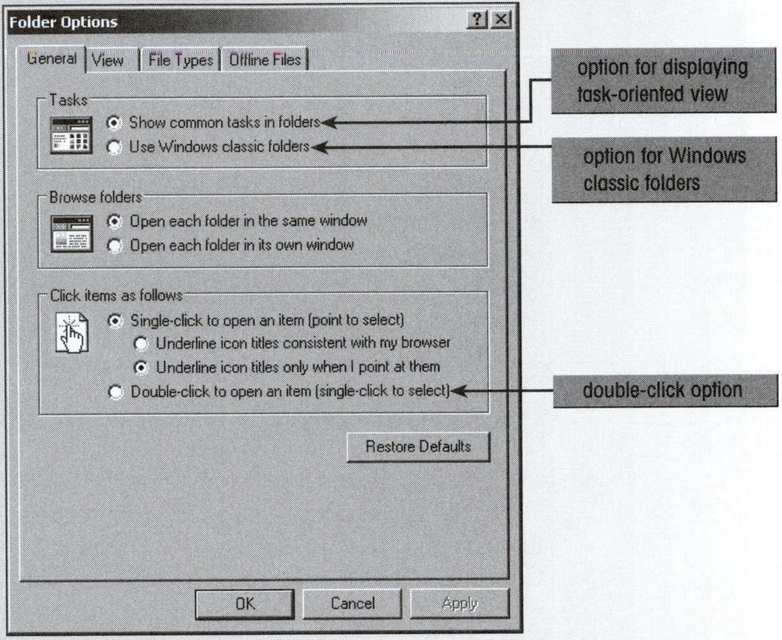

5. On the General property sheet, click **Use Windows classic folders** under Tasks, click the **Double-click to open an item** option button under the "Click items as follows" section if it is not already selected, and then click the **OK** button. You no longer see dynamic menus in the Control Panel.

6. Close the Control Panel, and then double-click the **My Documents** folder icon on the desktop. Windows XP no longer displays the task-oriented list and the links to Other Places on your computer in the folder window. See *Figure A1-13.*

Figure A1-13   WINDOWS CLASSIC FOLDERS VIEW

7. Close the My Documents window.

> ### REFERENCE WINDOW   RW
>
> <u>Changing to Windows Classic Style</u>
> - Right-click an empty area of the desktop, and then click Properties on the shortcut menu.
> - After Windows XP opens the Display Properties dialog box, click the Theme list box arrow on the Themes property sheet, click Windows Classic, and then click the OK button.
> - Right-click the Start button, click Properties, and after Windows XP opens the Taskbar and Start Menu Properties dialog box, click the Start Menu tab if it is not already selected.
> - Click the Classic Start menu option button, and then click the OK button.
> - Click the Start button, point to Settings, and then click Control Panel.
> - After Windows XP opens the Control Panel window, click the "Switch to Classic View" link in the Control Panel dynamic menu.
> - Double-click the Folder Options icon, and after Windows XP opens the Folder Options dialog box, click the "Use Windows classic folders" option button under Tasks on the General property sheet, click the "Double-click to open an item" option button under the "Click items as follows" section if it is not already selected, and then click the OK button.
> - Close the Control Panel.

You've modified the user interface so that it more closely resembles the Windows Classic view found in Windows 2000. Depending on your individual preferences, you might combine elements of Web style and Classic view.

 ## Changing to Web Style

To change your computer from Windows Classic style to Web style, you must reverse the changes you've made, namely:

- Apply the Windows XP theme
- Change the Start menu style
- Change to a task-oriented view of folders
- Select the option for single-clicking to open objects

If your computer originally used Web style (the default), you will likely want to switch back to that style. If your computer originally used Windows Classic style, you may want to read, but not complete, the following steps so that you can continue to work in Windows Classic style.

If you are working in a computer lab, make sure you have permission to change desktop settings. If necessary, ask your instructor or technical support staff before you continue with this tutorial. If you are not allowed to change desktop settings, read, but do not complete, the following steps. However, you should review the figures so that you are familiar with the features described in these steps.

To apply the Windows XP theme:

1. Right-click an empty area of the desktop, and then click **Properties** from the shortcut menu.

2. After Windows XP opens the Display Properties dialog box, click the **Theme** list arrow on the Themes property sheet, click **Windows XP**, and then click the **OK** button. Windows XP applies the Windows XP theme to the desktop.

   TROUBLE? If Windows XP does not display the original desktop wallpaper used on your computer, right-click an empty area of the desktop, click Properties, click the Desktop tab in the Display Properties dialog box, locate and select that desktop wallpaper in the Background list box, and then click the OK button.

Now you can change the Windows Classic Start menu style back to the Windows XP Start menu style.

To change the Start menu style:

1. Right-click the **Start** button, click **Properties**, and after Windows XP opens the Taskbar and Start Menu Properties dialog box, click the **Start Menu** tab if it is not already selected.

2. Click the **Start menu** option button, and then click the **OK** button. Windows XP removes the My Documents, My Computer, My Network Places, and Internet Explorer icons (if previously displayed) from the desktop and switches to the Windows XP Start menu style.

Next, change the Windows Classic folders view back to a task-oriented view and enable single-clicking.

To change to a task-oriented view of folders and enable single-clicking:

1. Click the **Start** button, click **Control Panel**, and then double-click the **Folder Options** icon in the Control Panel window. Windows XP opens the Folder Options dialog box.

2. On the General property sheet, click **Show common tasks in folders** under Tasks, click the **Single-click to open an item** option button if it is not already selected, click the **Underline icon titles only when I point at them** option button if it is not already selected, and then click the **OK** button. Note that Windows XP has restored the dynamic menus in the Control Panel window.

3. Click the **Switch to Category View** link in the Control Panel dynamic menu, and then close the Control Panel.

REFERENCE   WINDOW   **RW**

Changing to Web Style

- Right-click on an empty area of the desktop, and then click Properties on the shortcut menu.
- After Windows XP opens the Display Properties dialog box, click the Theme list box arrow on the Themes property sheet, click Windows XP, and then click the OK button. *Note*: If you want to apply a different desktop wallpaper option, choose that wallpaper option from the Background list box on the Desktop property sheet in the Display Properties dialog box before closing it.
- Right-click the Start button, click Properties, and after Windows XP opens the Taskbar and Start Menu Properties dialog box, click the Start Menu tab if it is not already selected.
- Click the Start menu option button, and then click the OK button.
- Click the Start button, click Control Panel, and then double-click the Folder Options icon in the Control Panel window.
- After Windows XP opens the Folder Options dialog box, click "Show common tasks in folders" under Tasks on the General property sheet, click the "Single-click to open an item" option button if it is not already selected, click the "Underline icon titles only when I point at them" option button if it is not already selected, click the OK button, and then close the Control Panel.
- Click the "Switch to Category View" link in the Control Panel dynamic menu, and then close the Control Panel.

Now you've restored your computer to the default Windows XP Web style. As you've seen, Web style simplifies the way you work with Windows XP, and allows you to use your Web browsing skills within the Windows XP user interface.

[UPDATE] Opening a Command Line Session

The process for opening a Command Prompt window is slightly different with Windows XP. The command interpreter will display a different Windows version number in the Command Prompt window, and the command prompt will show the full path to your user account directory instead of the root directory. :

> ■ **Page 24, Step 1:** The Programs menu is now listed on the Start menu as "All Programs". After you open a Command Prompt window, the command interpreter identifies the version of Windows XP you are using. In addition, the default operating system prompt or command prompt shows the path for the directory for your user account instead of the path for the root directory. *Figure A1-14* shows that Isabel is using the original version of Windows XP Professional, Version 5.1.2600. The path to Isabel's user account directory is located under the Documents and Settings directory. Yours will differ. So that your screen more closely matches the figures shown in the text, type CD \ and then press the Enter key to change to the root directory. CD is the Change Directory command, and you will learn more about it in Tutorial 4.

Figure A1-14	**COMMAND PROMPT WINDOW**

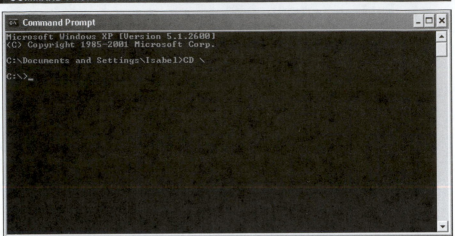

■ **Page 30, Step 1:** The Version command (VER) reports that you are using Windows XP and a specific version of Windows XP. As noted in the last bullet, Version 5.1.2600 is the original version of Windows XP.

Logging Off, or Turning Off, Your Computer

Once you have finished working with Windows XP, you can do one of two things: You can shut your computer down, or if you are connected to a network, you can log off your user account. If you are working on a company network, on a network in a computer lab, or on your own home network, you can use the Log Off option to display the Welcome screen or the Log On to Windows dialog box. Then you or someone else can log onto the computer and network later.

If you are working in a computer lab, do not shut down your computer unless your instructor or technical support staff has specifically requested you to do so. If you are unsure of what to do, check with your instructor or technical support staff. *Most computer labs prefer that you do not turn off the computers for any reason.* Typically, the computer lab support staff is responsible for turning the computer systems on and off.

To log off, or turn off, your computer:

1. If you want to log off your own computer, or if you are working in a computer lab and want to log off the computer you are using, click the **Start** button, click the **Log Off** button, and then click the **Log Off** button in the Log Off Windows dialog box. Windows XP displays the Welcome screen or a Log On to Windows dialog box.

2. If you are using your own computer and want to turn off the computer, open the Start menu, click the **Turn Off Computer** button, and in the Turn off computer dialog box, click the **Turn Off** button.

If you are working on a company network, it is a good idea to log off when you finish your work so that no one else can access files via your account. Also, when you are ready to shut down a computer at the end of the day, it is important to use the Turn Off Computer option so that Windows XP can save important settings to disk and properly shut down your computer.

DISPLAYING DIRECTORIES

Session 2.1

The first session in Tutorial 2 describes how to use the Directory command to display information about the directories and files stored on a disk. Because Windows XP defaults to a different directory when you open a Command Prompt window, you must change directories.

Displaying a Directory Listing

So that the view in your Command Prompt window match those shown in the figures, complete the following operation after you complete Step 2 on Page 53:

- **Page 53, Step 3 and Figure 2-1:** You must first switch to the root directory. Type CD \ and then press the Enter key to change to the root directory. Then, complete Step 3 on Page 53. Also, the Windows directory is likely to be named "Windows" instead of "Winnt".

Session 2.2

The second session in Tutorial 2 covers advanced command line switches and the use of wildcards in file specifications. As described in the next section, there are some minor differences that you might notice.

Using Sort Order Parameters

Note the following differences when examining Figure 2-12 and Figure 2-15:

- **Page 67, Step 2, and Page 68, Figure 2-12:** Although files are still organized by file extension, the order in which files are listed differs from that shown in the figure. For example, files with the "bmp" file extension are listed in the order "Palette #1.bmp," "Color Palette.bmp," "Colors of the Rainbow.bmp," and "Palette #2.bmp," instead of the order "Palette #2.bmp," "Palette #1.bmp," "Colors of the Rainbow.bmp," and "Color Palette.bmp" (as shown in the figure).
- **Page 70, Step 1, and Figure 2-15:** For files that are the same size, the file order differs. For example, the three files with a file size of 24,064 bytes are listed as "File0000.chk," "Break Even Analysis.xls," and "Sales Projection Models.xls" instead of "Break Even Analysis.xls," "Sales Projection Models.xls," and "File0000.chk" (as shown in the figure).

UPDATE Displaying Short Filenames

You might note the following minor difference when examining Figure 2-18:

- **Page 74, Figure 2-18:** In this figure, there are blank lines between some of the entries in the directory listing. These blank lines are caused by filenames that are longer than the width of the window and that wrap to the next line. You might see additional files displayed in the Command Prompt window.

UPDATE Displaying a Directory Using File Attributes

The following notes describe differences that you might notice when examining these figures:

- **Page 76, Figure 2-21:** You will not see a RECYCLER folder.
- **Page 77, Figure 2-22:** You will not see a RECYCLER folder, and if your computer does not have the MS-DOS startup configuration files Config.sys and Autoexec.bat, they do not appear in the directory listing.

WORKING WITH FILES

Session 3.1

As you work through Session 3.1 and Session 3.2 in Tutorial 3, you will discover that Windows XP is remarkably similar to Windows 2000 when performing file operations. However, you might notice one difference that is not unique to Windows XP, but might also be observed when using Windows 2000.

UPDATE Piping Output to the MORE Filter

The following note provides additional information on Readme files included with software products:

■ **Page 103, paragraph following the Reference Window:** If you use the Type command to view the contents of a Readme file with an "htm" or "html" file extension, such as the Readme.htm in the root directory of the Windows XP CD, you will see the HTML code in the text-based HTML file.

HELP Sorting ASCII Text Files

You might note a difference in the location of one of the files shown in the directory listing for Figure 3-13:

■ **Page 108, Step 2, and Figure 3-13:** Since the date you created the Templates.txt file more than likely differs from that shown in the figure, this file appears at a different position in the redirected input.

HELP Redirecting Output to the Printer

The command interpreter and your printer might not respond when redirecting output to your printer port:

■ **Page 115, Step 4:** If you enter this command and nothing happens, complete these steps:
  1. Close the Command Prompt window.
  2. Open the Command Prompt window.
  3. Change the background and foreground colors.
  4. Switch to the root directory, and then switch to drive A.
  5. Complete the directions in the first Trouble to print a copy of the directory listing.
■ **Page 116, Reference Window:** If you redirect output of the Directory command to PRN and nothing happens, close the Command Prompt window, open it again, redirect output of the Directory command to a file on disk, and use Notepad to print the contents of the file.

USING DIRECTORIES AND SUBDIRECTORIES

Session 4.2

As you step through both Session 4.1 and Session 4.2 in Tutorial 4, you will discover that Windows XP is remarkably similar to Windows 2000 when working with directories and subdirectories. If your Windows directory is named Windows instead of Winnt, you will see "Windows" in the command prompt path when working in that subdirectory or when viewing a directory listing for the Windows directory.

Stepping Down a Directory Tree

You will observe the following difference between the contents of your Windows directory and the one shown for Windows 2000:

- **Page 157, Step 6 and Figure 4-31:** Your System32 directory might contain close to twice as many directories and files as compared to Windows 2000.

Case 4: Investigating Advertising Images at Turing Enterprises

Because the total size of the files in the Wallpaper directory exceeds the capacity of a floppy disk, you must modify one step in this case problem:

- **Page 168, Step 10:** The collective size of all the files in the Windows XP Wallpaper directory exceeds the storage capacity of a floppy disk, and the Bliss.bmp file used by Windows XP as the default desktop wallpaper fills an entire floppy disk. Instead of copying all the files in the Wallpaper directory, copy five files of your choosing that are each less than 100 KB in size to the Windows Images directory on your floppy disk.

A

auditing

Tracking events, such as attempts to log onto a computer and to access files and other network components, so there is a record of all operations that affect the network

C

Category view

A new Windows XP view that organizes windows components into related categories

Credential Manager

A Windows component that secures and automatically provides your user name and password to applications (such as e-mail software), services (such as your ISP), and Web sites that request that information so that you do not have to repeatedly specify the same information

D

Device Driver Rollback

A Windows component that replaces a newly installed device driver that does not work properly with a previously working version of that same device driver

dynamic menu

A new Windows XP component of folder windows that displays a menu of options related to your current task or the contents of the window, and that provides links to other places on your computer

Dynamic Update

The process of downloading updates to Windows XP during the installation of Windows XP on a computer

F

Fast User Switching

A new Windows XP feature that enables a user to remain logged onto their user account with open applications and documents while another user logs onto their user account on the same computer

Filmstrip view

A new Windows XP view that displays thumbnail images of images contained within the files in the folder at the bottom of a window and that also displays a full-screen view of the currently selected thumbnail

G

group

A set of users, computers, contacts, and even other groups with a network domain

H

hop

One of a sequence of router connections between networked computers

I

Internet Connection Firewall

A new Windows XP component that protects your computer from intruders and hackers while you are connected to the Internet

Itanium

A processor that can perform up to 20 operations simultaneously, and that can preload data into virtual memory for faster access and processing

M

most frequently used programs list

The bottom portion of the left panel of the Windows XP Start menu that contains a list of the most frequently used programs you have used

N

Network Location Awareness

A new Windows XP service that allows the operating system and applications to determine when a computer has changed its network location

Network Setup Wizard

A Windows XP component that steps you through the process of creating a home network so that your networked computers can share peripherals (such as a printer), software, and files, and use Internet Connection Sharing to share a single Internet connection

Notification area

The right-hand area of the Windows XP taskbar with the digital clock and icons for applications loaded during booting (formerly called the system tray)

P

pinned items list

The upper portion of the left panel on the Windows XP Start menu that contains options for accessing the Internet and using your e-mail software, and that might can also contain shortcuts to other tasks

R

Remote Assistance

A new Windows XP component that enables another user who also uses Windows XP to remotely connect to your computer to assist you with a project or to troubleshoot a problem

Remote Desktop

A new Windows XP component that allows you to access and use another computer from a computer running Windows 95 or later

right

A task that a user can perform on a computer or within a domain, such as logging onto a computer locally

S

Show in Groups

A new Windows XP view that organizes the contents of a folder window in groups

Side-by-side DLLs

A new Windows XP feature that maintains different versions of the same DLL (Dynamic Link Library) program file used by different applications

skin

A design scheme for changing the look of Windows Media Player

system checkpoint

A representation of the state of your computer system at a specific point in time that includes changes to system files, device drivers, and system settings

System Restore

A Windows component that periodically saves information regarding changes to the configuration of your computer system, operating system files, and devices drivers, so that if you make a change to your computer and then encounter a problem, you can "roll back" your computer system to an earlier functioning state

T

taskbar grouping

A new Windows XP feature that combines all the taskbar buttons for documents opened with the same application into one taskbar button labeled with the name of the application.

task-oriented view

A view in which Windows XP uses dynamic menus to display links to common folder tasks and other locations on your computer

Tiles view

Large Icons view in previous versions of Windows

Trojan horse

A program that appears to be a bona fide program, but which is designed to retrieve information from your computer, such as user names and passwords, and then transmit that information to others who then can access your computer via an Internet connection

U

User State Migration Tool

A new Windows XP Professional tool for migrating a user's data, operating system settings, and application settings from one computer to another computer

W

WebTV

A Windows technology for viewing television program broadcasts over the Internet with a TV tuner card

Windows 9x

The operating system product line that includes Windows 95, Windows 98, and Windows ME

Windows Image Acquisition

A Windows technology for obtaining images from a scanner or digital camera

Windows Media Player

A Windows component for listening to music CDs with on-screen visualizations of sounds, creating music libraries, playing movies, and listening to Internet radio stations

Windows Messenger

A Windows instant messaging application that allows you to find out who is online, send an instant message, engage of a group of friends in an online conversation, invite someone who is online to play a game, dial a contact's computer, send one or more files to someone else, and, if you have a HotMail account, receive a notification when new e-mail arrives

Windows Movie Maker

A Windows component for editing and enhancing video and home movies

APPENDIX TASK REFERENCE

TASK	PAGE #	RECOMMENDED METHOD
Web style, changing to	189	See Reference Window "Changing to Web Style"
Windows Classic style, changing to	187	See Reference Window "Changing to Windows Classic Style"

Windows XP File Finder

As you complete the tutorials in the textbook with Windows XP, you will use the same data disks, folders, and files, and you will create the same folders and files as listed in the Windows 2000 File Finder at the end of the textbook. However, for the following end-of-chapter exercises, you will work with a different set of files or with additional files.

Location in Tutorial	Name and Location of Data File	Student Creates New File
Tutorial 4 Case 4	C:\Windows\Web\Wallpaper [Five files that are each less than 100 KB in size]	Windows Images (directory) [Directory Structure.txt]

* (asterisk wildcard)

A symbol used as part of a directory or file specification to substitute for any number of characters in the directory name, filename, or file extension, starting from the position of the asterisk

. ("dot")

A symbol for the current directory in a directory listing, which can be used as a shortcut to specify the current directory

.. ("dot dot")

A symbol for the parent directory of the current directory in a directory listing, which can be used as a shortcut to specify the parent directory of the current directory

? (question mark wildcard)

A symbol used as part of a file specification to substitute for a single character in the directory name, filename, or file extension

\ (backslash symbol)

A symbol for the -root directory, or top-level folder, on a disk

> (output redirection operator)

An operator that redirects the output of a command to a file, the printer port, or another device, instead of to the monitor

< (input redirection operator)

An operator that uses input from a source other than the keyboard, such as a file

>> (append output redirection operator)

An operator that appends the output of a command to an existing file

A

A:

The device name for the first floppy drive in a computer

absolute path

The use of the full path to identify the exact location of a folder or file, starting from the root directory

active content

Web content that changes periodically

algorithm

A formula or procedure for calculating or producing a result, such as determining an alias or MS-DOS name from a long name

allocation unit

(1) One or more sectors used by an operating system as the minimum storage space for a file or part of a file when it allocates storage space on a drive to the file; (2) a cluster

ANSI (American National Standards Institute)

A character set that supports characters from different languages

append output redirection operator (>>)

An operator that appends the output of a command to an existing file

application-oriented

An operating mode in which you open the software application you want to use, then you locate and open the document you want to use

archive

(1) To store less frequently used files on a storage medium, such as diskettes, recordable CDs, or Zip disks; (2) A file that contains one or more other files within it

Archive attribute

An attribute assigned to a file by the operating system to indicate a newly created or modified file, so that a backup utility can identify files to back up

ASCII

The abbreviation for "American Standard Code for Information Interchange," a seven-bit coding scheme for representing 128 character codes, including the uppercase and lowercase letters of the American alphabet, digits, and a limited set of symbols and control codes.

ASCII code

The numerical code for an ASCII character

ASCII text file

A simple file format in which data is stored as text

ASCII value

see "ASCII code"

asterisk wildcard (*)

A symbol used as part of a directory or file specification to substitute for any number of characters in the directory name, filename, or file extension, starting from the position of the asterisk

attribute

(1) An optional parameter for the COLOR command; (2) A special characteristic, such as System, Hidden, Read-Only, Archive, Directory, Compress, Encrypt, or Index, assigned to a folder or file by the operating system

B

backslash (\)

A symbol for the root directory, or top-level folder, on a disk

backward compatibility

The ability of an operating system to handle hardware and software designed for earlier types of computers, microprocessors, and operating systems

binary file

A file that can contain any kind of data, rather than just ASCII text

boot disk

A disk, such as a hard disk or a diskette in drive A, that contains the core operating system files needed to start a computer

booting

The process of powering on a computer system and loading the operating system into memory so it can configure the computer system and manage the basic processes of the computer, including providing support for applications

byte

(1) The storage space required on disk or in memory for one character; (2) a combination of eight binary digits, or bits, used to encode commonly used characters, including letters of the alphabet, numbers, and symbols

C

C:

The device name for the first hard disk drive in a computer

clock speed, or **clock rate**

The speed at which a microprocessor executes instructions, measured in megahertz (MHz)—millions of cycles per second

Clipboard

An area of memory where Windows temporarily stores data for copy or move operations

Clone

(1) an IBM-compatible computer that works like an IBM computer; (2) a computer program on one platform that works like another computer program on another platform

cluster

(1) One or more sectors used by an operating system as the minimum storage space for a file or part of a file when it allocates storage space on a drive to the file; (2) an allocation unit

command

An instruction to perform a task, issued by a user to a program

command history

An area of memory where Windows 2000 and Windows XP keep track of the last 50 commands entered at the command prompt

command interpreter, or **command processor**

A program that displays a command prompt, interprets commands entered at the command prompt, locates and loads the appropriate program from memory or disk, and then executes the program

command line interface

A text or character-based user interface with an operating system prompt at which you type commands in order to interact with the operating system and instruct it to perform a task

command line session

A window in which you use the command prompt and MS-DOS commands

command prompt

The operating system prompt (for example, C:\>) displayed on the screen or in a Command Prompt window to identify the current drive and directory and used as an interface for interacting with the operating system

command stack

A small area of memory used by the command processor to store the command history

computer virus

A program that gains access to your computer, makes copies of itself, and that can adversely affect the use or performance of a computer system, or even damage the computer

configure

The process by which the operating system loads and installs the software that it needs to interact with the hardware and software on your computer

console

(1) A video display device, or monitor; (2) An administrative program, or snap-in, for managing the hardware, software, and network components of your computer system.

control code

An ASCII code for the use of the Ctrl (Control) key with another key; e.g. Ctrl+i for the Tab code

current directory

In a Command Prompt window, the directory in which you are currently working, which is identified in the command prompt and which becomes the default directory for commands that do not specify an alternate directory

cursor

A blinking underscore character (_) or a small solid rectangle that identifies your current working position on the screen and marks where the next typed character will appear on the screen

customize

To set up a computer system to meet a specific set of user needs, such as loading antivirus software during booting

D

Date stamp

The date assigned to a file by the operating system

default directory

(1) The starting directory used by the operating system; (2) the directory in which a command operates unless the user specifies a different directory

default drive

(1) The starting drive used by the operating system; (2) The drive Windows uses to locate commands and files if no other drive is specified; (3) the current working drive

destination disk

The disk to which files are copied

destination file

A new file produced by the operating system during a copy operation

device

A hardware component

device driver

A file with program code that enables the operating system to communicate with, manage, and control the operation of a specific hardware or software component

device name

A name Windows assigns to a hardware component or "device"

dialog box

A component of the graphical user interface that displays information, lists objects properties and settings, or that provides options from which to choose as you perform a command operation

DIP (Dual In-Line Package) switches

A set of toggle switches that are mounted on a chip, which is in turn mounted on an add-in board, and that are used to specify the configuration for a hardware device

directory

A specialized file that contains information about files or other directories; also known as a folder

Directory attribute

An attribute assigned to a file by the operating system to indicate a directory or subdirectory

Directory listing

A list of directory and filenames, file sizes, file dates, and file times, and other information displayed by the DIR command

directory tree

A diagrammatic representation of the directory structure of a disk

disk order

The order in which the file system keeps track of files on a diskette or hard disk

document-oriented approach

An approach, or operating mode, in which you locate and open the document you want to use, and then the operating system automatically opens the program originally used to produce that document or the program currently associated with that document type

DOS

The abbreviation for *Disk Operating System*, the primary operating system software used on IBM and IBM-compatible microcomputers from 1981 to 1995

DOS prompt

The command line interface for interacting with DOS

dual-boot computer, or dual-boot configuration

A computer with two installed operating systems, one of which you choose during booting

E

end-of-file code (EOF), or end-of-file marker

(1) A control code, [Ctrl][Z], that marks the end of an ASCII file; (2) the code in the File Allocation Table that identifies a cluster as the last cluster in use by a specific file

environment variable

A symbolic name associated with a setting or sequence of characters (such as the name of the operating system), and stored in the Windows environment to make information available to programs

executable, or executable file

A file that contains program code which the operating system can load into memory and run

extended ASCII

A variation of the ASCII code that uses 8 bits to encode characters and contains values ranging from 0 (zero) to 255

external command

A command whose program code is stored in a file on disk

F

file

(1) A collection of data, such as a program or document, stored in a folder on disk; (2) the storage space on a disk that is set aside for the contents of a program, document, or data file

file extension

One or more characters included after a period at the end of the main part of a filename, typically used to identify the type of data in the file

file specification

The use of a drive name, path, directory name, filename, and wildcards to select one or more directories or files

file system

The features built into an operating system, and the data structures used by the operating system, for naming, organizing, storing, and tracking folders and files on disks

filter

A command that modifies the output of another command

folder

The graphical user interface term for a directory. See "directory"

format capacity

The storage capacity of a drive or disk

full format

A type of format used on new or formatted diskettes that defines the tracks and sectors on the disk; creates a boot sector, new File Allocation Tables, and a new directory file; and performs a surface scan for defects in the disk

full path (also called the MS-DOS path)

A notation that identifies the exact location of a file or folder on a disk by specifying the drive and folders (and, if needed, the filename) that lead to the desired folder or file

G

graphical user interface (GUI)

An interface that operates in graphics mode and that provides a pictorial method for interacting with the operating system through the use of icons, multiple windows, menus with task-related lists, dialog boxes, and a mouse

H

hardware

The physical components of a computer system

Help switch

An optional parameter (/?) which, when used with the command for an operating system or program, displays any available Help information included with the program

Help system

Information included within an operating system or program on its use and features

hexadecimal digit

A value in the hexadecimal, or base 16, numbering system

Hidden attribute

An attribute which indicates that the icon and name of a folder or file should not be displayed in a directory listing

hyperlink

A link between one object and another on a computer or the Web

I

icon

An image or picture displayed on the screen to represent hardware and software resources (such as drives, disks, applications, and files) as well as system tools (such as "My Computer") on your computer that you can open and use

initialization file

A file that contains system settings or settings used by the operating system or by a specific program when it loads into memory

input

The process of providing program instructions, commands, and data to a computer system so that it can accomplish a specified task

insert redirection operator (<)

An operator that uses input from a source other than the keyboard such as a file

insert mode

The default keyboard mode, in which characters typed at the command prompt are inserted at the position of the cursor, and characters to the right of the cursor are shifted to the right

internal command

A command whose program code is contained in the command interpreter program (such as Cmd.exe or Command.com) and is available once the command interpreter loads into memory; also known as a built-in command

Internet Connection Sharing

A feature of certain versions of Windows that allows other computers on a local network to access the Internet through a connection on one main computer

J

jumper

A small metal block that completes a circuit by connecting two pins on a circuit board and, in the process, controls a hardware configuration

K

kernel

The portion of the operating system that resides in memory and provides services for applications, as distinguished from operating system programs run temporarily for specific purposes

L

legacy devices

Hardware devices that do not support the Plug and Play standards defined by Microsoft Corporation and hardware manufacturers, and which require manual installation, including, in many cases, setting jumpers or DIP switches; also now known as non-Plug and Play devices

long filename

A folder name or filename of up to 255 characters, which can contain spaces as well as uppercase and lowercase letters and certain symbols

LPT1, or LPT1:

The device name for the first Line Printer Port in a computer; also known as PRN

LPT2, or LPT2:

The device name for the second Line Printer Port in a computer

M

macro

A set of stored keystrokes or commands that can execute an operation or set of operations automatically

memory leak

A gradual decrease in available memory caused by program code that remains in memory after you exit an application and that ties up that memory so the operating system and other applications cannot use it

menu

A list of command choices or task-related options presented by a program

MORE filter (or command)

An external command that displays one screen of output, pauses, and then displays a prompt, that permits the user to view subsequent screens when ready

MS-DOS mode

A shell that emulates the MS-DOS operating environment using the Windows 2000 MS-DOS subsystem

MSN (The Microsoft Network)

An Internet Service Provider (ISP)

multimedia

The integration of video, audio, animation, graphics, and text

multitasking

An operating system feature that permits the user to open and run more than one application simultaneously

multithreading

The ability of an operating system to execute more than one operation within a single application simultaneously, or to execute the same operation multiple times

N

non-Plug and Play devices

See legacy devices

NUL device

A special device (also called a "bit bucket") used by the operating system as a target for discarded data

O

object

A component of your computer system, such as a hardware device, software application, document, or part of a document

object-oriented operating system

An operating system that treats each component of the computer as an object and that manages all the actions and properties associated with an object

operating environment

A software product that performs the same functions as an operating system, except for booting the computer and storing and retrieving data in files on a disk

operating system

A software product that manages the basic processes that occur within a computer, coordinates the interaction of hardware and software so that every component works together, and provides support for the use of other software, such as application software

operating system prompt

A set of characters displayed on the monitor to provide an interface for interacting with the computer. *See* command prompt.

output

To transmit the results of a computer process to the screen or to storage media; also, the results of a computer process

output redirection operator (>)

An operator that redirects the output of a command to a file, the printer port, or another device, instead of to the monitor

overtype mode

A keyboard mode in which new characters overwrite existing text as they are typed in

P

paging file

See swap file

parallel directories

Directories located at the same level within the directory tree

parameter

An optional or required item of data for a command, entered as part of the command line

parent directory

The directory located one level above the current directory

partition

(1) All or part of the physical hard disk that is set aside for a drive volume or set of logical drives, or (2) to divide a hard disk into one or more logical drive volumes

path

The sequence of drive, folder, and file names that identifies the location of a folder, a file, or object on a computer. *See* absolute path and relative path.

PCMCIA (Personal Computer Memory Card International Association)

An organization that sets standards for connecting peripherals to portable computers

peer-to-peer network

A simple type of network in which each computer can access and share the same printer(s), hard disk drives, removable storage devices (such as CD-ROM, Zip, and DVD drives) and other drives, as well as software, folders, and files on any other computer

pipe operator

A symbol (|) that indicates that the output of one command is to be used as the input for another command

pipe, or piping

To use the output of one command as the input for another command

pipeline

A command line containing a sequence of commands and that uses a pipe operator to transfer the output of one command so that it becomes the input for another command

Plug and Play (PNP)

A set of specifications for designing hardware so that the device is automatically detected and configured by the operating system when the computer boots or when it is attached to, or inserted in, the computer

POST (Power-On Self-Test)

A set of diagnostic programs for testing the system components at start-up

Power Users

Advanced users who have developed a broad base of skills useful for many different situations, such as designing and automating the use of custom programs, troubleshooting problems, providing support for other users, and setting up computer systems from scratch; (2) members of the Windows 2000 or Windows XP Power Users Group who are authorized to install software and change some system settings

print queue

A list of all the documents that are scheduled to print, along with information about each print job

PRN, or PRN:

The device name for the first printer port in a computer; also known as LPT1

program-oriented approach

An approach or operating mode in which you open the software application you want to use, then locate and open the document you want to use

property

A setting associated with an object (for example, the Windows version shown on the General property sheet in the System Properties dialog box for My Computer)

Q

question mark wildcard (?)

A symbol used as part of a file specification to subsitute for a single character in the directory name, filename, or file extension

Quick format

A type of format in which the formatting program erases the contents of the File Allocation Tables and directory file, but does not lay down new tracks or sectors and does not verify the integrity of each sector on a previously formatted disk

R

Random-Access Memory (RAM)

(1) Temporary, or volatile, computer memory used to store program instructions and data; (2) the computer's working memory

Read-Only attribute

An attribute assigned to a file to indicate that you can read from, but not write to, the file

redirect

To change the source of input or the destination of output

relative path

A sequence of directory names that identifies the location of a file relative to the current directory

Restricted User

A user who is part of the Windows 2000 or Windows XP Users Group, but who cannot install software or change system settings

robustness

The stability associated with an operating system and the system resources that it manages and protects

ROM-BIOS (Read Only Memory Basic Input Output System)

A computer chip that contains the program routines for running the Power-On Self Test, identifying and configuring Plug and Play devices, communicating with peripheral devices, and locating and loading the operating system

root directory

(1) The first directory created on a disk during the formatting of the disk; (2) the name of the top-level directory on a disk

routine

A program executed during the booting process to check the availability and functioning of hardware components or to locate and load the operating system from disk

S

scan code

A code that is produced from pressing a key on the keyboard and that is, used by the operating system to determine which character to display on the monitor

scrolling

A process by which a program adjusts the screen view

sector

(1) A division of a track that provides storage space for data; (2) the basic unit of storage space on a disk, typically 512 bytes of data

server

A high-performance computer that manages a computer network with the use of network operating system software, and that provides access to software, hardware, and files on a network

shell

The interface provided by a program so that the user can communicate with the program. In the case of Windows, the graphical user interface and the command line interface are shells employed by a user to communicate commands, or requests for actions, that the operating system will then carry out

short filename

An MS-DOS folder name or filename (also called an MS-DOS-Readable filename, or alias) that follows the rules and conventions for 8.3 filenames (that is, names that allow up to 8 characters for the main part of the filename and then up to 3 characters for the file extension, all using capital letters only)

sort order parameters

One-character codes used with the DIR command and Order switch to control the way in which the DIR command displays a directory listing

source code

The original, non-executable code in which a program was written

source disk

The disk that contains files you want to copy

source file

The original file copied by the operating system during a COPY operation

spool

To store print jobs on disk until the printer is ready to process the print request

spool file

A temporary file that contains a processed print job request, complete with printer formatting codes

spooling

The process of storing a document for printing in a temporary file on disk and transferring the document to the printer as a background operation

standard input device

The device the operating system uses for input; by default, the keyboard

standard output device

The device the operating system uses for output; by default, the monitor

Standard User

A user who is part of the Power Users Group and who can modify computer settings and install software

string

A set of characters that is treated exactly as entered

subdirectory

A directory that is contained within, and subordinate to, another directory; also known as a subfolder

surface scan

(1) A part of the formatting process in which the formatting program records dummy data onto each sector of a disk and reads it back to determine the reliability of each sector; (2) the phase during which the operating system examines the surface of a disk for defects

swap file

A special file created on a hard disk by the operating system for use as supplemental RAM; also known as a paging file

switch

An optional parameter, or piece of information, that is added to a command to modify the way in which a program operates

syntax

The proper format for entering a command, including how to spell the command, required parameters (such as a drive), optional parameters (such as a switch), and the spacing between the command, the required parameters, and any optional parameters

system architecture

The internal design and coding of an operating system

System attribute

An attribute that identifies an operating system file or folder

system disk

A disk that contains the core operating system files needed to start a computer; also known as a boot disk

SystemRoot

The directory that contains the installed version of the Windows 2000 or Windows XP operating system

systems software

The programs that manage the fundamental operations within a computer, such as starting the computer, loading or copying programs and data into memory, executing or carrying out the instructions in programs, saving data to a disk, displaying information on the monitor, and sending information through a port to a peripheral device

T

target disk

The disk that receives a duplicate copy of the contents of another disk

target file

A new file that results from a copy operation

taskbar

A gray horizontal bar on the desktop that displays a Start button for starting programs or opening documents, a Quick Launch toolbar, buttons for currently open software applications and folder windows, and a system tray with the current time and icons for programs loaded into memory during booting

task-switching

The process of changing from an open task, or process, in one window to another task in another window

template

A file that contains the structure, general layout, formatting, and some of the contents of a specific type of document, such as spreadsheet templates for analyzing a company's performance and projected growth

text file

A simple file type consisting of lines of ASCII characters, each terminated with an end-of-line code, and, in MS-DOS and Windows, typically a pair of codes--CR (Carriage Return) and LF (Line Feed)

text mode

A simple and fast video display mode for displaying text, including letters, numbers, symbols, and a small set of graphics characters using white characters on a black background

thread

A segment, or unit, of program code within an application which Windows can execute more than once at a time, or at the same time as other segments of program code in the same program

throughput

The speed with which a device processes and transmits data

time stamp

The time assigned by the operating system to a file

toggle key

A key that alternates between two related uses or functions each time you press the key

track

A concentric recording band around the inner circumference of a disk that stores data and which the operating system creates when formatting the disk

U

Unicode

A 16-bit coding scheme that can represent 65,536 character combinations, which can represent all the characters within the alphabets of most of the world's languages

universal serial bus (USB)

A computer interface with fast data transfer rates and which supports connections to multiple devices

user interface

The combination of hardware and software that lets you interact with a computer

utility

An auxiliary program included with operating system software for performing common types of tasks, such as searching the hard disk for files that can be safely deleted, or for monitoring or optimizing the performance of your computer

V

virtual DOS machine (VDM)

A complete operating environment for one program that is created each time a user opens a DOS program

virtual memory

(1) Space on a hard disk that an operating system uses as extra memory to supplement the memory available in RAM; (2) the combination of RAM and the swap file used as memory

volatile

Dependent on the availability of power, and therefore temporary (such as RAM)

volume

A physical storage device, such as a diskette, or a logical storage device, such as a partition on a hard disk

volume label

An electronic label or name assigned to a disk

W

Web style

A Windows user interface and operating environment that allows you to work on your local computer in the same way that you work on the Web

wildcard

A symbol in a directory or file specification that substitutes for all or part of the directory or filename

window

A bordered working area on the screen for organizing your view of an application, document, drive, folder, or file

Windows environment

An area of memory that stores information in environment variables for use by programs

wizard

A program tool that asks a series of questions about what problem you are experiencing, or what you want to do and the settings you want to use, then provides suggestions to solve the problem, or completes the operation or task for you

write-protect

A technique for protecting a disk so the operating system or any other program cannot record data onto it

TASK REFERENCE

TASK	PAGE #	RECOMMENDED METHOD
ASCII file, add a blank line to the end of an	113	See Reference Window: Appending Output to an ASCII Text File
ASCII file, append output to the end of an	113	See Reference Window: Appending Output to an ASCII Text File
ASCII file, search an	111	See Reference Window: Searching ASCII Text Files with the Find Filter
ASCII file, sort the contents of an	109	See Reference Window: Sorting the Contents of ASCII Text Files with the Sort Filter
ASCII file, view the contents of a	100	Type TYPE, press the Spacebar, type the filename, and press Enter
Asterisk wildcard in a file specification, using the	82	See Reference Window: Using the Asterisk Wildcard in a File Specification
Command Line session, open a	25	See Reference Window: Opening a Command Line Session
Command Prompt window, clear the	40	Type CLS and then press Enter
Command Prompt window, close a	43	Type EXIT and then press Enter
Command Prompt window, customize the	29	See Reference Window: Customizing the Command Prompt Window
Date, viewing or changing the	33	See Reference Window: Viewing or Changing the Date and Time
Default drive, change the	56	See Reference Window: Changing the Default Drive
Default drive, Listing a directory of the	54	See Reference Window: Listing a Directory of the Default Drive
Directory, create a	137	See Reference Window: Creating a Directory
Directory listing by date, displaying a	70	See Reference Window: Displaying a Directory Listing in Order by File Date
Directory listing by file attribute, displaying a	79	See Reference Window: Displaying a Directory Listing by File Attribute
Directory listing by file extension, displaying a	69	See Reference Window: Displaying a Directory Listing in Alphabetical Order by File Extension
Directory listing by file size, displaying a	71	See Reference Window: Displaying a Directory Listing in Order by File Size
Directory listing in alphabetical order, displaying a	65	See Reference Window: Displaying a Directory Listing in Alphabetical Order
Directory listing, displaying short filenames in a	74	See Reference Window: Displaying Short Filenames in a Directory Listing

TASK REFERENCE

TASK	PAGE #	RECOMMENDED METHOD
Directory listing, pausing a	63	See Reference Window: Pausing a Directory Listing
Directory listing, redirecting output to a file on disk	100	See Reference Window: Redirecting Output of a Directory Listing to a File on Disk
Directory tree, displaying a	155	See Reference Window: Displaying the Directory Tree of a Disk or Directory
Directory tree, saving a	161	See Reference Window: Saving a Directory Tree to a File
Directory tree, stepping down a	157	See Reference Window: Stepping Down the Directory Tree
Directory tree, stepping up a	158	See Reference Window: Stepping Up a Directory Tree
Directory, change a	140	See Reference Window: Changing the Current Working Directory
Directory, changing to another	156	See Reference Window: Changing to Another Drive and Directory
Directory, create a	137	See Reference Window: Creating a Directory
Diskette, copying a	42	See Reference Window: Copying a Diskette
Diskette, format a	38	See Reference Window: Formatting a Diskette
Drive, changing to another	156	See Reference Window: Changing to Another Drive and Directory
Drive, list a directory of another	55	See Reference Window: Listing a Directory of Another Drive
File attributes, displaying in a directory listing	79	See Reference Window: Displaying a Directory Listing by File Attribute
File, create a copy of a	117	See Reference Window: Creating a Copy of a File
File, delete a	122	See Reference Window: Deleting Files
File, rename a	120	See Reference Window: Renaming Files
Files, copying to another directory	144	See Reference Window: Copying Files to Another Directory
Files, copying within a directory	154	See Reference Window: Copying Files within a Directory
Files, moving from parent directory	150	See Reference Window: Moving Files from the Parent Directory
Full screen view, change to	25	Press Alt+Enter
Group of files, moving a	142	See Reference Window: Moving a Group of Files to Another Directory

TASK REFERENCE

TASK	PAGE #	RECOMMENDED METHOD
Help on DIR command switches, displaying	62	See Reference Window: Displaying Help on Directory Command Switches
Help, displaying	40	Type the command, press the Spacebar, type /?, and then press Enter
Log off Windows 2000	23	See Reference Window: Logging Off, and Logging On to Windows 2000
Log on to Windows 2000	23	See Reference Window: Logging Off, and Logging On to Windows 2000
Pipe output of a command to the More filter	103	See Reference Window: Piping the Output of the Type Command to the More Filter
Question mark wildcard in a file specification, using the	84	See Reference Window: Using the Question Mark Wildcard in a File Specification
Redirect input from an ASCII file to the More filter	105	See Reference Window: Redirecting Input from an ASCII Text File to the More Filter
Redirect output to a printer	116	See Reference Window: Redirecting Output to a Printer
Root directory, change to	140	See Reference Window: Changing the Current Working Directory
Screen, clear the	34	Type CLS and press Enter
Short filenames, displaying in a directory listing	74	See Reference Window: Displaying Short Filenames in a Directory Listing
Start Windows 2000	22	See Reference Window: Powering on Your Computer and Starting Windows 2000
Time, viewing or changing the	33	See Reference Window: Viewing or Changing the Date and Time
Wide directory listing, displaying a	64	See Reference Window: Viewing a Wide Directory Listing
Wildcard, using the asterisk	82	See Reference Window: Using the Asterisk Wildcard in a File Specification
Wildcard, using the question mark	84	See Reference Window: Using the Question Mark Wildcard in a File Specification
Windowed view, change to	25	Press Alt+Enter
Windows environment, viewing and changing settings in the	87	See Reference Window: Viewing and Changing Settings in the Windows Environment
Windows version, display the	30	Type VER and then press Enter

File Finder

Location in Tutorial	Name and Location of Data File	Student Creates New File
Tutorial 1 Review Assignments	Data Disk #1 Data Disk #1	
Tutorial 2 Review Assignments Case Problem 1 Case Problem 3 Case Problem 4	Data Disk #1 Data Disk #1 Data Disk #1 Data Disk #1 Data Disk #1	
Tutorial 3	Data Disk #1	Templates.txt Sales Templates.txt Five Year Plan Draft.xls Computer Training Proposal.doc 2003 Sales Summary #1.xls 2003 Sales Summary #2.xls
Review Assignments	Data Disk #1	Spreadsheet Solutions.txt Spreadsheet Solution Files.txt Backup of Spreadsheet Solution Files.txt
Case Problem 1	Data Disk #1	Stratton Graphics.txt
Case Problem 2	Data Disk #1	Bayview Travel.txt Financial Analyses.txt
Case Problem 3	Data Disk #1	Five Year Sales Projection.xls Company Balance Sheet.xls Loan Analysis.txt Bank Loan Analysis.txt
Case Problem 4	Data Disk #1	Turing Balance Sheet.xlsl Turing Client Invoices.xls Turing Weekly Worklog.xls 2003 Trips Summary #1.xls 2003 Trips Summary #2.xls Turing Budget Projection.xls Mediterranean Excursions.ppt
Tutorial 4	Data Disk #1 ~WRC0070.tmp File0000.chk Data Systems Budget.xls Hardware.ppt Application Software.ppt Software.ppt Using the Mouse.ppt Colors of the Rainbow.bmp Color Palette.bmp Palette #1.bmp Palette #2.bmp Addressing Cells.xls Fonts.xls Format Code Colors.xls Formatting Features.xls Andre's Employee Payroll.xls Loan Payment Analysis.xls Invoice Form.wk4 Weekly Worklog.xls Daily Sales.xls Savings Plan.xls Product List.xls Sales.wk4 Balance Sheet.xls Commission on Sales.xls Client Invoices.xls 2002 Sales Summary #1.xls 2002 Sales Summary #2.xls	Presentations (directory) Designs (directory) Training (directory) Business Records (directory) Company Projections (directory) 2003 Sales Summary #1.xls 2003 Sales Summary #2.xls Treefile.txt
Review Assignments	Data Disk #1 File0000.chk ~WRC0070.tmp Colors of the Rainbow.bmp Color Palette.bmp Palette #1.bmp	Images (directory) Word Templates (directory) Presentations (directory) Lotus Templates (directory) Excel Templates (directory) [Directory Structure.txt]

File Finder

Location in Tutorial	Name and Location of Data File	Student Creates New File
Review Assignments (continued)	Palette #2.bmp Projected Growth Memo.doc Proposal.doc Hardware.ppt Application Software.ppt Software.ppt Using the Mouse.ppt Invoice Form.wk4 Sales.wk4 Commission on Sales.xls Client Invoices.xls Weekly Worklog.xls Software Quotes.xls Andre's Employee Payroll.xls Daily Sales.xls 2002 Sales Summary #2.xls Advertising Income.xls Break Even Analysis.xls 2002 Sales Summary #1.xls Data Systems Budget.xls Five Year Growth Plan.xls Five Year Plan Template.xls Product List.xls Product Sales Projections.xls Regional Sales Projections.xls Sales Projection Models.xls 3 Year Sales Projection.xls Savings Plan.xls Loan Payment Analysis.xls Fonts.xls Formatting Features.xls Format Code Colors.xls Addressing Cells.xls Balance Sheet.xls Sales Projections.xls Employees.xls	
Case Problem 1	Data Disk #1 File0000.chk ~WRC0070.tmp Colors of the Rainbow.bmp Color Palette.bmp Palette #1.bmp Palette #2.bmp Projected Growth Memo.doc Proposal.doc Hardware.ppt Application Software.ppt Software.ppt Using the Mouse.ppt Invoice Form.wk4 Sales.wk4 Balance Sheet.xls Client Invoices.xls Commissions on Sales.xls Daily Sales.xls Data Systems Budget.xls Employees.xls Loan Payment Analysis.xls Product List.xls Software Quotes.xls Weekly Worklog.xls 3 Year Sales Projection.xls Advertising Income.xls Break Even Analysis.xls Five Year Growth Plan.xls	Spreadsheet Templates (directory) Business Records (directory) Projections (directory) Sales Summaries (directory) Training (directory) [Directory Structure.txt]

File Finder

Location in Tutorial	Name and Location of Data File	Student Creates New File
Case Problem 1 (continued)	Five Year Plan Template.xls Product Sales Projection.xls Regional Sales Projection.xls Sales Projection Models.xls Sales Projections.xls 2002 Sales Summary #1.xls 2002 Sales Summary #2.xls Addressing Cells.xls Andre's Employee Payroll.xls Fonts.xls Format Code Colors.xls Formatting Features.xls Savings Plan.xls	
Case Problem 2	Data Disk #1 Colors of the Rainbow.bmp Color Palette.bmp Palette #1.bmp Palette #2.bmp File0000.chk Projected Growth Memo.doc Proposal.doc Hardware.ppt Application Software.ppt Software.ppt Using the Mouse.ppt ~WRC0070.tmp Invoice Form.wk4 Sales.wk4 2002 Sales Summary #1.xls 2003 Sales Summary #2.xls Sales Projections.xls	FY 2002 (directory) 2002 Sales Projections.xls FY 2003 (directory) 2003 Sales Projections.xls 2003 Sales Summary #1.xls 2003 Sales Summary #2.xls [Directory Structure.txt]
Case Problem 3	Data Disk #1 Projected Growth Memo.doc Proposal.doc File0000.chk ~WRC0070.tmp Invoice Form.wk4 Sales.wk4 Hardware.ppt Application Software.ppt Software.ppt Using the Mouse.ppt Fonts.xls Software Quotes.xls Colors of the Rainbow.bmp Color Palette.bmp Palette #1.bmp Palette #2.bmp	Computer Courses (directory) Images (directory) [Directory Structure.txt]
Case Problem 4	C:\Winnt\Web\Wallpaper Boiling Point.jpg Chateau.jpg Fall Memories.jpg Fly Away.jpg Gold Petals.jpg Ocean Wave.jpg Paradise.jpg Purple Sponge.jpg Snow Trees.jpg Solar Eclipse.jpg Water Color.jpg Windows 2000.jpg	Windows Images (directory) [Directory Structure.txt]